FOUR RED
SWEATERS

FOUR RED SWEATERS

Powerful True Stories of Women and the Holocaust

Lucy Adlington

HARPER

NEW YORK · LONDON · TORONTO · SYDNEY

HARPER

HarperCollins books may be purchased for educational, business, or sales promotional use. For information, please email the Special Markets Department at SPsales@harpercollins.com.

FIRST EDITION

Designed by Jamie Lynn Kerner

Library of Congress Cataloging-in-Publication Data has been applied for.

ISBN 978-0-06-337513-0 (pbk.)

ISBN 978-0-06-337516-1 (simultaneous hardcover)

25 26 27 28 29 LBC 5 4 3 2 1

This book is dedicated to Jock, Anita, Chana, and Regina, and to all the girls forced to find their way in a harsh world, with love and friendship to guide them.

In memory of Elsie Walton, 1936–2024 – dear friend, trusty companion, dedicated history sleuth, superlative storyteller, and provider of the finest lemon drizzle cake ever baked. With love.

CONTENTS

FOUR RED SWEATERS.

Four girls – Anita, Jock, Chana, Regina.
Four stories knitted together.

I got it and wore it incessantly until the liberation –
always well concealed of course.
– ANITA LASKER-WALLFISCH[1]

Step out of the light and into a dimly lit room in the museum. As you walk – softly, no rush, no talking – you glance through glass walls. You see clothes held up by invisible supports or neatly laid on plinths. Coats. Dresses. Overalls. Among the greys and blues and browns you spy red. Not burlap or cotton or heavy-duty wool like the other garments on display, but soft angora.

A sweater. Just a sweater.

The red dye has faded over time, that's obvious. Without shame it shows a light sprinkling of moth holes, yawning openings at the elbows and a dense patch of yellow darning stitches. Hardly the sort of garment that usually graces a museum gallery, neither being stylish nor boasting the label of a famous designer. But this is not a fashion museum. It is one of the exhibition galleries of the Imperial War Museum in London, a place that explores the impact of conflict on ordinary people. To reach the red sweater you travel through a history of the Holocaust told via photographs, film clips, sounds, documents and objects such as this. The sweater is a simple item, holding a remarkable story.

Cellist Anita Lasker-Wallfisch donated the sweater to the museum's collection. It saved her life in Auschwitz.

Anita's red sweater is set alongside more recognisable prison wear, including the infamous blue/grey stripes now synonymous with suffering in the Nazi Third Reich. It is very bright in comparison, and so familiar it jolts to see it on display: the sort of everyday item you might own and never really think about. When cold, we reach for something woolly – a smart pullover, a chunky knit, or a cosy cardigan. If you're wearing wool right now you might feel its light itch against your skin, or the tickle of a label against the nape of your neck. Acrylic mix, cashmere, mohair, lambswool, angora . . . wool has been next to human bodies for millennia.

In the perverse world of Nazi concentration camps, inmates daring to take care of themselves by wearing an extra layer were brutally beaten. Frostbite and frozen bodies were the norm; warmth was a luxury. Acquiring something as simple as a sweater signalled defiance in a prisoner. A will to live. The desire to own something normal that reminded them of their pre-war life before roundups and deportation. Wearing a sweater re-humanised inmates who'd been told they were nothing more than numbers, or vermin, or fuel for crematoria fires.

Anita took the red sweater from a mountain of plunder in a barrack not far from one of the gas chambers in the Birkenau extension of the Auschwitz camp complex. Thirty such wooden barracks were laid out in three rows of ten. Each one was piled up to the rafters with clothes and accessories – sweaters, dresses, shawls, socks, shoes, coats and furs. It was considered theft for inmates to take anything from the barracks because according to Nazi law, every single garment, every last stocking or watch or waistcoat belonged to the SS. The original owners, brought on a one-way trip to the camp, were all murdered save for a few, like Anita, who, against the odds, managed to hold on to life.

Looking through the display glass at Anita's sweater you'll see your own face like a ghost next to the red. Projected behind the sweater are shadowy silhouettes of people, like a human skyline, reminding us that if the garments on display are now body-less, they once clothed living beings.

Everyday objects connect us across history. We can associate ourselves with something as recognisable as a sweater, then realise, with a chill, that what we think of as 'history' actually happened to real people. It didn't flicker past in black and white, as vintage film footage or photos suggest. It was in full colour. A series of present-tense moments for those who experienced it.

As you look at the sweater, you might wonder about nineteen-year-old Anita in Auschwitz, pulling it over her head for the first time. Or wonder about the girl who wore it before it was stacked with other plunder. About the woman – assuming it was a woman – who knitted it. About the shop that sold the balls of yarn and the machines that twisted it . . . even the angora rabbits that shed the fur to make the yarn. They are all part of the story. Sadly, many of these questions can never be answered. The Nazi system of genocide deliberately severed people from their belongings and the individual associations they held, before murdering them and destroying memories. Whoever first made and wore the sweater are lost to history, but the sweater has been found and could be one of the only pieces of evidence that they'd ever been alive. For Anita as a young girl, the sweater offered a chance to survive, whatever its previous history.

Meeting Anita as an older woman, it's clear her resilience is still as bright and bold as the red of the sweater. Through Lasker family letters, photographs and Anita's own words, it is possible to discover just what qualities and what twists of fate brought Anita to the sweater in the Auschwitz warehouse, and from there along the path to liberation.

From viewing Anita's red sweater in the darkened Holocaust gallery, come back into the light and behind the scenes – to the Imperial War Museum's research room. Here, by appointment, you can pull on the sheath of nitrile gloves to handle another precious garment. When not on tour it lives inside layers of protection, including an acid-free cardboard box and layers of specialist tissue paper. This scarlet sweater belonged to a girl called Jochewet Heidenstein, known as Jock.[2] It was part of an unexpected journey that saved her from ever experiencing the striped uniforms and shaved heads of Auschwitz.

The sweater is so vulnerable when you examine it closely. The pattern of blue and white around the neck and across the chest is still lovely and bright, but some of the buttons on the shoulder are shattered. It's easy to see how it was stretched out of shape as Jock kept growing, and where it was nibbled by moths once Jock finally grew out of it.

It was donated with a scant biography and an almost empty album of photographs. The few remaining photos are passport-style images showing pre-teen schoolgirls with big smiles and glossy hair. A note with the album states, *I don't think any of the girls survived.*

From the first time I saw Jock's sweater I knew I had to find out more of her story, if that was possible. What I eventually uncovered about her life was both sorrowful and uplifting. From just a name and a garment I traced a history of a loving family wrecked through persecution, with the remnants slowly knitted together again for quietly victorious post-war lives. I was able to track Jock's closest living relatives and spoke with them about family memories.

'Did you know Jock left her sweater to the Imperial War Museum?' I asked.

They did not know. They were amazed to learn of this precious relic.

Jock's sweater dates from 1938, when she was just twelve years old. It was shop-bought, not handknitted. In fact, it was one of three. One for each of the Heidenstein sisters: Jock, Rita and Gisela.

'Our parents bought each of us the same jumper,' Jock noted when the time came to part with her sweater so it could go into an exhibition. 'At times, the three of us would go out together, all wearing them.'[3]

This was in Berlin.

Picture Jock in her red sweater in the winter of 1938, with an energetic group of friends from the local Jewish girls' school, all heading out to the lake at Wannsee for ice-skating. Jock's middle sister, Rita, wanted to skate too, but Jock shooed her away. This fun was just for the big girls.

In January 1942, a villa on the shores of Lake Wannsee was used to host a meeting where details were finalised for the so-called Final Solution – the establishment of a Jew-free Europe via systematic genocide. Skating on the ice of Wannsee Lake in 1938, Jock knew nothing of this future, but she was old enough to be aware of anti-Jewish menace in Berlin. She'd grown up with threatening and demeaning graffiti. The signs saying *Don't Buy from Jews*. The cascade of anti-Jewish legislation that stripped her and her family of their German citizenship.

Jock, just a child, couldn't have understood how lethal the threat would become. Then came the horrific violence of November pogroms in 1938. Synagogues burned. Homes violated. People terrorised. When Jock's father was dragged off the street and taken to a concentration camp, it was all too obvious that the only way to be safe was to be somewhere beyond Germany's border. Jock's escape came due to the Kindertransport, a desperate initiative to save ten thousand Jewish children from Europe before it was too late. In January 1939, Jock's mother packed a suitcase, just one small item of baggage holding only the things a Jew was permitted to take out of the country. There was no room for ice skates, of course, but space for a photograph album. And the fancy red sweater.

The sweater tethered Jock to the lost life in Berlin, to the family and friends who couldn't flee with her. It is truly a forget-me-not garment. Her desperate journey pulled her away from everything she knew and everyone she loved, all in hope of a safe haven.

Chana Zumerkorn's red sweater, gifted to her brother, Josef.
Yad Vashem/Holocaust Remembrance Center

Some three thousand miles away from London, another red sweater is kept safe in the archives at Yad Vashem, the World Holocaust Remembrance Center in Israel. It's as bright as Jock's sweater, but with a high roll-top neckline and stylish tucks at the shoulder that give a fashionable puff effect, rather like the blousy sweater styles of the late nineteenth century. It has become worn on the edges and under the arms. Mended in places, unravelling in others. The shabby condition is hardly surprising considering the journey this sweater endured and the hardships of its wearer. It is not representative of how absolutely precious the sweater is.

'The wanderings of the sweater were my wanderings,' wrote the man who'd treasured it for over seven decades, Josef Zumerkorn.[4]

It was donated as part of an initiative by Yad Vashem to rescue personal items from the Holocaust era. The project is known as Gathering the Fragments. Among the photos, documents and memorabilia donated, Yad Vashem received a letter from Josef, a resident of Petah Tikva in Israel. He wrote, 'At home I have a red sweater given to me by my dear sister who was born in Lodz.'[5]

Seventy-two years after last seeing his sister, Josef was ready to share the story of the sweater – a bittersweet story he'd kept secret even from his family.

Josef's sister, Chana Jochewet Zumerkorn, was still a teenager when war broke out in Europe – just. She was nineteen going on twenty. She lived with her family in the great industrial city of Lodz, in eastern Poland.

Whatever dreams and plans Chana had at nineteen, the German occupation of her homeland disrupted everything. Her brother, Josef, argued for leaving: going somewhere – anywhere – had to be better than life under the Nazis. Chana felt tied to Lodz. It was her home. She stayed with her parents. Things were bad, but Lodz people were resilient. Surely they could endure a few months or years of war?

Fenced into a ghetto and forced to work for a meagre bread ration, Chana's fight for survival became bound up in loops of yarn and the click of needles. She took on work as a stocking-maker. Lodz was, after all, a city of mills, looms and shoddy dust. A city of textile transformation, from fleece to fashion.

Lodz Jews were soon considered essential to support German military ambitions, not least in the knitting industry. Invasions required kit. Boots marching into Finland, Norway and Russia needed thick socks, as did the sea boots of the German navy, or the fur-lined boots of the air force. Frostbite could take a man out of action every bit as effectively as a bullet or shrapnel fragments. Socks were essential, as were gloves, scarves and sweaters, and so the imprisoned Jews of Lodz were ordered to make them. Regular deliveries of old clothes and rags came into the city, to be renovated into new garments. Where had these clothes and rags come from? Few dared think about the answer to such a question.

'Only work can save us from the worst calamity!' announced Chaim Rumkowski, the Jewish head of the ghetto.[6] And so Chana knitted. Every stitch kept her alive a little longer.

Chana was one of many thousands knitting during the war. She knitted with the possibility of liberation; the chance that things couldn't get any worse than ghetto life. Seventeen-year-old Regina Feldman had all such illusions stripped away one bitter night in late 1942. While Chana laboured in a Lodz knitting factory, Regina[7] wasn't so far away in Poland, digging ditches for German forced labour enterprises. Jews were considered suitable – and disposable – for whatever work the expanded Reich required. From happy days as a school student in a friendly town, Regina was now exhausted and demoralised. Starving. Freezing. No warm woollens. Then orders came to muster for a journey.

With only the clothes on their backs, Regina and her family clambered into horse-drawn carts. Their destination was a neat compound near the village called Sobibor. As the new arrivals lined up, they heard Strauss waltzes playing over loudspeakers. The compound was lit with lamps as bright as daylight. A man in SS uniform stepped onto a podium. He ordered women who could knit to step forward. It wasn't exactly a rare skill among girls and women at this time, but most were reluctant to move. Why single themselves out? There could be safety in the crowd.

Golda Feldman shoved her daughter forward, saying, '*You* can knit.'[8]

Regina was one of just twelve girls who stood out from the lines.

And the rest of the new arrivals?

'That was the last time I saw my family,' Regina later mourned.[9]

The camp complex at Sobibor was one of the Nazis' dedicated extermination centres. A final destination for an estimated quarter of a million Jewish people. The function of the camp was to be kept secret, on literal pain of death. Regina, as one of the few Jews kept alive in the camp, was knitting a red striped sweater for one of her SS tormenters when she first witnessed the reality of Sobibor – a terrifying glimpse of women and children stripped of all their clothes in a one-way procession to their death.

The red sweater Regina created no longer exists. Or if it does, by a miracle, survive, stashed in a drawer or attic or vintage collection, its woollen stitches would give no clue as to the extraordinary story it holds. The burgundy-red wool was unravelled from other sweaters brought to Sobibor in transports from across Europe. The unravelled wool would be washed and re-wound, ready to knit something new, as if the original owners had never existed. In Regina's case the yarn she knitted with was all that tethered her to life in a place choked with death.

Staying alive was an act of resistance all in itself, but the prisoners in Sobibor had even greater defiance in mind.

On 14 October 1943, Regina and her friends set down their work. They were primed for action, in coats and woollens of their own. On that cold autumn day the inmates of Sobibor fought back in an incredible uprising and mass escape attempt. Guns were taken up in place of needles . . .

From frozen Polish forests, to sleepy English villages, Australian suburbs and the Manhattan skyline, this book tells the story of four red sweaters. Or rather, the stories of four girls who made, wore or cherished them: Anita, Jock, Chana and Regina.

Like Anita's well-worn sweater, there are gaping holes in the stories, as well as attempts to fill in the gaps. Gathering the fragments was sometimes like reaching into a rag bag of unravelled yarn and snipped threads. When pieced together the stories give a unique look at wartime history and fractured lives. The woolly sweaters seem so ordinary, but there is nothing ordinary about what these girls experienced, whether adapting to life as a refugee, or scrambling over barbed wire as an escapee. The girls themselves never met, yet their lives are still connected through their experiences – and through the red sweaters. They were once all young, Jewish and eager to live. A few different loops of fate might have had them passing each other in the street, sharing a classroom at school or going to the same music concert. Instead the girls are connected through their need for resilience in the worst circumstances. Their stories span the years of war, as well as post-war revival, when those still alive could knit for fashion as well as survival; for their babies, not SS persecutors.

Each element of these stories gives an insight into a horrific escalation of hatred against Jewish people; into the ways in which a process of dehumanisation, dispossession, degradation led to mass murder. They are part of what we now call the Holocaust. But the sweaters are not just emblems of atrocity, and they are far more than evidence of inhuman crimes. As the stories will make clear, they embody *love*. A love of life. Deathless mother love. Deep bonds of sibling love and loving friendships.

The woollen yarns may be fragile, but the love endures, indestructible as long as the knowledge of it is kept alive.

PART ONE

Salvaged

End of the Old, Beginning of the New

People had an air of hurrying somewhere without quite knowing where they were going.
– PAUL TABOR, JOURNALIST IN BERLIN[1]

Adolf Hitler never met Jochewet 'Jock' Heidenstein.
He never heard her name or saw her face. She was not presented to him, paraded past him or brought to his attention in any way. One time, near her house, there were crowds cheering on the streets as a sleek, black motor convoy went past. That was as close as Jock ever got to the man who destroyed her childhood. He was one of the most famous figures of the twentieth century. She was nothing to him – a nobody in history.

Of course, it wasn't history then. It was present tense: Berlin, in the 1930s. A city of industry, enterprise and energy, captured in endless photographs and film footage. Aeroplanes circled to land. Trains steamed into stations. The streets seemed frantic with trams, vans, carts and cars. On the river Spree, barges shifting heavy loads. On the boulevards, people heading to work, shopping, having a hasty lunchbreak. Sometimes smiling at the camera, sometimes keeping heads down, eyes on the ground ahead. At night, electric lamps and headlights. Concert halls dazzling with talent. Cinemas promising adventure and romance. Everywhere confident architecture. Everywhere red flags with black swastikas.

To find Jock Heidenstein in 1938 your Berlin map would take you away from the centre of political power at the Reichstag and the monolithic ministry buildings. Heading east from the Spree into the Mitte district – perhaps dawdling in front of the marvellous shop window displays on Leipzigerstrasse, and dodging deliveries in the fashion district around Hausvogteiplatz – there would be a growing awareness of residential blocks among the cafés and shops. Lace curtains at the windows. Multiple doorbells in the porches. With the right instructions you'd find your way to number 83a Linienstrasse, and the home of the Heidenstein family.

One day in 1938, Jock's mother, Mania Heidenstein, opened the door of 83a and went shopping. It was hardly world-stopping news, but in Jock's quiet history, it was tremendously important. Mania was out buying new clothes.

That year, Mania was only thirty-six years old. More or less. On her marriage registration her birthday is noted as 4 April 1902. When she completed the forms for the German Minority Census in May 1939, she'd shed a year, and is listed as born in 1903. Either way, at thirty-six, Mania was young enough to have the energy to take care of her children, but old enough to know her family was under threat. Adolf Hitler – the man who never met the Heidensteins and knew nothing about them – presided over policymakers intent on wrecking their stability. While Mania's children might have been aware of tensions, the parents understood that age-old bigotry was playing out again. The Heidensteins were Jewish.

If, by chance, Mania was caught on camera in Berlin of the 1930s, we'd never know it. She'd be one more figure on the street. Just another woman in a tilted hat, long coat and sensible shoes. There is no one now who would recognise her. No photographs survive of Mania Heidenstein. Even her children found their memories of her dear face eventually grew hazy until they had no recollection of her at all.

Mania had five children. The oldest was Jochewet Chana, called Eva at home, and later known as Jock, although not until after she'd left Germany. Jock was a Berliner, born and bred. She came into the world on 29 July 1927, a summer baby, eleven months after her mother and father married. There is no surviving record of her first smile, or the way in which her parents cradled her. No footage of her first steps, or the first proud day at school. There was, however, love. This love would be captured in a single garment. A warm, red sweater.

One of the few recollections Jock recorded in later life was a reference to her and her sisters wearing their red sweaters together. 'Our parents bought each of us the same jumper,' she said. 'At times, the three of us would go together all wearing them.'[2] The three sisters were welcomed into the Heidenstein family at nicely spaced intervals following Jock's birth. Rita was the middle girl, born in spring – 2 May 1929. It was a celebration for the Heidenstein family, before the country's economy was hit by aftershocks of the Wall Street stock market crash in the coming autumn.

After Rita came Gisela. By the time of Gisela's birthday – 14 October 1931 – Berlin, like many cities, was suffering a tumult of political conflicts and economic crises. For families like the Heidensteins, money was tight. By 1938, when Jock, Rita and Gisela got their matching red sweaters, financial constraints were even harsher. That the sisters needed warm clothes wasn't in question. Berlin winters were inhospitable, for all Jock loved to go ice-skating on the lake at Wannsee. That the girls could have *new* clothes was significant.

Throughout the 1930s, the Jewish Winter Aid agency fought a compassionate battle against hunger and cold, to support those who were cold and hungry. By 1938, it seemed that almost every Jewish family in Berlin was in need. Winter Aid representatives were clear – 'The need for clothes is enormous.' Tens of thousands of people were supplied with garments in 1936 alone, all available through donations from the Jewish community. Their gifting was called an 'act of love.' This wasn't to suggest Jewish families were neglecting their responsibilities. On the contrary. There was nothing but praise for parents who were somehow keeping their children healthy and neat, and 'who give their very last to the children.'[3]

In the wider German community, family care was praised as the central focus for a mother. Women's organisations supported a strong gender divide in family roles. Despite the fact that many women might be the main or only earner in a family, men were still considered the official 'breadwinner' and head of the household. Particularly under Hitler's National Socialist government, women were praised for maintaining a happy husband, clean house and a brood of healthy children. 'There is no area in which human beings are so precious and so indispensable as in the household and in the family,' gushed the editorial of *German Housekeeping* magazine – *Deutsche Hauswirtschaft* – in January 1939. By 'human beings' they meant non-Jews. The Nazi regime had long since decided that Jews in Germany were not at all precious or indispensable. In fact, a torrent of anti-Jewish legislation swept away any sense of security for even the most integrated families. Buying new clothes when Jewish incomes and livelihoods were being battered was an act of optimism, even defiance.

Mania certainly had to keep on top of the clothing situation as her girls grew and her family expanded. The Heidensteins at 83a had another new arrival in August 1935 – a little brother for Jock, named Michael. By the time the next brother David was born, in June 1937, being Jewish in Germany meant being stripped of German citizenship. One of the few fragments of evidence to prove the little boys ever existed is a list of people whose citizenship has been revoked, and whose assets are required to be declared. The list includes baby Michael's name.

Michael's birth year coincided with the passing of a series of laws to elevate those categorised as having 'German' blood, and discriminate against those considered of lesser races, namely Jews, Black people and Romani. The Heidenstein children were German born and bred. They'd known no other home. Under these so-called Nuremberg Laws they were demoted to subjects, not citizens. The men who crafted the laws, who printed them, who posted up the proclamations, who supervised the typing of record cards, and who stamped a 'J' for Jew on all new Jewish passports, these men knew nothing about baby Michael or his siblings. All they cared for was pressuring Jews to leave the country and exist elsewhere. Or even – and the thought was there, even before the killings began – even not to exist at all.[4]

Whatever the dehumanising Nazi attitude to Jewish families, with grotesque propaganda likening them to spawning rat hordes, all Mania's children were precious to her. Brought up in an Orthodox Jewish family, she honoured the traditional role of mother and homemaker. Unknown to Mania, the purchase of new sweaters in 1938 would be one last tangible gift to her daughters.

Even before the war, finding quality goods in local shops wasn't always easy. Jock's sweater was knitted from nice quality yarn, with a strong, fast dye. As Hitler's government pivoted resources towards rearmament and invasion, supplies of consumables for civilians were squeezed. From 1936, Reich Plenipotentiary Hermann Goering oversaw the structuring of the Four-Year Plan. Part of the plan was to enhance Germany's industrial infrastructure while reducing reliance on foreign imports. Boosting resources was everything. Nothing could be wasted. Most of Germany's fleeces were imported from Argentina and Australia. Foreseeing that war in

Europe would threaten supplies from abroad, initiatives were encouraged to find alternatives to natural fibres. Domestic sheep farming couldn't produce enough wool for all the country's needs.

Scientists were already pioneering synthetic yarns. Semi-synthetic fabrics such as rayon – essentially derived from wood pulp – were an important part of the fashion world, given fancy brand names and promoted as a modern alternative to silks and wools, rather than a poor substitute. Artificial fabrics such as rayon – glamorised as Art Silk – were fabulous for dressmaking or home furnishing. New fabrics were the future: this was the ideology promoted in the Third Reich. However, when it came to warmth, wool was still by far the better option. Garments based on cellulose yarn were prone to alarming bouts of shrinkage, and their insulating properties were not as good as wool. Except wool was in short supply.

Textile manufacturers lamented the loss, declaring, 'We experts are in despair, we are also ashamed that we must sell such rubbish.... Woollen goods are unprocurable.'[5]

This was something of an exaggeration. There were still ways to buy wool, and Mania was better placed than many to restocks drawers and wardrobe, since the Heidenstein family led lives steeped in clothes. Mania's husband was a clothes dealer.

Perhaps it's hard for consumers in the twenty-first century to understand just how much an investment clothes were for most individuals across human history. Even elite fashionistas made sure their cast-off garments were passed to relatives and household servants, or sold on. As late as the nineteenth century, ordinary clothes might be bequeathed in a will, such was their value. The most sumptuous ensembles would be unpicked and remodelled into new styles. Sad fabrics were revived with new dyes and optimistic trims. Surplus garments were cut down for children's wear, then torn into rags. Rags were recycled into new yarns. 'Too good to throw away' was the recycling refrain from German homemaking magazines such as *Deutsche Hauswirtschaft*.

Inevitably an industry grew up to trade used clothing and recycle even the shabbiest scraps of fabric. This was the trade that paid the rent on the Heidenstein home at Linienstrasse 83a and funded the purchase of three red sweaters for Jock, Rita and Gisela.

Jock's grandfather Josef was the foundation of the family business. Josef Heidenstein is first listed in Berlin directories in 1916, at a time when the Great War was devouring men and resources. In his fifties during this conflict, he was too old for military service. His energies were needed to maintain his livelihood.

In the early twentieth century, many second-hand clothing dealers worked small scale, as travelling pedlars going village to village, door-to-door with bundles and trays of goods. Life as an itinerant pedlar was hard and dangerous, particularly for women and for Jews in antisemitic areas. Jews could be forced into the work due to poverty and discrimination against them in other professions. That said, pedlars were welcome in many homes as they brought news, gossip and much-needed consumables, from needles and buttons to bolts of cloth and balls of yarn. Travelling pedlars feature in many European fairy tales as otherworldly harbingers of wonder, change or calamity.

Another familiar figure of the trade was the 'rag-and-bone' merchant, who laboured buying, sorting and selling cast-off clothes, refuse and scrap metal. Communities were quite familiar with the street calls of the rag-and-bone man, and the stereotypical image of a shabby figure with an overloaded cart.[6]

Josef Heidenstein, Jock's grandfather, was no wandering pedlar. He was settled, established and respectable. He had earned the distinction of being a wholesale rag dealer.[7] Kinship networks were very important in the textile trades, and it was no different for Josef. Once they were old enough, some of his sons were able to join him in the work. First the senior son, Jock's uncle Wolf, thirty-seven years old when she was born. Not long afterwards, Chaim, born 1897. Chaim was Jock's father.[8]

What did Chaim look like? At least we have hints of a description, unlike for his wife, Mania. As a student Chaim bought a ticket on the SS *Seydlitz*, sailing from Bremen to New York City in October 1923. On the passenger list Chaim is described as 'Hebrew,' not Polish. Being Jewish superseded nationality. Other men are simply 'German.' To be Christian was the norm; to be Jewish meant 'other.' Bremen immigration authorities also noted that Chaim was five foot nine inches tall, with a fair complexion, green eyes and black hair. There are no surviving photographs to show the details of his face. No one left alive who could remember how he looked.

Chaim stayed in New York long enough to learn something of the vibrant "rag trade" there. On his return to Berlin he lived for a while with Josef and Wolf. He met Mania – by chance or arrangement, no stories of their courtship survive – and they married. The children didn't see as much of Chaim as they would have liked. He was often away on business. Although the Heidenstein wholesale warehouse was down near the river Spree in Berlin, Chaim's work meant travelling a good deal. He had strong trade links with Amsterdam in the Netherlands – a great hub for clothes dealing.

There was also the issue of unprovoked violence against Jewish men. Chaim stayed away from home so he wouldn't be found there and taken away.

On a financial level, Josef, Chaim and Wolf each had to work to avoid being overwhelmed by Nazi laws against Jewish trade. Jews were to be excluded as competition to 'Aryans' through a combination of bullying, extortion and theft. Even so, Chaim had built a fairly comfortable life for his family. Nazi prejudice against Jewish businesses was enabled through adverse laws at a government level and enacted at a domestic level. The laws could not have been so effective without general compliance from those who did business with Jews, such as individual dealers deciding to overcharge Jewish merchants and cheat them of payments, or individual housewives, sorting old material and rubbish for recycling being told 'the nearest non-Jewish commodity trader should take care of this.'[9] By 1939, all Jewish dealers had been excluded from the German rag-and-bone system, with a great loss of expertise and a third fewer dealers.[10] Chaim's feelings about such blatant discrimination are not recorded. We can only imagine his frustration and sorrow.

Was this pervasive anti-Jewish hostility in Berlin one reason that Mania and Chaim decided to buy matching sweaters for their daughters – an unconscious desire to bind them together against the will of a regime working to fracture their lives? However the decision was reached, one day the three Heidenstein girls got their new sweaters.

New garments meant checking price tags instead of haggling at a second-hand stall in the market. It meant the chime of a bell as shop doors opened. The welcome – or scrutiny – of shop assistants when going inside. The pleasure of browsing shelves and rails; of admiring cabinets and displays.

Where was Jock's red sweater sold? Unknown. It has a white cotton label at the back of the neck, but this just gives a number, presumably a size reference, not a shop name or design brand. From specialist couturiers to cheap market stalls, Berlin could be a shopper's paradise, particularly when the seasonal sales opened to a scrum of bargain hunters. There were department stores like brilliant palaces. Boutiques with chic quality. Earnest local shops catering to those wanting style on a budget.

There was a catch to all this choice. One of the very first public actions of the newly empowered Nazi Party, in April 1933, was to organise a national boycott of Jewish-owned businesses. Due to sound investment, entrepreneurial energy and excellent industry experience, the majority of Berlin fashion talent and capital was Jewish. The backlash to this boycott from Germany's international trade partners was more powerful than expected, not to mention the disappointingly lukewarm response from many shoppers. Undeterred, the Nazis stoked existing bigotry with increased anti-Jewish propaganda and legislation. Walking the streets of her home city, Jock Heidenstein would have been used to the sight of Nazi uniforms standing guard outside Jewish shops. They were not there to protect the owners from harassment, but to intimidate those who might dare defy the bigotry and support the business. One girl remembered one such brave act of defiance in a Jewish man's shop: 'My mother really had nothing to buy, but wanted to show him, I'm still coming. So she bought two small spools of thread.'[11]

The persecution became so flagrant it would be common to see shop windows defaced with dripping paint. There were crude, daubed Stars of David to signal the Jewishness of the store, and equally crude slogans, including the near ubiquitous *Nicht Kauf bei Juden* – Don't Buy from Jews.

It took courage for non-Jewish shoppers to face bullying and even denouncement to the police for shopping in the 'wrong' place. It took even more courage for Jews to be operating businesses in the face of such brazen harassment, with no protection from laws or police.

It would be nice to imagine Mania and Chaim out with the three girls, with toddler Michael and baby David . . . although that was a lot of little humans to manage on a busy street. In an ideal world, Jock and her family could have enjoyed such a family expedition. In reality, wherever the Heidensteins got the three red sweaters, they had to negotiate hostile public spaces.

Would it have been better to knit the sweaters at home? Deft knitters could be inspired by patterns printed in women's magazines and crafting publications. In fact, the 1930s was a glorious era for fashionable knitwear. Previously considered best suited for underwear or sporting activities, knitted garments enjoyed a surge in popularity from the Great War onwards. Fancy socks, waistcoats, cardigans and sweaters were seen on film stars and royalty. In France, the surrealist designer Elsa Schiaparelli started a trend for jumper tunics with eye-catching motifs, while Sonia Delaunay created sweaters that were woollen works of art. If Mania felt up to the task, there were printed patterns for ski sweaters, toboggan woollies, lace-effect tops or blouse styles with fancy bows. She could try moss stitch, basketweave, cable patterns or stripes. The choice of yarns was exciting too, from colourful plain wool to spangly silver twists and silky angora.

Unfortunately, even knitting wools were saturated with antisemitism. Germany's largest wholesale supplier of yarn was the Bavaria-based company Quelle. Quelle's printed boast was 'Can't be beaten in terms of performance! In one year around 600,000 pounds of knitting and needlework wool sold to German housewives!'[12] Quelle offered a lovely range of hues, including cherry, rust, blood and brick reds.

Quelle was founded by Grete and Gustav Schickedanz in 1927. They were enthusiastic supporters of Nazi ideology and profited enormously from aggressive state-sanctioned takeovers of Jewish businesses. There was widespread distribution of their attractive booklets of yarn samples. Prospective knitters and crafters could turn the pages to finger little twists of yarn, all at competitive prices, alongside alluring promises, such as, 'The wool is much more beautiful than the small samples can show.' In the early 1930s, Quelle sample books declared they were the biggest German mail order company with *Christian-Aryan* owners.

'Aryan' was a designation conceived by racial obsessives to

create a hierarchy of purity. According to this theoretical hierarchy, Aryans were 'pure-blood' German/Nordic types. Not Jewish. For Quelle to link Christian and Aryan hammered the message home even further: very not Jewish.

By 1937, the Quelle company was engorged with Jewish businesses acquired by devious tactics that were technically legal due to antisemitic laws. That year the Quelle yarn booklet had a somewhat slimmer range of woollen yarns available, but the front page still proclaimed 'Purely Aryan Enterprise.' Their wool was Jew-free.[13]

Perhaps Mania wasn't a confident knitter, the yarn was unobtainable, or perhaps she had her hands full with a household of five children. Whatever the reason, her daughters each had a shop-bought sweater. They matched. Sometimes they went out together wearing them. As life in Berlin became increasingly fraught, they went out less and less. Home became a haven.

Home is often the centre for remembrance of childhood. There can be hazy sense memories – echoes, aromas, warmth or chill – and there can be visual recollections of sudden, incredible clarity. Regular experiences, such as daily life at home, can be so familiar that only something unusual will have a strong impact. Well-known sounds and sensations may not even be consciously registered. Photographs, objects and recordings can help regain a sense of what we once knew so well. Without these cues, how is it possible to hold on to the memories of lost loved ones, if relationships are severed during childhood? Jock Heidenstein at least had her red sweater in later life. Something uniquely associated with people and places.

Any visualisation of past lives is imperfect. Elusive. Fragmentary. Like standing in a dark street looking at a tiny chink of light beyond curtains drawn across a window. Small details are all we have to visualise the Heidenstein family before the war. Jock's former home survived the war, at least, unlike many of its inhabitants, and it gives a good sense of place even now. Built in 1912 83a is still a handsome edifice, with intact masonry embellishments. Originally, numbers 83 to 85 were headquarters for the German Metalworkers' Association. They chose the quiet end of the street, where the road narrows and no trams run. The Mitte district was a hub for many Jewish families originally from Poland. Jock's family had lived at several addresses in the general area before settling at 83a. Now the building has a rooftop swimming pool. In 2023 a four-room apartment of 85 square meters was listed for sale at a cool 625,000 euros. It wasn't quite so upmarket during Jock's time there. Back in 1938, when the family lived in flat II on the left side, 83a housed a mix of tenants, including a shoemaker, carpenter and author. The small apartments could be home to extended families. Jock's school friend Hella lived in flat III with six other people. The only reason there weren't more was because Hella's grandparents had recently died and other relatives had fled Germany.

On Saturdays, the Heidenstein flat would be rich with the aroma of *schmaltz*, garlic-infused goose fat spread, redolent of the family's Polish origins. Jock's sister Rita remembered it eventually became too dangerous to eat schmaltz on the Sabbath – the smell singled them out as Jewish. Apartment 83a no longer holds traces of the Heidenstein pattern of life. Everything is dispersed.

In the early years of the regime, the hate enabled by Nazi rule could, to some extent, be kept at bay through loving family inter-actions and the comfort of religious practices. For Jock growing up there were plenty of uncles, and lots of women to call *Tante* – auntie: Tante Rosa, Tante Lotte, Tante Esther and Tante Tauba. Tauba was married to Jock's uncle Wolf. Tauba and Wolf had suffered the tragedy of multiple bereavements, from stillbirths to deaths of an infant. They had one surviving son, Juda.[14] Esther, a dressmaker, was married to Uncle Juda. They all lived nearby, but their homes had once been towns and villages in eastern Poland. They'd come to Berlin to start new lives, through work and through children – a few of the many thousands who hoped for greater safety, opportunities and financial security.

Home, shops, school, streets . . . Family, friends, prayers, treats . . . Even if Jock's home life might have seemed somewhat small and ordinary, she was still connected across borders and generations. From 1938, her world would get a whole lot wider. One constant for Jock during the coming disruption would be her little red sweater.

In knitting terms, change could mean undoing old work and making something different. *German Housekeeping* magazine celebrated change as 'The end of the old, and beginning of the new.'[15]

New might represent hope or improvement, but there is always loss with unravelling, even if something can be salvaged. For twelve-year-old Jock Heidenstein change was catastrophic. Her small, ordinary life would come to seem magical compared to the shock of being hit by events that make history.

2

Winter Can Get Grim

I felt extremely grown up.
– ANITA LASKER-WALLFISCH[1]

While the Heidenstein family had no record of their home life – no 'proof' of how things were before disaster struck – in another German Jewish home a picture was taken of a family gathered together for a sacrosanct ritual: the taking of coffee and cake. The photograph captures this ordinary pleasure. We see a family around a table with white crockery and a pretty scalloped tablecloth. Enjoying patisseries is Anita Lasker, her parents and her two sisters, Marianne and Renate.[2]

It's a lovely scene. The coffee and cake appointments were enlivened with jokes, storytellings and readings. Simple pleasures.

Many months and many partings later Anita's mother wrote, 'We never knew how marvellous everything was back then!'[3]

Even before war made peacetime seem extra magical, Anita enjoyed life at home. She came from a comfortable middle-class family that thrived on culture and activity. Another photograph of the apartment on Kaiser Wilhelmstrasse shows a pleasant, spacious room with light drapes, framed paintings, patterned rugs and crystal vases of fresh flowers. Permanence and impermanence in harmony. This was before the Nazis renamed the address as Strasse

der S.A. – *Street of the Storm Troopers*. The S.A. – *Sturmabteilung* –
were prominent strutting in all German towns. Their uniform of
brown shirts and ties came to signal thuggery and freedom from
consequences.

Anita had a growing awareness of these Brown Shirts and the
regime they represented. In happy contrast to ominous politics, the
Lasker household was always alive with song and music. Marianne,
the oldest sister, played piano. Renate, next in age, was a violinist,
like their mother, Edith. Then there was Anita, the youngest, on
cello. Given Anita's emerging talent as a musician it was decided she
should take a break from school to focus on music lessons. The diffi-
culty was finding a suitable teacher in Breslau brave enough to tutor
a Jewish child, when those in power were discouraging all interac-
tions between Jews and non-Jews. It was decided Anita would go
to Berlin. Here she'd be taught by cellist Leo Rostal, a man who'd
worked his way to a sound reputation, starting out playing for an
orchestra at the famous Adlon hotel in the heart of the city.

In spring 1938, Anita took the train from the elegant Breslau
station feeling confident and very grown up. She was kitted out in
clothes made by her mother, who had a great talent for sewing as
well as music. Anita was twelve when she set off, and turned thirteen that summer – only two years older than Jock Heidenstein.
If life were a film she might have met Jock during the Berlin stay.
As it was, their lives would be linked in different ways. If they did
happen to pass in the street, or brush shoulders in a shop or at a
concert, they'd never know of the future connection through two
red sweaters.

Once in Berlin, Anita took lodgings in an old-fashioned apartment on Augsburgerstrasse on the western side of the city, hosted by
a woman who provided two hours of schooling each morning, and
almost daily meals of meatballs with brussels sprouts. Now, the
street is mainly modern. There is little evidence of the 1930s in the

architecture, the nail bars and posters advertising superhero films. Back in 1938, Augsburgerstrasse was a base for Anita to explore. Zoo Station, the Tiergarten Park and Charlottenburg were all fairly near. She diligently visited her new cello tutor and not so diligently bunked off music practise to wander through the wonderland of the nearby department store, Kaufhaus des Westens – Department Store of the West – known as the KaDeWe. Offering sensational fashions, the KaDeWe was a shopper's paradise and a browser's dream. Few of those admiring displays of luxury fashions would have been aware that the Jewish owners of KaDeWe had already been ousted from the business. Jewish employees were also ejected on racial grounds.[4]

Anita Lasker and cello.
Anita Lasker 1938; private property

A photograph from this time in Berlin shows Anita in a dark dress with the very fashionable detail of a zip at the front. She poses with her cello, fingers on the strings and bow set to create a chord. Her eyes are down, her expression serious. Another moment captured that would quickly be gone once the bow moved and new notes sounded. Five years after this photo was snapped Anita took up a cello she'd never held before, for an audition that would save her life. In that future moment, poised with her bow in Auschwitz, she would be glad of all that she'd learned in Berlin.

For Anita, used to freedom at home, wandering the displays of stores such as the Berlin KaDeWe was far more fun than being stuck in formal lessons. Back in Breslau Anita had attended a small private school. She may have become used to the hiss of insults on the street, being called *dirty Jew*, and spat at. It was still a shock to hear children in her own class whispering 'Don't let the *Jew* have the sponge' when it came to clean the chalkboard. What could she possibly reply to that? She was a Jew, although not so religiously observant as Jock. The Lasker family attended synagogue for high holidays only and considered themselves utterly assimilated with German society. Hitler's Germans thought differently. Their concept of nationality and community was strictly defined by social and racial exclusions.

Anti-Jewish bullying in school was intensive under the aegis of the Third Reich. Jewish children were harassed by teachers and so-called friends. Ultimately they were ejected from mainstream education. They were not seen as fit to sit beside non-Jewish children. This was one of many steps to push Jews out of education, out of work, out of sight. Real friends formed protective groups, with a core of loyalty and camaraderie. In Berlin Jock Heidenstein was lucky to have such support from girls at school. For Jock, school was a haven, not a battleground. She was enrolled at the new Jewish Girls' School on Auguststrasse, just a few minutes' walk from home. There was no official uniform, so Jock could wear her red sweater when the weather turned chilly.

The modern visitor to Berlin can follow her route to school, turning right at the doorway of Linienstrasse 83a then crossing to Auguststrasse through the rose bushes of Koppenplatz. Since it was very much a Jewish area in the 1930s, these streets might have been free from Nazi harassment. Jock wasn't short for good company en route, or at school. Among her friends were Hella and Mimi Sternlicht, and Helene Spitz Kiwowicz. All these girls had Polish-born parents, like Jock.[5] Their names and young faces are kept alive through tiny passport photographs, showing bright smiles and bobbed hair. What jokes they shared, what games they played – these are not recorded and there is no one left to remember them. Their voices no longer echo in the Jewish School for Girls, but the building still stands. The intimidating façade – dark brown-red bricks and unadorned windows in neat geometric rows – looks over the narrow pavement from 11 to 13 Auguststrasse. It's not hard to imagine a press of girls pushing against the wide front doors and passing through the entrance with no thought for the stylish geometry of the mosaic tiling within. The stone steps reaching four floors high must have clattered with boots and shoes, hands rubbing along the parallel metal bars of the stair rails. There were fourteen classrooms in total for 330 girls, a courtyard hidden from the street and a pleasant roof garden. It was all incredibly modern when new, and it still has an airy, light feel.

The school was built the same year Jock was born. 'Insanely well built' in the words of one of the modern owners.[6] It has outlasted her and all the original pupils. The architect, Alexander Beer, had a daughter, Beate, just two years older than Jock. As he drew up plans for the impressive Jewish school, did he envision a time when Jews would be barred from other schools and universities? When all the bricks and mortar and modernity in the world couldn't stand against hate? His architecture now houses chic art spaces and artisan eateries. It is strange to go inside; to image Jock and her friends clattering across the mosaic floors and up the stairs to class.

There are no longer any desks and chairs in the Auguststrasse building. No ink pens or textbooks. No sums on boards or chalk dust. No trophy cabinets or ledgers with daily registration marks.

No vaulting horses in the gym. No staff. No pupils. A few photographs on a hallway wall recall its former life, showing classrooms full of pupils – bright faces without names.

Relics from the school are scattered among personal possessions of survivors. One solitary end-of-term report card exists in the archives of the Jewish Museum in Berlin, for a girl called Meta Wollny. Meta was fourteen in 1936, when she got good marks in needlework and Home Economics, but not so impressive in History and German Comprehension.[7] Her behaviour is described as 'good'; attention only 'moderate.' Meta's report is exactly the sort of card Jock would have taken home to hand over to parents, with pride or trepidation, depending on that term's results. We don't know how Jock's report would compare. Did she focus on her lessons, or was it hard to keep general anxiety at bay?

Whatever tensions Jews in Berlin felt, in November 1938 they were about to get far worse. The night of 9 and 10 November saw an orgy of violence against Jewish people and property so extreme it sent shockwaves around the world. For Anita Lasker, the warning came via a telephone call on 9 November. *Come home*, her mother said.

'It was no time for a family to be separated,' Anita later reflected. She admitted she perhaps hadn't made the best of her time in Berlin, but added, 'I had no way of knowing how short-lived the opportunity was going to be.'[8]

No one should have to fear a knock on the door.

In happier times, visitors to Jock's home at 83a Linienstrasse would be welcomed in. There were aunts and uncles, of course – Esther, Tauba, Lottie, Rosa, Juda and Wolf – as well as school friends coming to call, or Chaim's business friends from the world of clothes-dealing. By November 1938 Jock wasn't permitted to answer the door. Rita, just nine years old, had lighter brown hair than

Jock. She didn't look like the Nazi stereotype of a Jewish girl. She was the one who opened the door when they heard a knock. She was the one who went out into the neighbourhood to run errands.

A knock was the prelude to arrest. It could come at any time, day or night. Rita was coached to say her father wasn't home, if anyone asked. Chaim spent his days riding the elevated train around Berlin, just another man in a hat and coat. If he wasn't home, the Gestapo couldn't find him.

His fear was justified. In late October 1938, Polish-born Jews living in Germany were being rounded up and transported to the Polish border, where they were simply abandoned with their bags and bewilderment, since the Poles refused them entry. Victims of this travesty, termed the *Polenaktion*, had their German citizenship revoked but were considered denationalised by Poland if they'd lived abroad for more than five years. Chaim thought of Berlin as his home, even though he'd been born in Poland. Even if he and Mania had discussed going back to Galicia, where Mania's family still lived, it was one thing to plan a careful emigration and transfer belongings, quite another to be hoisted out of life and into a hasty refugee camp with seventeen thousand other ejected individuals.

Luckily the Heidensteins weren't caught by the Polenaktion. Chaim also managed to avoid arrest during the storm of anti-Jewish violence on 9 November. Back in Breslau, Anita Lasker's father faced the same threat as Chaim and other Jewish men. Dr Alfons Lasker was usually an optimist. He thought the best of people and felt secure in his professional status as a lawyer. However, when a non-Jewish friend from the apartment upstairs told him serious things were going to happen, he took notice. He got in the friend's car and was driven around Breslau until the following day, when the attacks seemed to have subsided.

Whether in Berlin, Breslau or any other city, town or village in Germany, it was the noise of smashing glass that most people remember about the 9 November pogrom. Bricks and iron bars smashed house, shop and synagogue windows. The frenzy continued inside, leaving display cases, door glass and mirrors in fragments. Anything obviously Jewish that could be smashed, was deliberately broken into thousands of pieces. There was so much shattering, 9 November became known as Kristallnacht – night of broken glass. The attack was nationwide – an organised campaign of terror and destruction. Jewish homes were raided, families terrorised, sheets slashed and clothing torn. Children were told to hide in wardrobes and under the bed.

What wasn't broken was stolen. From the grand department stores to little local shops, nowhere was safe. The famous KaDeWe store where Anita had wandered gazing at wonderful things, this too was trashed and plundered, one of over seven thousand shops destroyed. Through broken shop windows loot came flying down onto the street for anyone to snatch up – fabric lengths, furs, coatracks, even sewing machines. What wasn't smashed or stolen was burned and defaced.

Berlin, a major trading metropolis, had shown that racial hatred and greed was now the main currency. The outrages were nothing new: in June 1938 journalist Bella Fromm fumed in her diary about the havoc along Berlin's most popular shopping street, Kurfürsten-dam. Elsewhere she noted 'loot from the miserable little shops was strewn over the sidewalk and floating in the gutter.' It was the ex-tremity and shamelessness of the violence that made 9 November so significant.

Non-Jewish Germans were puzzled by the violence, disturbed by it . . . or they gloried in it. Some shrank small for fear of being caught up in the brutality; some stepped out boldly to participate. Hysteria overtook whole communities of people who'd otherwise consider themselves decent. Those who did plunder had nothing to fear from police. It was not a crime to steal from Jews. When the fire brigade were called out to hundreds of arson attacks they only intervened if it looked like the fire would spread from the Jewish target to non-Jewish neighbouring buildings.

The violence continued through the night and into the next day. In the Heidenstein home Jock's sister Rita woke to the sound of breaking glass and an awful burning smell. From that day she felt a fear that never, ever left her.

Alexander Beer, architect of Jock's school on Auguststrasse, was woken in the night and told to come and witness the destruction of the beautiful synagogue on Prinzregentestrasse. It was plundered then torched. One of 101 synagogues to be destroyed by fire. Just one block along from Jock's school, inside the New Synagogue on Oranienburgerstrasse, a Nazi mob set a bonfire of Torah scrolls and furniture. Remarkably, a local police officer halted the destruction, declaring the synagogue a national landmark. The gilded dome still sparkles, intact, but the rampant destruction across the country sent a very clear message from the Nazi government: they would condone, co-ordinate and carry out spiritual and material damage against Jews in Germany.

As a little girl, Rita Heidenstein liked to slip into the New Synagogue. Being Orthodox, it wasn't her usual place of worship, but she loved to wonder at the space, the brilliance and the stillness. Now it smelled of smoke and desecration. The synagogue congregation very quickly rallied to restore the building's interior and restart services, but Rita's sense of safety had cracked like the glass of broken windows.

Then they took her father.

It all happened so fast. One moment Chaim Heidenstein on the street; the next, rounded up and – gone. Rumours crackled across the Jewish community. Why and where had the men been taken? It wasn't just Chaim. Chaim's brother, Wolf Heidenstein, was also

dragged away. Thousands of men were snatched in the days following Kristallnacht. Most were taken north of Berlin to a concentration camp in the town of Oranienburg, known at that time as
Sachsenhausen. It was a little over a half-hour drive from Linienstrasse, but a world apart. The route took Chaim away from all the
places he'd lived and worked since coming to Berlin as a younger
man. Away from Mania and his five children.

There were few woolly sweaters in Sachsenhausen in November 1938. Chaim and 6,000 other Jewish men began their life in
the camp with a twenty-four-hour-long roll call, out in the open.
Warmth? That was for SS staff, in their long winter coats and knitted boot stockings, and maybe a flask of schnapps. Warmth was for
men with hair, not shaved heads like the prisoners. Warmth was
forbidden for inmates: no earmuffs, scarves, socks or vests. Whatever the men had been wearing at the time of their arrest was taken,
inventoried and stored. Rudolf Höss – future commandant of
Auschwitz concentration camp – became administrator of prisoner
belongings in Sachsenhausen during Chaim's incarceration there.
Jock's father – called Papa by his children - was issued with a basic
uniform of cotton drill cloth. Ill-fitting, with distinctive stripes, the
uniforms were intended to degrade him into just one humiliated
figure in a homogenous mass of suffering. If Chaim were caught
acquiring winter clothing, such as the cement bag coats and caps
fabricated by men doing forced labour at construction sites, he
would be punished brutally. This winter torture wasn't enough for
Rudolf Höss. One night he ordered 800 prisoners to stand outside
in freezing weather. By morning there were 140 corpses on the roll
call square, and countless men suffering frostbite.[9]

Höss looked back on his time as adjutant in Sachsenhausen
with a chilling lack of self-awareness, writing, 'I was not suited for
service in the concentration camp because I had too much compassion for the prisoners.'[10]

Jewish men rounded up after the November pogroms were sent to three of the sixty-eight barracks. The only heating was from a small heater that burned wood or coal – supplies permitting – and from the fug of 400 bodies crowded into hastily erected buildings, each meant for only 150. There were three-storey wooden bunks, sometimes two men per mattress on each tier. One thin blanket per man. One bowl and one spoon for the lukewarm murk that passed as coffee or soup. All work, all errands had to be 'at the double.' Running was not a good way to keep warm without decent nourishment. Frequent, random beatings warmed the abuser, not the poor body on the end of the whip or fist or boot. No parcels were permitted, so Mania Heidenstein couldn't even send food and clothing for her husband.

The children were unremittingly anxious. Why couldn't their Papa come home?

SS administration buildings created a physical buffer zone between the camp itself and the town it was built in. Every element of appearance and design reinforced the lie that all prisoners were lesser. Other. It might have been comforting for civilians in the adjacent town to think themselves a world apart from the harrowed men in stripes marching to forced labour, but they were only one new legislation away from being 'othered' themselves.

Bricks, concrete and barbed wire gave Sachsenhausen its physical existence. Made it seem permanent, inevitable, therefore justifiable. Every element was designed to consolidate power for some and generate suffering for others. When snow fell on the roll call square, shovels could easily have been issued. Instead, prisoners had to clear the snow with their bare hands.

How could Chaim and his brother, Wolf, be expected to endure this institutional cruelty? Because they had to. Because they couldn't possibly believe it could last. They were innocent, after all. Just men trying to live and work in the city. Their crime was simply existing as Jews.

Kinship networks helped, and we can hope Chaim found mutual support with Wolf. Since many of the new Jewish prisoners were from Berlin and surrounding areas, there was also a chance that Chaim would recognise friends from his neighbourhood and dealers from the rag trade. Having connections in the camp could mean getting a place on one of the indoor work squads, rather than in the brutal conditions of the brickworks and other factories. There was even a tailor's workshop at Sachsenhausen, although Chaim was a dealer not a maker, so he couldn't take advantage of shelter in this indoor work squad.

Chaim had been torn from family, home, work and place of worship, but he could at least hold in his heart the knowledge that Mania and the children were safe at home, and that the Jewish community would rally round to support them.

Don't ask what's happened to people who disappear.

Don't ask.

This was the rule for nine-year-old schoolgirl Ulla Mahlendorf. Ulla was the same age as Rita Heidenstein. She remembered the noise of the Kristallnacht pogroms in November 1938. She saw a classmate's house smashed up, with only glass and paper debris left scattered.

Ulla was German but not Jewish. She could tuck her concerns away, comforted by the propaganda that told her Jews deserved everything they got and then some.[11] In the Jewish community, there were endless, frantic questions – Where were the men? Why had they been taken? When could they come home? Rumours were the only answers at first. Those left behind faced the task of cleaning up after the pogroms and holding a fractured community together.

While the Nazis discouraged criticism of pogrom damage through their usual tactics of opinion monitoring, censorship and menace, they couldn't confiscate every camera. One image from

Berlin shows a clothes shop owner called Martha Jacobowitz in a patterned frock and smart street shoes sweeping up glass with a brush, dustpan and bucket. A young boy helps her. Behind her are the broken security grills of the shop. Grotesque jags of glass cling to the window frames. Two men in hats and long coats look on. Martha, like Mania Heidenstein, had been born in Poland, coming to Berlin to shape a better life for herself. Now she was sweeping up pieces of that hope.[12]

The November pogroms in Germany saw very public violence and also contamination of very private spaces – homes that had seemed safe. Feathers had to be stuffed back into pillow slips, clothes re-hung in the wardrobe and scattered lives re-ordered. Sweeping, cleaning, mending, tidying . . . these tasks were primarily seen as women's work.

At some point in 1938 Jock Heidenstein took needlework classes, all part of her education as a girl. Jock was a good knitter, but judging by the garments she produced, sewing was definitely not her forte. Still, she persevered. She pieced together a small apron of red-and-blue-checked cotton.[13] An apron was often the first thing girls learned to sew at school. It fitted them out for future domestic roles. Men might be issued with military kit, but the apron was the ultimate female uniform.

Third Reich propaganda and policies idealised and enforced gendered roles. Male, female. Public, private. Proactive, submissive. Hitler set out separate spheres for men and women right from the first. Men were to be heroes on the battlefields. Women's heroism came through never-ending sacrifice and suffering for the family. Organisations such as the National Socialist Women's League – the *Frauenschaft* – helped promote housework and childcare as inevitable, beatific roles for women, through peer pressure, publications and mass education programs such as Mother Schools and thrift classes. It wasn't a question of choice. Aside from leadership in women's organisations under Nazi rule there was no longer any female representation in politics, unless it was as fashionable females attending public functions with their husbands. The Nazi emphasis on separate gender roles wasn't even a reflection of social reality. Although women undertook most domestic roles, they absolutely laboured in factories, on farms and in offices. They just weren't praised for it unless it suited a Nazi narrative.

Gertrud Sholtz-Klink, leader of the Frauenschaft, emphasised the social importance of women's voluntary endeavours, declaring, 'Each of us has an unbreakable bond to the community.' For the Nazis, 'community' deliberately and maliciously excluded Jews.[14]

'There is no area in which human beings are so precious and so indispensable as in the household and in the family!' was the bright declaration from the *Deutsche Hauswirtschaft* editorial in January 1939. Such a statement showed a callous indifference to households broken up by Nazi policies. Jock's mother Mania certainly was both 'precious' and 'indispensable' once her husband had been forcibly taken. Society lauded men as breadwinners and protectors, as sturdy bulwarks against the outside world. Where did that leave the women without men? Jewish husbands and fathers had already had their roles battered by successive laws restricting or stealing their livelihoods. Jewish wives and mothers had to draw on all their personal and community resources to reshape their roles.

The ultimate lie was that the Nazis prized motherhood. They did not. True, Hitler did emphasise the mother's heroism, declaring, 'Every child she brings into the world is a battle, a battle she wages for the existence of her people.'[15] His vision only included so-called Aryan women. In reality, there was no existential war for German nationhood, except in Hitler's mania-fuelled rhetoric. The real battle, one that Mania Heidenstein was absolutely prepared to fight with whatever resources she could muster, was for mothers to save their Jewish children from Nazi persecution.

Help was there. The Jewish community had long, necessary experience taking care of those in need. Under Third Reich domination, the need was endless. Economic assistance programs gave legal advice, moral support and loans for Jewish workers harassed from their jobs or simply banned from employment. As early as 1933, companies in the Berlin textile trade arranged collections of clothing and fabrics to support the most beleaguered dealers stay in business. Groups such as the Jewish Women's Association assisted professional women network for opportunities. Money was raised to help beleaguered Jews emigrate.[16]

Winter was always hardest for people in need. Excluded from the national Winter Aid programs, Jews in Germany established their own Jewish Winter Aid, with many tens of thousands of people registered. A large proportion of these were in Berlin. They were able to help the community thanks to money levied from synagogue donations, collection tins and community taxes. Self-employed workers such as Chaim Heidenstein would have chipped in, perhaps not realising that one day his family would be receiving help rather than donating it. Clothing collections were all part of the scheme, to help warm those who most had need – all in defiance of Nazi oppression.

At least in the bitter winter months of 1939 the Heidenstein girls had the comfort of their matching red woollen sweaters. Red as a colour has many meanings in human society. Although some associate it with blood, or passion, in Europe there have also been historic links with protection – a superstition that red clothing, such as cloaks, could ward off danger. After the open violence of Kristallnacht, Mania knew it would take more than warm red sweaters to keep danger at bay. She, like thousands of others, had to be active in trying to salvage what she could from the wreckage of Jewish life in Germany.

It was the same for the Lasker family in Breslau. Anita Lasker's father, Alfons, actually travelled to Berlin after Kristallnacht to see if there were more openings in the bureaucracy of emigration there. In between appointments to apply for visas he wrote letters to contacts in England. He had one main focus: get his daughters to safety. Marianne, Renate and Anita were all at Breslau, anxiously waiting to learn if there was a way out, perhaps via a dynamic network of people trying to organise the legal escape of at-risk minors. This exodus initiative for children became known as Kindertransport.

Without a father present, Jock and her sisters had to rely on the extended Orthodox community to try to find a way out. Luckily, there was talk of a rabbi from England who might be able to help – a charming maverick named Dr Solomon Schonfeld.

'Winter can get grim,' sympathised a magazine article from 1943, with tips on how to stave off the cold when wool, food and fuel were limited.[17]

Four years before this advice, Jews in Berlin knew only too well how grim things could be. It is hoped that in winter 1938 Chaim was warmed by the awareness that plans were under way to rescue Jewish children from Germany, and that his daughter Jock would possibly be among them.

When You Hear Your Name, Please Come Forward

The children must be rescued as fast as possible.
– *Jewish Chronicle*, 18 NOVEMBER 1938

You're packing for a journey. Destination, uncertain. Length of stay, unknown. The suitcase isn't for you. It's for your child. You cannot go with them. What will you pack?

In January 1939, Mania Heidenstein had this task. Her oldest daughter, Jock, was leaving Germany. On one level packing was a series of practical decisions. What would fit? What would the Germans permit? Then there was the question of lugging it. Jock later wrote of her journey, 'I remember bringing with me a suitcase, which had to weigh no more than what could be carried by the child.'

Jock was a strong, healthy girl. She could heft a case. Even so, how do you fit what's needed into a single case or rucksack?

Entwined with any practical decisions about packing were soul-gutting, heartbreaking emotions. Every action Mania took would twist her inside. Taking clothes from drawers, wrapping shoes in paper, tucking little treasures into rolled socks – all these things would be so ordinary and yet so staggering: a mother is sending a child away. The other children watched. Jock's brother Michael, known as Meschi, was particularly awestruck by the suitcase. Even this four-year-old knew it meant something important.

An open-ended one-way ticket to the unknown was a far cry from Anita Lasker's six-month stay in Berlin for cello lessons. Nevertheless Anita's parents were willing to repress their initial, natural instinct to keep the family together. Like Mania Heidenstein, they too wanted to get their girls to safety, even if this meant fleeing Germany entirely. England, Holland, Brazil, Shanghai – anywhere out of the Third Reich would be acceptable. The main things was to *get out*.

Telegrams, letters, international calls, newspaper pleas – every form of communication was co-opted to shout round the world – HELP US. Rejection was the norm. Most countries had tight refugee quotas despite the desperate need. In the months following Kristallnacht Anita's father tried all possible agencies and embassies in his attempts to secure visas to leave. He typed reams of letters, labouring over English where required, in courteous yet insistent requests for support. Any complacency about the situation in Germany was over. The November pogroms had seen to that. However, Dr Lasker's optimism was still strong. The eldest Lasker girl, Marianne, was working to secure the paperwork needed to emigrate to Palestine via England. She was a very capable eighteen-year-old and eager to take up the challenge of life on a kibbutz. Surely something could be done for Renate and Anita too? Maybe for the whole family, together?

A week after Kristallnacht the pleas for help intensified. Having a job in place was a requisite for emigration in many countries, including Great Britain. Among advertisements for woollen materials, new suits and quilted bedspreads, the English newspaper the *Jewish Chronicle* featured long lists of appeals:

> 'unexpectedly without income, seeks immediately any kind of work'

'seeks position immediately'
'urgent appeal for existence.'[1]

In Germany those hoping to emigrate were doing everything possible to prepare for a new life, wherever this might be. The Breslau *Jewish Community Bulletin*, available at the Lasker's local synagogue, had the usual ads for new fashions and rooms to let, laced with special offers promoting both rainwear and tropical clothes for emigrants. A series of lectures was advertised, including talks on 'Emigration issues,' 'Necessary knowledge for the emigrant,' 'Jewish migration.' Occupational training was offered to would-be welders, dressmakers, carpenters and electricians – all trades considered useful for a migrant. Even the prayer for the Jewish New Year included a wish for 'accelerated, intensified and regulated emigration.'[2] The focus was clear: Get out.

Kristallnacht broke more than glass. It cracked the complacency of all those who said things weren't so bad; that all the unpleasantness would blow over. Now, after such a shameless orgy of violence, there could be no solid excuses for not recognising the danger and doing something about it.

'You are asked not only to feel but to act,' implored Eleanor Rathbone, one of the many dynamic advocates for rescuing victims of Nazi persecution.[3]

Emotions ran high in Britain, one of the possible havens for refugees, both from those calling for humanitarian action and those warning against inundations of Jews. A compromise emerged from government debates. There would be a loosening of red tape for a limited number of applicants, dropping the need for emigration visas and passports, but only for unaccompanied minors.

As rumours of a scheme to save children spread, through posters, pamphlets, newspaper ads and word of mouth door-to-door, the pressure was on to make it work. There were well over sixty thousand German Jewish children at risk yet only ten thousand places in England. The British government enabled the initiative and established a fund of money. Beyond that all the work and money-raising was left to an array of charities, religious groups and committees, staffed by eager, earnest, ordinary people. The acronyms of all these organisations were confusing enough, let alone their overlapping roles and conflicting methods. Then there were all the different bureaucracies that had to be negotiated before any ideals could be turned into reality. The resulting maelstrom of paperwork had to be sent across the Channel and back, without the benefit of email or even a fax machine. The stalwart aid workers fought injustice and persecution armed only with typewriters and telephones.

Berlin was home to the HQ of the Central Organisation of Jews in Germany – *Reichsvertretung der Juden in Deutschland*. The Children's Immigration department – *Kinderauswanderung Abteiling* – had the unenviable job of scouting for and selecting children who would be placed on the Kindertransport. They were a remarkable and talented team, and one of several Jewish-run departments turning emotion into action. Across the English Channel were equally dedicated counterparts seeking out foster homes or hostels for when the children began to arrive.[4] Inevitably, there was, at first, an intense muddle of conflicting strategies towards a common goal. Luckily for Jock Heidenstein, she – and other Orthodox children – had a particular champion. Called a conquering hero by his admirers, and unprintable epithets by those he crossed, there was perhaps no one more tireless, more capable of cutting through administrative chaos and, to the authorities, no one more exasperating than the man who'd help save Jock: Rabbi Dr Solomon Schonfeld.

Dr Solomon Schonfeld was used to taking responsibility. His father, Victor, was Chief Rabbi of the Orthodox community in England, having worked his way up from a small-town family on the Danube in Hungary. His mother, Ella, had been a city girl from Budapest. It was lucky she had a strong character, because she had plenty to contend with – Victor died in 1930 leaving her with seven children, the youngest not even a year old. There wasn't much time for sentiment with a large household to feed and take care of. Remembered as impressive yet daunting, Ella Schonfeld was the sort of person who never asked her grandchildren how they were, only if they'd done their homework.[5] After Victor's death, their twenty-eight-year-old son, Solomon, was appointed Chief Rabbi in his father's place, taking over the role of religious leader, mentor, breadwinner, and organiser. Inheriting his mother's forcefulness worked to his advantage, particularly when matched with his own impetuous generosity. He was an unstoppable force – and did not consider laws or bureaucracy to be unmovable objects.

One of Dr Schonfeld's sons summed it up well: 'He got a feel for what was going on and decided something had to be done about it.'[6]

Both impulsive and wayward at times, Dr Schonfeld inevitably needed a superb support staff to ensure his grand schemes and promises could actually be carried out. Everyone he knew ran the risk of being drawn into his plans, or at the very least inconvenienced by them. Dr Schonfeld's sister Asenath – known as Senath, and described as 'mad and wonderful' – even undertook a marriage of convenience with a Jewish refugee named Ernest Petrie, to enable him to escape Europe. On one occasion his brother Akiva – now Sir Andrew Schonfeld – returned home from term at Oxford to find one refugee sleeping in his bed and another one underneath it. 'My father just took over the house,' remembers Schonfeld's son Jeremy, without rancour.[7]

Schonfeld's administrative team included his wife, Judith Hertz. Her name can be seen in paper trails of refugee

documentation, and she was responsible for the children's department of the Chief Rabbi's Religious Emergency Council – the
CRREC. Being such a meticulous, well-educated woman, a gradu-
ate of Somerville College, Oxford, her husband's flamboyant Scarlet
Pimpernel style could be frustrating at times. Dr Schonfeld laid out
his ideas on gender roles for men and women, yet appreciated the
intelligence and dynamism of women in organisations he headed.
When he emphasised that 'the family is the foundation-stone of real
civilisation,' his concept of family was broad enough to include the
care offered by those who fostered, people in hostels and every child
who needed a father figure.[8]

Dr Schonfeld focused on the religious poor. Funds were raised
from the Orthodox community, where Schonfeld was known, well
embedded and very well liked. In 1938, when he quite literally went
door-to-door asking how many refugees each household could welcome, there would be few who could resist his charm and positivity.
He embraced what were seen as traditional English values, such as
'fair play' and 'mucking in.' In this sense he saw the Nazis as bullies,
and you had to stand up to bullies. Schonfeld truly did 'muck in,'
racking up thousands of miles as he crossed Europe gathering both
strays and support. His networks stretched across the US, Siberia,
Shanghai and Palestine.

One thing is obvious: despite all his many responsibilities, Dr
Schonfeld took the time to get to notice everyone who came under
his aegis, including child refugees. When asked if his father liked
children, his son Jeremy replied with energy, 'Oh yes! He was a real
twinkler – very playful and a hugger, and recognised them even
when they were older.'

This was one of the champions responsible for helping bring
Jock Heidenstein to England. Because of Dr Schonfeld's advocacy,
and the stamina of countless quietly heroic aid workers, Mania

Heidenstein had to help pack a suitcase: Jock had been allocated a Kindertransport place.

And here is Jock: the earliest photograph of her known to survive. Just an ordinary girl, only eleven and a half years old, looking

Jochewet 'Jock' Heidenstein
Courtesy of Tamar Abrams

straight at the camera for a passport-size picture. She has a nice expression, a pleasant face – perhaps a hint of mischief? There is nothing, absolutely nothing, that should single her out for persecution, yet because she was Jewish the Third Reich decreed her unfit to keep her German citizenship and live in safety.

Her new identity card needed a photograph. The camera flashed, and there she is, preserved on the brink of leaving one life for another. When uncovering a person's history it makes all the difference to see a face to go with the name. As gazes meet, we make a connection. Suddenly Jock seems more real, even to those who've never known her. Her face is captured. Her thoughts and emotions at that time – unknown.

Certainly nothing about her departure would be easy. Official approval was required every step of the way. On the German side of bureaucracy, Kindertransport applicants had to provide sheafs of paperwork, including health certificates, school certificates and financial statements. Staff were overwhelmed with thousands of applications each month, not to mention the deluge of desperate parents visiting the office in hope of influencing outcomes. Who can blame them? But what a torment, to be urging the very thing that will break up the family and take children away from parental protection.

Jock's photograph was stamped and authorised by a German registrar on 11 January 1939, marked with a swastika carried by the Reich eagle. Apart from that, her paperwork to leave was remarkably banal looking, considering its importance. She was given the number 2241.

On the English side of administration, all documents had to be checked, and there was the not-so-small matter of money. Each child had to have a guarantor willing to pay fifty pounds. One reason for anti-immigrant sentiment was a fear – baseless or otherwise – that refugees would either be a burden on England's patchy welfare system, or that they'd 'take' jobs from English people. Fifty pounds in 1939 is the equivalent of roughly two thousand pounds in 2024 – a sizable amount, particularly for families cut off from any form of income. Once again the Jewish community rallied round to pay what they could. The English government also created a special fund to support aid agency work. Elaine Blond, of the famous Marks family – as in, Marks & Spencer shops – helped raise money and awareness. She lamented, 'However fast the money came in it was never quite enough.'[9]

Of course, all of this expense could have been spared had Jewish people been left to live their lives at home. Ironically, for all the National Socialist regime wanted to pressure Jews to leave the country, there was a strict ban on taking money or valuables out of Germany, which meant most refugees would be starting out in a strange land with almost no resources. The items they chose to pack in their single suitcase took on great significance.

Among the precious items Jock packed for travel was a tiny album, the sort of cloth-covered book popular with girls for collecting mottoes, messages and sketches. It was bound in blue, green and yellow floral fabric. The pages are cream. Inside the cover is a carefully written message from Jock's friend Helene Kiwowicz: *In Memory of Your Friends*.[10]

Helene inserted her own passport photograph, showing another bright face, with a flip of hair and a white cotton collar. Among the other pictures is Hella, a girl with quite a grown-up face and wonderfully arched eyebrows. Her photo carries the words, *A Memento of Hella Sternlicht*.[11] Hella's sister Mimi was also one of Jock's friends. The message written by Mimi Sternlicht on her picture is illegible, so slanted and uncontained it almost falls off the photo paper. Mimi's face is sweet, and young. She's adorable. One photo has no name, just a little blond girl with the friendliest smile ever wearing a snazzy wool coat with a fur collar. Martl is the most glamorous. Her hair is sleek and rolled in a very chic style. On the back of her photo is a sentimental sigh in ink – *The date, oh I don't know, I think it's called forget-me-not. Your Martl*.[12]

In memory of . . . a memento of . . . forget-me-not . . . The simple messages carry a world of emotion.

Helene, Hella, Mimi . . . none of these girls got places on the Kindertransport. Their photographs were not stamped and approved for travel cards. Why was one child selected over another? There were simply more names than places. As Norbert Wollheim, one of the German Jewish organisers, recalled, 'Everybody was trying to get out.'[13]

Wollheim and his colleagues described their office as besieged. The letters poured out of post sacks, and the telephones never stopped ringing. While they desperately wanted to save as many children as possible, they still had to filter applications. The zeal of aid committees in trying to get children out cannot be overstated. The malicious obstruction of Nazi officials was a reminder just why Jews needed to leave in the first place. Jock's name was added to a list of children who could be salvaged. Anita Lasker's name was not, although other children from Breslau won the refugee lottery.[14] With a deluge of desperate requests for travel permits, mostly it all came down to sheer luck – who could go and who was forced to stay.

Jock's friends presented her with the little photo album on 15 January 1939. Jock's train was due to leave Berlin the very next day.

What to pack? What, of your familiar home life, to fit into a small case? Jock looked around her belongings, ready to make some difficult choices. There were strict limits on what Jews could take from the country, even when escaping to start a new life: only a restricted amount of basic household items and a change of clothing. No valuables. No large cash sums, just small change. Of course, suitcase contents also depended on how impoverished the family had become thanks to the Third Reich's squeeze on Jewish incomes.

Jock didn't have a lot of worldly goods. She took what seemed important. She had her travel pass, her birth certificate and a folder with her school reports, since she intended to continue learning in England. There was also a treasured manicure set, and her newly gifted photograph album from Helene, Mimi, Hella and Martl.

'I remember bringing with me a suitcase, which had to weigh no more than what could be carried by the child,' she later recalled. 'Inside it had some special things. Otherwise the contents consisted only of clothing which, incidentally, I very soon grew out of.'[15]

Every wise parent on a budget knew that clothes had to be big enough to grow into. Children in thrifty households understood they'd start a new school term in sweaters with too-long sleeves, and that winter began with voluminous coats, deep hems on skirts and tucks that could be let out. Being swamped by new clothes was a rite of passage in poorer households. For child refugees in oversize clothes there was an added implicit message – these clothes not only had to last because new things were pricey, but also due to the very real fear that parents might not be around to buy the next batch. With growth spurts in mind, some mothers also gave their daughters hurried lectures about puberty and tucked folded cotton sanitary napkins in among the clothes.[16]

Among Jock's grown-out-of garments was a blue cotton blouse that she had sewn herself, at school. It didn't take up much room in the suitcase: just a very plain blue T-shape, enlivened by three bands of optimistic crochet at the neck in royal blue and coral pink, and fastened at the front by a zip that's more-or-less stitched straight. In fact, the blouse never fitted, so Jock never wore it. However, she kept it all her life.[17]

Inevitably, adults sending children to England wanted them to make a good impression – no holes in socks, unravelling sweaters or cracked shoes if possible. There was only so much space in a case after all; why shouldn't the children take their best things? On the other hand, looking *too* smart reinforced an anti-immigration narrative about refugees not truly being in need of financial support or hospitality. One thing was certain: having the right clothes would help children fit in with their new foster families, while having the wrong clothes would signal the children as outsiders. Rejected by their own country for being Jewish, they would be 'othered' all over again. There was an implicit tangle of social rules to navigate.

Jock's blue blouse is one of many clothing mementos of the Kindertransport. Many museums and private collections now have a poignant selection of souvenirs of the journey away from home. There are religious items such as prayer books and tallit shawls.

Practical objects such as sewing kits, cutlery, fountain pens or German-English dictionaries. Useful linens such as pillow slips and tablecloths, individualised with bright embroidery. Aspirational belongings, including sheet music, drawing books and even ice skates – objects that speak of the life the refugees hoped to have once they reached safety. Dolls, cuddly toys and teddies for comfort. Handkerchiefs for tears or runny noses.

All ordinary. None valuable. All priceless.

In the normal jumble of peacetime life, everyday pens, pillow slips and pullovers would be used until lost, damaged or discarded. Tired woollens would be scrapped or knitted into something new. Jock's red sweater is a notable exception. It was not unravelled. Unlike her life.

Did she wear it for the journey, or fold it into her suitcase? Either way, it made the selection when the suitcase was packed. It would travel to England with her. And then the summons – short notice – time and place of departure. The suitcase lid was squashed flat; the clasps were fastened.

Trains waited under the great arched roofs of Berlin train hubs

Sweater bought for Jock Heidenstein in Berlin.
Imperial War Museum (EPH3909)

such as the Haupthanhof or Friedrichstrasse station. Jock's departure date was 16 January 1939. It was night. A time of bright lamps, dark shadows and cold breaths.

One of the criteria for approving a child's application to escape Germany was parents' willingness to let them go. The fact that parents would be separated from their children in such conditions is testament to both their love and their desperation. Who could feel *willing* at the station, untwining little arms from around their necks, or letting go of small hands for possibly the last time?

There were few fathers bringing children for departure. Those who hadn't yet been arrested were keen to avoid it. Jock's father, Chaim, was a few miles north of Berlin, enduring a bitter winter in Sachsenhausen. As for Mania, German police blocked her from waving her oldest daughter off from the platform. Families were not allowed up to the train, under pain of having the child taken off the transport. Parents and children were ordered to keep their emotions, their grief and distress, for the relative privacy of a nearby room that organiser Norbert Wollheim had rented. God forbid German citizens might be disturbed by such obvious evidence that Jews were human, not vermin, as the propaganda would have them believe. Witnessing Jewish distress, some non-Jews might have dared to feel critical of a regime that forced a child out of the country just to survive. Or perhaps bystanders just didn't want to be disturbed at all. They preferred to hide in the fantasy that as long as they were safe it didn't matter what happened to others.

There were many ordinary people facilitating the exodus of young people aside from the Jewish helpers. German officials who were unlikely to see themselves as complicit in any crimes. Those who reviewed passenger lists; who checked tickets and searched luggage, did they see children under all the coats, scarves, hats and bag straps, or did they just see Jews? Were they relieved the children were travelling to safety, or glad to see the back of unwanted offspring? Only doing their job, or savouring the moment? At the end of the shift, when they'd trudged home and peeled off their own woollen layers, what did they report about their day?

It was business as usual for the Third Reich. Train after train – successive departures.

All too soon came the moment when Norbert Wollheim, who ultimately oversaw twenty transports from Berlin, would stand on a chair to declare, 'Now it's your last goodbye.'[18]

Emotions were bound by the constraints of a railways timetable. Sometimes there was uncontrollable crying; sometimes an unnerving silence. Then whistles blowing. Steam billowing. Pistons turning. Childhood – ending.

'We'll follow you in a few weeks!' was a repeated cry from parents.[19]

Jock, along with ninety-two other children on her transport, was given into the charge of six adult escorts. She let go of her mother's hand, and climbed into a carriage with her suitcase. Perhaps her heart was beating hard under her red sweater. Perhaps, in fine older-sister fashion, she took care of younger children sharing her compartment, who maybe reminded her of Rita, Gisela, David and Michael. Mania returned home, but probably not to sleep. There was one less place to set at the table for breakfast the next day.

Jock's suitcase didn't stay stowed for long. Any children feeling a sense of adventure during the journey were brought back to reality when Nazi officials came on board and harassed every compartment of Jewish children. They pulled luggage down, tipped out the contents and snatched up whatever took their fancy. All those carefully packed clothes and love tokens, treated like rubbish. Nazis had no respect for people or property when it came to Jewish emigrants. As one English aid worker put it, 'The armed guards liked to give a lasting impression of their authority.'[20] One girl making the crossing to England had a brand new red dressing gown in her suitcase. Luckily, her mother had the foresight to give it a good pummel in the laundry, so it lost its new sheen and passed inspection: new clothes were not permitted for children on the transports.[21] Jock's red sweater wasn't considered an infraction of this rule, looking neither new or valuable – at least, not valuable in the Nazi sense of the word. To Jock it was priceless.

The adult escorts were helpless against Nazi officials. They knew that Jewish children might be removed from the train on a whim, or the whole transport denied passage. They were at risk of arrest themselves, only allowed to travel to England on condition that they returned within a few days. Jock's guardians for the journey on 16 January were six selfless individuals. Being a child, Jock may never have given them a thought beyond following their tall forms through crowds at stations and ports.

There was Dr Erna Davidsohn, an experienced paediatrician ejected from her profession for being Jewish. She ensured the passage of several transports to Britain and Sweden. Despite being described as 'a person of impeccable character' and 'extremely trustworthy and reliable,' she was consistently refused a visa to escape herself.[22]

With Dr Davidsohn was a head teacher called Dr Fridolin Friedmann, a special education worker called Irma Zancker and committed volunteers Dora Zegall and Dorothea Magnus. Not forgetting Else Hoffa of Hamburg, who had the distinction of being Germany's first professional head gardener. She gave up rose gardens and water lilies for the task of saving children, although it was by no means certain if any of the escorts would be able to save themselves.[23]

Jock's train left, heading for Hamburg, in time to take a ship across the English Channel to Southampton. The ship was a luxury liner called the SS *Manhattan*, only eight years old when Jock came on board. On the night voyage there wasn't chance to enjoy the sun deck, swimming pool or gymnasium.[24] The children lunched before embarkation, enjoying food and delicious cocoa at the Jewish Domestic Science School. Then they were taken by bus through snowy Hamburg and to the port, with views of electric trolley buses and winter sales in the shop – everything going on as normal.[25] Among all the adults helping Jock's group some well-meaning but misguided souls decided to arrange a party for the sea crossing. Containing large groups of children is a challenging task at the best of times, like herding cats. Adding ice-cream into the mix on board was asking for trouble given the Channel's notoriety for choppy waters. Some children never made it as far as the party. Wolfgang Dieneman, already disorientated by the transition from normal citizen to outcast, was highly disgruntled to be sick on the boat over, complaining, 'My sister had ice-cream and enjoyed herself.'[26] Hot chocolate, plus party food, plus twenty-four hours of choppy sea – this nauseating combination meant that many children disembarked not only grubby from travel, but also marked with evidence of pungent seasickness.

How did Jock feel coming down the gangplank into England? By the time she arrived at Southampton, the newspapers, so keen to cover the poignancy of the first Kindertransport arrivals in Harwich, in December 1938, had moved on to new dramas. There were no photographers to capture her first steps in a new country, or her red sweater. She had a ride across the town of Southampton on a double-decker bus, then her first English breakfast – hot porridge with a lovely crust of brown sugar – then a train to London and the start of a new life. She would be allocated to a foster home far from her real home and her real family. Strangers had put up the fifty pounds needed to guarantee a place.

'I will now read the list of names,' was the routine spiel for child distribution at the pre-arranged dispersal point. 'When you hear your name, please come forward.'[27]

Jock stepped forward into her new life. One child out of nearly ten thousand saved by the Kindertransport. One child out of many tens of thousands still at risk.[28]

A young boy leaving Berlin later said, 'Those who stayed behind envied us.'[29] It was certainly stressful for Anita Lasker's family, stuck in Breslau, still thwarted in all their efforts to find safety. Anita's mother recognised the futility of expecting the whole family to be salvaged together. Her focus was all on getting her three girls to safety, writing, 'If only there were some prospects for the children.'[30]

Soon it wouldn't only be Jewish children in Germany endangered by Nazi policies. After gaining the Sudetenland, Austria and part of Czechoslovakia, Adolf Hitler had his eye on Poland next. The children there would need very different survival strategies.

4

We Do Not Know Where It Will End

*Hast du schon von Mutti Post bekommen? – Did you get
any post from Mummy yet?*
– RITA HEIDENSTEIN TO HER SISTER GISELA,
12 AUGUST 1939

What does it mean, to *belong*?

Is it a sense of place, of time or continuity?

When we are uprooted, can we keep enough sense of self to
know where we are from, as well as where we have been replanted?

'I want to be thought of as completely English,' said one girl
saved by the Kindertransport. Even after making England her home
for many years and becoming a naturalised citizen she was aware
that she would always be different from what she called *real* English people. In her mind, the simple act of knitting set her apart. 'I
still cannot knit the English way,' she said, 'and for that reason will
never knit in public.'[1] She couldn't trust that she wouldn't instinc-
tively revert to the method learned at home.

The difference between German and English knitting is slight
but noticeable to those in the know. The English technique is to
hold working yarn in the right hand while the German – or Con-

tinental – style uses the left. That's it. Yet it was enough to generate feelings of unease in the girl who wanted to fit in so badly she would only knit in private. The state of belonging is precarious. It can break as easily as a broken yarn.

Jock Heidenstein was a keen knitter all her life, whichever hand held her yarn. In the mid-twentieth century it was so normal for girls to knit they probably never registered it as a particular skill. Anita Lasker, when asked in later life about her knitting skills, was almost bemused at the question. 'Of course I can knit!' she exclaimed, as if it were the most natural yet inconsequential thing in the world.[2]

Knitting might seem too ordinary to merit attention, but this everyday act of looping yarn on needles was a powerful generational link at a time when too many families in Europe were being divided. It would be a mother, grandmother, sister or aunt who first helped little fingers hold the knitting needles, who first showed how to cast on, keep tension and make a row of stitches. Childhood letters between Jock and her two sisters, Rita and Gisela, are sprinkled with references to knitting.

'I am knitting ever such a lot,' wrote Jock.

'I have knitted a pair of socks and a cardigan,' Rita informed Gisela, with no small pride.[3]

When Jock first came to England, housed first in Rabbi Schonfeld's family home in London, then with a sponsor not so many streets away, it was deep winter.[4] Temperatures in the city dipped to minus 7°C with a light crust of snow on pavements, parks and rooftops. Woollen underwear and wool accessories were vital for warmth. Layering was the key to combating the cold. British shoppers pulled on boots and galoshes when shopping for long johns and jersey combinations, or they pulled their armchairs closer to the fire while knitting homemade woollen knickers and vests. In January 1939 many Londoners might have been sporting woolly hats, gloves and scarves gifted at Christmas. Humble woollies were not scorned as presents.

Jock had only a meagre stock of clothes in her single suitcase, including an old taffeta dress from Berlin which had to be made over into a skirt and bolero once she'd grown out of it. Her sister Gisela had a dress of the same fabric. Their mother obviously liked her daughters to be connected through their clothes, including the three red sweaters they'd all owned in Berlin.

Months passed. Spring warmth meant Jock would put away her snug jumper. Back in Berlin, spring did not produce a thaw in Jewish persecution, although by summer Jock's father, Chaim, would miraculously be released from Sachsenhausen concentration camp, along with her uncle Wolf. They could not be sure if the respite was temporary or permanent. They knew Germany wasn't safe for any of them. Mania was especially anxious to get the remaining children to safety: Rita, Gisela, David and Michael needed sanctuary somewhere.

Jock's school friends were also hoping to follow her across the Channel. Almost every day Mimi Sternlicht came to the Heidenstein home to ask about Jock and to say how much she wanted to go to England.

While other Berliners enjoyed spring sunshine in the beautiful Tiergarten perhaps, or splashed out on new spring fashions promoted with 'Aryan-only production' labels, Mimi and all Jewish people in Berlin were tangled in a nightmare of harassment, impoverishment and emigration dead ends. Hopes rose and fell as rumours of possible exit visas billowed like smoke then vanished. It was the same for Anita Lasker's family in Breslau.

The bureaucracy of borders kept them trapped in Germany – a country that had made it clear they certainly did not belong. Thanks to the heroic efforts of Kindertransport volunteers, rescue trains kept running through spring and summer of 1939. In a multitude of locomotive cabs firemen shovelled coal to burn into steam that pushed pistons and turned wheels. In each tethered carriage refugees waited for the moment when the border would be crossed and they could leave the Third Reich behind.

Lines drawn on a map meant the difference between fear and freedom. For all those who made it out of Germany, there were countless more hoping against hope that they would find a place. One joyful, sorrowful day, Mania Heidenstein learned that her youngest daughter Gisela was on a list for England.

It's not only place that gives a sense of belonging. *People* make all the difference.

Berlin was Gisela's hometown. All she'd ever known. She might have thought she was leaving all love behind when she gave one last wave to her family. In fact, there were kind souls on the journey who let her know that not all people would be hostile to Jews. Once across the border between Germany and Holland she got comfort and chocolate from Dutch women waiting for the train. One set of strangers – the antisemites in Germany – considered this seven-year-old girl to be an enemy, another – the Dutch volunteers – saw her as a tiny human in need of care. Gisela's journey demonstrated how humans could choose to veer towards hostility or helping.

It was Gisela's first time out of Berlin. First time to see the sea. First time on a ship – the boat from Holland to Harwich in England. From the port another train took her to London. She was a small girl, dwarfed by the massive railway architecture of the mustering point at Liverpool Street Station, and by the adults hustling all around her. She did not understand what was happening, but she knew her name at least. When it came to her turn to be called, a middle-aged lady called Mary was there to collect her. In appearance Mary Reid looked to be a quintessential English spinster – plain-faced and practical. In fact, she had a rather messy past featuring a divorced husband, abandoned lover and two estranged children. Only her own resilience and the support of the Salvation Army had dragged Mary out of the anaesthesia of alcohol.

Despite these offences against respectability, Mary was both extremely capable yet very warm-hearted. Her task that day in 1939 was to take little Gisela Heidenstein from Liverpool Street station to 209 Victoria Park Road in Hackney, east London, where Mary reigned as housekeeper and accountant. It was the home of Mrs Deborah Adler, known to friends and family as Debbie.

Debbie was a refugee herself, at once an alien to London and embedded in London life. She was technically born in Russia, as Deborah Dimant. She knew firsthand how borders could be disrupted. Her sense of home and place came under siege during multiple conflicts as Russia was engulfed in world war and revolution, and the new state of Latvia emerged out of the grasp of Russian and German empires.[5] One Dimant brother was conscripted into the Russian army, the other fled to England. Debbie did the same. Finding her feet meant a lot of adaption. For one thing, she anglicised her name to fit in better, from Dimant to Diamond. Refugees had to make these distortions to try to fit in. They had to be fractured from their past to earn a new future.

It helped that Debbie was an incredibly talented seamstress and could pick up work doing dressmaking and repairs. As a young woman she created all her own clothes – wonderfully fashionable concoctions of silk, gauze and beading. Shopping in Hackney one day, she entered the shop of H. Adler, kosher butcher. After a formal courtship, Herman Adler the butcher and Debbie the dressmaker married in 1919. Far from being a purely decorative wife, Debbie ran the butcher's with Herman. For special occasions she still shimmered in sequins and silk, with rosettes on her shoes, and sheer silk stockings. Everyday clothes were cotton wash frocks with thick stockings and sensible shoes.

'She worked hard,' said her daughter Betty, 'and it showed.'[6]

Getting carcasses for the shop involved a 3 a.m. start to make it to Smithfield meat market. It wasn't just work to earn money. Debbie's work involved supporting her community – both Christians and Jewish – and helping anyone in need.

After Herman's death from cancer in 1935, Debbie took over the whole business, as well as management of Adler properties, and the upbringing of two daughters, Betty and Lillie. It wasn't surprising she needed a housekeeper. She found Mary Reid at the Salvation Army, a Christian charity that she supported all her life, despite being Jewish. Mary was ferociously teetotal, no doubt because of past experiences. Mary wasn't the only one to find a refuge in the house behind the butcher's on Victoria Park Road. Debbie Adler was a proverbial port in a storm. Her home had once been grand enough to need a team of servants, answering summonses from bells in the basement. By the 1930s Debbie had to be more hands-on, with only Mary for help. She welcomed other refugees from Latvia – an energetic jumble of friends, relatives and children. In one quiet corner of the house was a mute woman of indeterminate origins who'd sit and sew and smile. Debbie's home at 209 Victoria Park road was a haven for those in need.

One Thursday in early summer 1939 Debbie acquired another stray – Gisela Heidenstein.

Even decades after the event, Debbie's older daughter, Betty, broke into tears remembering Gisela's arrival. Betty said she came home to find a little girl in the house, chatting away in German.

'She was terribly excited,' Betty recalled. 'She had no idea how tragic it was to leave her parents and come here.'[7]

Once installed at number 209, Gisela opened her luggage to show everyone what she'd brought, but the first thing she wanted to do was write to her mother and father, to let them know she'd arrived safely.

Always, there was the human desire to connect. At seven years old Gisela's writing was simple but earnest. In the letter remnants, there are repeated pleas in round pencilled words – *Please write to me*.

Please write to me . . .

The Heidenstein sisters absolutely did write. Their surviving correspondence makes for very poignant reading. The phrasing is at once polite – 'How are you? I hope you are well. I am well' – yet deeply loving. Mostly written on paper torn from school exercise books, the letters reveal a great deal about their excellent upbringing with Mania and Chaim, and about their mutual affection.

Rita began one letter to Jock, using her family pet name, 'Dear golden, sweet, beloved Eva.'

Gisela was called 'darling sister.'

Messages ended with 'lots of love and kisses.'[8]

Little Gisela certainly seemed to have swapped one loving home for another. Adler family photos show her being hugged by Mary Reid, the housekeeper, and by her new foster sisters, Betty and Lillie, not to mention Debbie's two nephews, Bernard and Kenneth Diamond, aged nine and five. In July, Gisela is seen with Bernard and Kenny at the open-air pool in nearby Victoria Park. In August she's at the seaside with a cotton print dress and breeze-blown curls. She's never alone in the photographs. Her pal Bernard became a perpetual playmate.

In this golden English summer there was no need for her red sweater – the one bought in Berlin to match Rita's and Jock's. Gisela's surreal new life needed knitwear of a different kind: sun suits and swimming costumes. She was too young to remember a time when Jews had been allowed to paddle or swim in German public parks. Now, in England, she was free to have fun, as all children should be.

Gisela 'Stella' Heidenstein with Bernard Diamond, summer 1939.
Courtesy of Diana Young

Photographs of Gisela evoke happy summer days at the lido or the seaside, kitted out in swimwear knitted by her friend Bernard's mother, and cheery cotton frocks. When the butcher's shop was closed for Sabbath, a big gang of family and friends would travel out to the east coast to picnic on clifftops. In the evening there'd be games of Monopoly, Snap and Solo whist.

It was all so wonderful . . . but it wasn't home. True, Gisela often wrote, 'It is very nice here,' but then she would add a wish such as, 'I hope that we will get together one day with our parents.'[9]

How did her mother, Mania, feel to receive letters talking of the cinematic delights Gisela was introduced to, such as Donald Duck cartoons, *Gone with the Wind* and slapstick comedies? Letters that mentioned gardens filled with roses, picking marigolds, learning Hebrew for the first time? Undoubtedly it was a relief to know that her youngest daughter had found such a haven with the Adler family, but what a painful contrast with the tense situation in Germany, and how searing to realise your child is beginning to belong in a different world; that she has crossed a border that you cannot follow. Several thousand enterprising Jewish women did gain visas to England as domestic servants, whether they'd been doctors, physicists or philanthropists before that. Mania might have hoped for the same, had she not been committed to the care of her little boys David and Michael, and Rita too.

Gisela had gone where her mother could not follow. Her summer passed in new experiences, learning new skills. Betty Adler was snapped by a roving camera, sitting in a deckchair in the sunny back garden, knitting, with a backdrop of roses on a trellis. Not long afterwards Gisela was delighted to report by letter to her parents, 'I can knit. I have knitted a dress and hat for a doll. They are very beautiful.'[10]

Gisela may not yet have been at the sweater level, but doll clothes were the perfect starter projects for first-time knitters, once they'd graduated from potholders and patchwork squares. In addition to all she'd brought in her suitcase, Gisela now had something that belonged to her new life. It didn't take long for this new life to push the old life away. Her first letters were written in German. Debbie spoke to her in Yiddish, which was similar to German. Yet within three weeks, surrounded by English friends, Gisela was chatting in English too. Somehow her foreign-sounding name was dropped and she became Stella, not Gisela, much as her big sister Jochewet became Jock.

Mania was helpless to object to these changes, knowing her daughters had to adapt to their new life, but she did write to Rita noting that 'Gisaly,' the affectionate diminutive version of Gisela, had become Stella. 'That name sounds so foreign, doesn't it?' was Mania's gentle comment.[11]

The assimilation was so swift that when middle sister, Rita, made it to England on a Kindertransport, Gisela/Stella struggled to communicate with her. Belonging in England came at a price.

She was forgetting her mother tongue. New words replaced the language of her first seven years of life. New memories pushed old ones aside.

Rita's transit to England was so stressful, in later life she came to believe she'd made it out of Berlin on the last possible train before all the borders closed to escapees on 1 September. In fact, she arrived in July. Who knows what frantic bureaucratic manoeuvrings had been necessary to take her from Mania's last embrace? On 26 July 1939, Rita's journey ended at a ladies' convalescent home in Sussex known as Wyberlye, a handsome country house owned by a Jewish-friendly organisation called the Grand Order of the Sons of Jacob.[12]

Despite being established as a haven for poor Jews, Wyberlye seemed grand enough to the fifty German girls billeted there, with private woods, a tennis court and golf course.[13] Rita was particularly impressed by a piano in one of the sitting rooms, and a friendly cat. 'We couldn't get over what a wonderful place it was,' remembered one of a Rita's classmates, Ester Müller.[14] A group photo taken at Wyberlye shows girls ranging from eight years old to seventeen, mostly in bright summer clothes. There are a few smiles, but many faces are apprehensive.

Even though Wyberlye was by all accounts a wonderful hostel, and Rita made friends with other German girls sharing dormitories in the converted coaching stables, it wasn't home. Of course she was homesick, like the other girls. How could she hope to belong? She was well looked after at the hostel, with food and clothing supplied by the Sons of Jacob, but she was hungry for more than food: for contact with her parents and siblings. Above all she wanted photographs. Reminders of those she loved and who loved her.

The Sons of Jacob vowed that the children housed at Wyberlye would be taken care of until there was a resolution of their homelessness – 'whether by restoration to their natural parents, or otherwise,' promised the Grand President.[15] As rumours of war intensified through the summer of 1939, a reunion with Mania and Chaim seemed an achingly improbable dream. Hitler's generals and economists strategized, surrounded by monumental architecture and mushrooming sycophants. Not for a moment did they spare a thought for ordinary families such as the Heidensteins. For the Nazis it was as if they didn't – or shouldn't – exist.

Existence in Nazi-controlled territories was unbearable for Jewish people. Those who could get out, fled. By July it was getting more and more difficult to find homes or hostels for children who made it to England. The Anglo-Jewish community rallied time after time.

In all the efforts to house young people – seen as the 'innocent,' acceptable face of immigration – few people had time to ask why government policies wouldn't broaden to save the equally innocent parents too, or to consider the emotional damage caused by family fragmentation. Refugee committees did agree that it was probably easier for children to be psychologically stable if they were placed in actual homes, like an echo of their former family lives. The problem was, there were thousands of refugees, and not everyone was willing to welcome a stranger.

It was particularly hard to find Orthodox homes. Rabbi Dr Solomon Schonfeld saw it as a very personal mission to ensure a continuity of religious practice. He was infuriated at the idea that Jewish children would be unable to follow their faith, or worse, would be baptised as Christians in their new foster homes. Saving lives was crucial, of course, but Schonfeld believed that doing so at the cost of Jewish heritage would mean a different kind of erasure. Integration brought loss as well as belonging.

Originally Jock Heidenstein had been intended for the care of Debbie Adler in Hackney. However, although the Adlers observed high holidays and the Sabbath, and enrolled Stella in Hebrew classes with Bernard and Kenneth, they were liberal while Jock was deeply observant. Jock's sense of belonging came through carrying and continuing her faith, regardless of borders. For this reason, Dr Schonfeld decided Jock should be placed with Orthodox Jews, and Stella took Jock's place in the Adler household.

One day the Adler girls took Stella to see her sister Jock, heading up from Victoria Park to the very Jewish area of Stoke Newington. When they arrived at Jock's foster home, Jock was on her knees scrubbing the floor, a task usually reserved for housewives or charladies. When Jock sat stitching an apron back at the Jewish school in Berlin, she could hardly have imagined a future in which she wore it to clean an English house. One stricture of the Kindertransport was that girls were not to be accepted purely so they could act as unpaid servants. Abuse of this rule was not unknown. Nor were other kinds of abuse, either physical or neglectful.

Jock must have been delighted to see her little sister, although she looked embarrassed to be caught doing housework.

'How lovely!' she exclaimed, admiring their frocks, made by Debbie Adler.

Betty Adler felt sorry for Jock, commenting, 'She never looked happy, never dressed nicely . . . She had a hard time.'[16]

Jock kept her feelings and experiences private.

On one occasion Dr Schonfeld visited the Adlers with Jock, enquiring if Stella would prefer to move to an Orthodox household. Stella would not. She had found somewhere to belong. She was becoming more liberal and more English week by week. Life in number 209 crowded out memories of Linienstrasse 83a. Now she was familiar with the patterns of life in the Adler household, such as washing in a tin bath, Sunday dinners with chicken soup and a roast, and Debbie Adler's homemade pasta noodles drying on the back of chairs.[17]

In their earnest and effortful correspondence – what young child naturally writes long, chatty letters? – Rita adopted Gisela's new name, Stella. Learning English was harder.

'I am very surprised that you do not know any German at all,' Rita complained to Stella in December 1939. 'I can never read your letters. But one of our big girls translates it.'

Stella was distressed not to be able to write in German to their mother, and asked Rita to copy her English letter into German before it went on to Berlin. From writing in German – *Ich kann stricken* – Stella evolved to English only – *I can knit* – albeit with a seven-year-old's grasp of spelling. To Rita she wrote, 'I can knit and I have knitted Kenny a skuf.' Her pal Kenneth Diamond had a cold, it seems, but Stella's scarf would remedy that: 'the wool I am knitting with is blue. It is very nice wool.'[18]

Five-year-old Kenny Diamond probably had no strong feelings about this nice blue scarf, or memories that he'd ever been gifted it. It would be a tiny detail in a busy childhood and an eventful life. Perhaps Stella's gift was the usual tactic of someone who's crafted a garment and doesn't quite know what to do with it. There is no proof that the scarf was ever finished. At that age, many an ambitious project begins as a scarf and ends as a far smaller item, such as a pencil case or purse. Perhaps the scarf was a token of Stella's appreciation to the Diamonds and Adlers for taking her in and loving her as one of the family. Gratitude was important. For refugees, the situation was always precarious. Bureaucrats had begrudgingly permitted them temporary lives in England. If they lost their sponsors or billets they would be homeless and helpless.

'I hope you are a good girl,' Jock wrote to her little sister, Stella.

Rita echoed the sentiment, writing to Mrs Adler, 'thank you for taking care of Stella and being so kind to us all.'[19]

When Stella inevitably acted up and misbehaved – what child

wouldn't? – Jock took on a parental role, writing long lectures about Stella's responsibilities towards her host family.

'I hope that you quite realize what you owe and we all owe to our dear Mrs Adler. I am sure that you understand and appreciate your good home, and the love with which you are being treated. Treasure it and respect it dear, and try to retain it for good and always. Never let go of it for a moment.'[20]

Bernard and Kenny Diamond were wonderful friends. There was also local boy Sidney Cohen, happy to join in with games and cinema trips. Stella did not talk about her past with them; about her life in Berlin. They could not take the place of her little brothers David and Michael. Stella was understandably worried about them. Mania reassured her by letter, 'They are all well.'

Mania hadn't given up hope of escaping Berlin with her husband and their two little boys. She wrote to Rita in August 1939, 'We want to get out and come to you in the quickest way possible.'[21] Chaim wasn't in great health after his long ordeal in Sachsenhausen. 'He's having stomach trouble,' she wrote in one letter, while Chaim pencilled 'Hellos and kisses' onto another letter for Jock in July 1939. After his experiences in Sachsenhausen concentration camp it would be agonising to think of Mania or the children suffering in such a place, and being powerless to protect them.

Little Stella was right to be worried. Those who said it couldn't get any worse were wrong.

Meanwhile, in Breslau, Anita Lasker's father was writing too. Letter after letter. To consulates, to relatives in America, to possible sponsors. There was great joy in the Lasker household in Breslau when Anita's oldest sister, Marianne, secured a precious work visa for England. She arrived there around the same time as Stella Heidenstein. Edith Lasker wrote to her daughter begging, 'Do whatever you can for your sisters and for us. You have got the photographs – show them around! One really has to try everything.'[22] Then, more joy – Renate, the middle Lasker girl, had a place confirmed with an English couple. Her train was due to leave on 10 September. Alfons Lasker crafted a letter in careful English, full of gratitude, and also with a request for information on how to provide the correct English school uniform.

'My wife could do it herself, if you kindly would send us a sketch and a pattern. We should be thankful too for some instructions about stockings, shoes, hat, and the like,' he wrote.[23]

In vain.

On 1 September 1939, Germany invaded Poland. Hitler had already demonstrated that one of his artistic talents was re-drawing borders, those imaginary lines marked on maps to suit the power structures of the moment. Poland's borders were violated. They couldn't keep invaders out. Germany's borders, in contrast, became as effective as prison bars. Renate Lasker's Kindertransport train never left the country. She was stuck in Breslau with Anita. Two days later Britain declared war on Germany. Jock Heidenstein and her sisters were stranded in a country that considered them enemy aliens.

'We do not know where it will end,' mourned a writer for the Dutch magazine *Libelle* on 1 September 1939, in an article between ads for knitting wool and knitting patterns. Jews across Europe would all too soon learn what sort of ending the Nazis had planned for them. To survive, luck, resilience and ingenuity would be needed more than ever.

Weather the Storm

Sending you hellos and a hundred thousand kisses, your
Mother who loves you.

– MANIA HEIDENSTEIN TO HER DAUGHTER RITA,

1939

Anywhere can be safe.

Until it's not.

So much is about luck. The luck of being born in the right place, to the right family, with the right passport, the right appearance, sex, health, religion . . .

A storm can ravage any relationship, or any community. When winds, rain, snow or floods surge, people take shelter. They emerge and re-build. Luck comes into it, as does privilege – who has the safest shelter, or who lives on the highest ground, or who can afford insurance. In a regime driven by hatred, the storm damage comes from people, not weather, from violence within communities; from violence of invasion. Is anywhere safe from such hatred?

Jock Heidenstein had been buffeted by luck – good and bad – throughout 1939. Living as a child refugee in London felt precarious at times. When the daughter of her host family fell ill, Jock had to pack her red jumper, her knitting needles and other meagre belongings to go stay with a refugee rabbi.[1] It was hard to hold on to a sense of home when her sisters were living such different lives – Stella in the quite up-market home of the Adler family and Rita in a country house hostel – and when her parents were still trapped in Berlin with little brothers David and Michael.

News came in precious letters, only a few of which have survived the tumult of war and subsequent decades, stored in a modest Tupperware tub by Heidenstein descendants. Through letters and postcards Jock learned that her dear relatives were scattering across Europe all looking for safe havens. Some, naturally enough, went to Poland, the homeland of their ancestors. Her uncle Leo – one of her father Chaim's many siblings – made it over Germany's eastern border into Poland. In 1933, when the Nazi Party came to power, Leo Heidenstein fell afoul of the law for harbouring communists in his home. He had worked his way up from being a rag dealer in Berlin to owning his own ready-to-wear clothing shop, which had to be abandoned when he fled to Krakow, in the Lower Silesia region of Poland.[2] Jock's aunt Esther had already left Berlin to be with her husband Juda in Krakow too. Could Jock's parents return to their native land, even if it meant putting more miles between them and their daughters in England? Would it be safer there?

Jock's mother Mania had extended family in Poland still, the Finks, including a cousin of the same name and age as Jock – Jocheved Eva Fink. Eva Fink lived in a small town about sixty miles from Lviv. It was a different world from Jock's life in London. The Finks were well rooted in their community, considered to be scholarly, with highly respected rabbis. This esteem could not guarantee stability. In their homeland, borders were fluid and could change on a political or military whim. If a house could be part of the Austro-Hungarian Empire, then Polish, then Russian, then German, what did that make the inhabitants? Mania Heidenstein was no stranger to dislocation. During the Great War, before Jock was born, the Fink family, like countless others, packed what they could carry to flee the country. Mania knew life was precarious. On the brink of another war she was just as desperate to get to safety with her husband and two boys.

She wrote to Jock and Rita begging them to speak to anyone in any refugee committee or congregation who could help get visas, and they took up the challenge. The girls heard of a scheme whereby adult Jewish refugees could enter the country as servants. 'You can tell them that your parents are young, healthy, hardworking and industrious,' Mania insisted in one letter.[3] Three days after this letter was written, Germany invaded Poland. Britain declared war on Germany. There would be no foreseeable reunion for Jock and her parents in England.

The declaration of war changed everything. Anti-German feelings in Britain spilled over onto innocent refugees. Jock's little sister, Stella, got bullied at school for being German until Lillie Adler, her new foster sister, stuck up for her. Like many thousands of other children, Stella was evacuated from London, due to fears of imminent German bombs or gas attacks. Stella and Lillie were sent to the Norfolk countryside and held, waiting for someone to take them in. One by one other children were picked from the group of evacuees. Stella wasn't picked because she was German. Lillie wasn't picked because it was assumed she was German too.

A woman breezed in calling 'Am I too late to have anyone?' She was told there were only two foreigners left. The little girls waited for revulsion or rejection. 'All right, I'll have them!' said the woman, and off they went to spend an idyllic period in the gardener's cottage of a big estate. Stella's letters talked with delight of shopping, cycling and getting caught in the rain. Once again humanity had triumphed over bigotry.

In Berlin, Mania treasured every word from her daughters. She was often overcome with emotion at the terrible situation: 'I'm finishing my letter with many tears in my eyes, so many that I can't write any longer. All of you stay healthy and strong for me. May the dear Lord protect you from anything bad.'[4] She could only parent from a distance, chiding Jock to write more often, consoling a homesick Rita, and warning Stella not to get sunburned. 'Take care of yourself, your parents are unfortunately so far away and can't see and hear and watch for what would be best for you,' she wrote.[5]

All Jock's mother could do was send letters and love. Deep, unceasing, unconditional love.

It wasn't just the separation from parents and siblings that left Jock isolated. Her maternal grandparents were in Poland. On her father's side, her Heidenstein grandparents, known affectionately as 'Omama and Opapa' – crossed the border into Belgium. Grandma Sara travelled first. Grandad Josef, more at risk because Jewish men were being harassed and rounded up for camps still, took a more circumspect route. He fled to Danzig first, then made his way to Antwerp via boat. Aged sixty-nine and seventy-three respectively, Josef and Sara were far too old to be starting over in a strange place without their usual resources, particularly as Sara was mostly bedridden with a bad cough. Luckily, they could live with their daughter Lotte – Jock's aunt – and Lotte's husband, Jacob Kapelner.[6] Antwerp also had a strong Jewish community near the main station, with support for incomers. They knew how to rally round any unfortunates blown in by the storm.

Love between the generations was strong. Jock's aunt Lotte wrote from Antwerp to say, 'Omama and Opapa are very worried about you all. They talk of you dear children very often and pray that they can be together with you again some day.'[7]

With exquisite innocence Jock's sister Stella wrote to her grandma and grandad in Antwerp: 'I hope that you like Belgium. I hope that the weather is nice and that you can go outside for lovely walks.'[8]

There could be nothing lovely about impoverished refugee life far from home, without any income beyond charity support. At least the Belgium border was believed to be a sound protection against Nazi persecution.

It was hard for the Heidenstein sisters to keep track of their loved ones left in Europe. 'Is Mummy in Belgium?' Stella wrote to Rita. At such a young age she understood nothing of geopolitics, only that she wanted to see her mother again.

Mania did not make it to Antwerp with David and Michael. Was it too much upheaval, or a simple matter of bureaucratic obstruction? They certainly knew Berlin wasn't safe. The Heidenstein brothers were too young to appreciate how serious things were in the world outside their home, but they definitely absorbed some of the tension from adults around them, no doubt listening in to their talk. Before the outbreak of war Mania wrote to Stella – calling her 'my little golden doll' – to say that Michael wanted to come to stay with her and Aunt Adler. At only four years old Michael had worked out that going to England was some kind of prize. He apparently promised to be 'very good' since, as Mania reported, 'it says in the newspaper that he needs to go over there to you and your sister.'[9]

It's heartbreaking to think that children absorbed the idea that their escape to safety was somehow dependent on being 'good,' when it was entirely the result of other people being bad. Their father, Chaim, was far from blind to the danger of staying in Berlin, but he was also conflicted about sending the boys away on their own.

The decision was taken out of his hands: the Gestapo re-arrested Chaim and he once again faced the nightmare of Sachsenhausen. Mania carefully avoided mentioning the concentration camp in her letters to England, apart from the forlorn comment that 'Papa's emigration process went too slowly,' and oblique references such as, 'He is doing very well … May the dear Lord just keep him healthy.'[10]

Mania's energies were devoted to finding safety for the boys.

Her letters to England became increasingly frantic as she scrabbled to find routes to Amsterdam, Palestine, Bolivia, Tangier . . . anywhere safe. If anywhere was safe. She needed money and luck, both of which were in short supply that autumn.

Jock didn't give up hope that a miracle would happen, and her parents could be saved. After all, she experienced her own kind of miracle during the years of war. She found a haven; a place of sanctuary with faith and friendship. In a little English town, she gained a sense of stability and belonging, even as a refugee. When London was being emptied of children at the start of the war, Jock was evacuated to a place called Shefford.

Where was Shefford? At the end of a long bus journey from London, heading north then branching out into increasingly leafy lanes in the county of Bedfordshire. In many ways, Shefford wasn't so different from countless rural towns in Germany, Belgium or Poland. There was a station, farms, schools, shops, churches, inns and cemeteries. But there was no synagogue in Shefford. No Jews in Shefford, until buses from London pulled up and tired children tumbled out, chattering in English and German.

Meeting them at their destination was a charismatic man emerging from a little Ford 8 car loaded with kosher food, large saucepans and a hamper of plates and cutlery. It was none other than Rabbi Dr Solomon Schonfeld, the man who'd helped get Jock to England in the first place. The children arriving in Shefford were pupils of the Jewish Secondary School – JSS – founded by Dr Schonfeld's father. Now, as Britain faced the threat of attack, the founder's son was determined to make sure that the whole school not only survived but thrived.

Jock mustered for evacuation at 6 a.m. on Friday, 1 September 1939, the very same day German troops invaded Poland. Many miles away, her relatives in Poland, including her cousin Eva, waited to find out what this would mean for them. Jock just waited for the bus, along with 550 other Jewish children assembled in a school playground in North London. Jock was prepped with her faithful suitcase and her warm red sweater. Also, food for two days and a blanket. An identification disk dangled round her neck. Before the school left, everyone said a prayer for those travelling. A third of them were recent refugees, already familiar with dislocation. Some had mothers to see them off. Not Jock.

Although views from the bus had shown lovely fields of crops and cattle – a far cry from Berlin or London – first impressions of Shefford were not encouraging. It was an old market town with buildings that had slowly sagged over centuries. Jock's name was called off a long list, and she was taken to yet another new billet in the village of Stotfold, just outside Shefford.

The next day, when the Jewish children emerged from their billets, it was obvious they were outsiders, and not just because they were city kids evacuated to the country.

'We looked different,' remembered Mella Lowy, one of Jock's good friends from the school, 'we were clumsily, unsuitably dressed, and above all we spoke if at all with a terrible accent and ludicrous lack of grammar.'[11]

Like Jock, Mella had Polish ancestry and had escaped her native Germany via the Kindertransport. They'd escaped London, but there was nowhere safe from antisemitism.

'But you have no horns!' exclaimed one local woman to the Jewish boy billeted at her house, genuinely taken aback that he didn't look like the demonised Jewish stereotype she was expecting.

The school's headmistress, Dr Judith Grunfeld, settled in a billet filled with flowers and nick-nacks. Jock and the others called her the Queen, out of a mixture of intimidation, respect and reverence.

It was here on 3 September that Grunfeld's host, calmly knitting without any show of emotion, passed on the news that, 'Oh yes, it's war all right.'[12]

War meant tension. Enemies. Heightened wariness. Shefford locals were suspicious to hear German spoken in the street. They wondered if these young strangers could be spies? They were even more puzzled at how to feed the incomers, since apparently the children couldn't eat bacon at breakfast or shellfish for dinner. 'Kosher' was an unknown concept to most folk in the area, not to mention the Orthodox rules on what must and must not happen during the Sabbath or high holy days.

Dr Schonfeld understood the mistrust, writing, 'The country people had heard only vaguely of Jews, had never lived with them.'[13]

How easily the community could have rejected the children as 'other.' Mistrust and anger were instinctive first responses in many billets. Over time Shefford folk grew to appreciate the positivity, integrity and common humanity of everyone in the evacuated school. It wasn't long before they felt proud of their 'Children of Israel,' as a local vicar biblically labelled them, and loyal to everything the school tried to achieve. Familiarity bred acceptance.

Dr Grunfeld, never one to miss an opportunity for verbal flourishes, declared that 'goodwill sprang up in the village like flowers in the sun.'[14]

The children themselves desperately needed the familiar Jewish environment of school, the comfort of faith, the distraction of study and all the fun of nurturing friendships. It wasn't quite home, but it was like a family.

Once she was settled, Jock took out her needles and got knitting.

Classes, theatre, music, devotion, football and ping pong – JSS school life was a wonderfully vibrant affirmation of life and faith. Frieda Korobkin, at school with Jock, expressed the sense of belonging in her memoirs, writing, 'It was the place where I did not feel utterly powerless; where I was able to express myself.'[15]

From lonely skivvy work in her London foster home, Jock now found herself part of a glorious system of team endeavour, where school 'House' groups vied to win points for how well they could clean the school. Among her papers saved from her school years Jock kept a list of House points and duties. They were an army of dutiful, even joyful workers now. She also kept many of her exercise books, some with missing pages where the paper had been torn out for letter writing, for there were many letters and notes still carried by posties between the Heidenstein sisters. She laboured over learning English and Hebrew, determined to become proficient at both, and to continue the deep religious dedication instilled by her parents. Faith was her anchor.

And she kept knitting.

No matter how engrossing her homework or exam revision, Jock was always lifted by the gift of a letter from home and her 'darling mother.'[16] She was especially elated with an update about her father.

'Have you heard the wonderful thing about my Daddy?' she wrote to Mrs Adler in January 1940.[17]

The 'wonderful thing' Jock celebrated was news that her daddy had a chance of release from Sachsenhausen.

Unfortunately, there was a catch. A whole snag of catches. Not only did the prisoner have to provide proof of imminent emigration – impossible to do without a visa and the money to back it – the Nazis also demanded a fee. For his entire life Jock's uncle Oscar – Chaim's brother – kept a crumpled sheet of paper announcing the extortion: pay the Nazis two hundred dollars for your loved one's release.[18] It was a staggering amount. Bludgeoned into poverty by anti-Jewish economic legislation, how could Mania hope to raise such a sum? Oscar was in Palestine by then, distraught that in no way could he get the money together. The failure haunted him for the rest of his life.

Even Jock's little brother Michael, aged four, understood how poor they had all become. Mania reported, 'Meszi always tells me that when he is big, he is going to go earn money and bring me all of it, I should have what I need.'[19]

The hopeful news about Jock's father's potential release from Sachsenhausen concentration camp was diluted to generic terms in Mania's letters to Jock – *Papa is well. Papa sends his love.*

For all she was safe and nurtured in Shefford, such anxiety inevitably took its toll on Jock, and on all the refugees with parents still in Europe. These children were tinged with a noticeable melancholy. They looked and often acted older than their years, forced to grow up too soon. One friend called Jock a 'wise old owl.'[20] If wise, it was a wisdom gained from sad experience. Another friend said Jock had a 'sobering and even motherly influence,' although with enough sense of fun to be pitting her wits against teasing boys, and enough courage to stand up to the school bully.[21]

Jewish Secondary School, Shefford, September 1941. Jock Heidenstein is second from the right, on the second row down.
Courtesy of Tamar Abrams

Jock, seen here in a JSS group photograph from the new autumn term 1941, is taller than her friends, with a full figure, a serious face and a generous cloud of dark hair. Set back a year because of language difficulties, Jock seemed almost matronly compared to the younger girls in her class. She went through puberty, and all the awkwardness of dealing with period cramps and acquiring sanitary towels from the chemist, without her mother to nurture and guide her.

'They looked like girls who had become women too soon,' Mella Lowy said of her school friends without parents.[22]

None of the JSS children had school uniforms – no homogenous blazers with embroidered insignia. There was no money for these luxuries. Their sense of identity came from shared goals and a collective spirit. Their clothes mostly came from the Committee for Refugees. Each girl was allowed to choose one hand-me-down winter dress from donations provided by Jewish families in London. Those with pocket money could save up for a bus trip into the nearby town of Bedford, to browse the bargains at Woolworth's, or turn over second-hand clothes sold at a cluster of junk shops there.

Pupils had to launder their own clothes. Jock's red sweater would first be soaked in cold water, then rubbed with soap to remove stains. Since she had so few clothes, it was washed over and over. The colour didn't fade too much, but the neat ribbing around the waist and cuffs began to go limp. As Jock grew, the jumper had to stretch with her.

The Jewish Secondary School in Shefford, spread in a miscellany of halls, huts and meadows, with ad hoc catering, a rowdy boiler and donated books, represented a much-needed place of safety for twelve-year-old Jock. Wanting to share the experience, she went with Rabbi Schonfeld to Debbie Adler's house in London, where little sister, Stella, was back from her evacuation to Norfolk, to persuade her to come to the school. No luck. Stella loved her new family and life in Hackney.

More pressing was to find a place for middle sister, Rita. All refugee girls were ousted from Wyberlye hostel in early 1941 when the property was requisitioned by the military. They were spread among foster families. Rita found herself with a nice couple leading a simple life. Rita wrote to Jock about the garden where she lived, and about the cat, about gramophone records, and learning first aid with the Girl Guides. She was safe enough, but there was no room for her to follow the faith and traditions of her family in this Christian household.[23] Jock pressed hard month after month for the JSS to find her a place. Eventually, she succeeded.

Rita came to Shefford to join the JSS by July 1942, aged thirteen. One of her first experiences at school was meeting a very naughty pupil called Henry Mayer. Henry informed the new girl, 'I am going to marry you.' Rita wasn't impressed with his gleeful confidence, but she added him to the list of her young admirers, entirely oblivious to the role he'd one day play in her life.[24]

In between study, friends, prayer and housework, Jock knitted. A lot.

The Heidenstein-Fink family was scattered. Postcards and letters helped keep them connected. Every letter received was a sign of life, particularly when the news from Europe was increasingly grim. On 10 May, English newspapers headlined the Nazi invasion of Belgium. Amazingly, Jock's grandparents, Sara and Josef, were able to gain places on a crossing to England just before the Germans took Antwerp. Jock's aunt Lotte came with them, and two cousins. They survived Luftwaffe strafing and mines in the English Channel. Their escape was partly thanks to luck, and mostly due to the efforts of Rabbi Dr Schonfeld's team, who never gave up on their efforts to bring Jews to safety.

Lotte's husband Jakob didn't get out in time.

And Mania? David and Michael? Chaim?

'Dear Papa is still not at home, and I am very heartsick because of it,' Mania Heidenstein wrote to Rita.[25]

'Papa can't write,' were Stella's pencilled words on one undated scrap of correspondence.

The words were truer than she knew.

In June 1940, Mania wrote to her daughters in England to let them know she'd finally had a letter from Papa: 'His first question was how our dear children are doing. He also wrote that he is doing well. May the dear Lord just grant us that we may have our dear father healthy at home again.'[26]

Tragically, Chaim Jakob Heidenstein, father to five children, husband to Mania, Polish Jew, devout member of the Adas Yisroel in Berlin and successful clothing dealer, was dead and cremated before Mania read and relayed this last letter. His death in Sachsenhausen camp was recorded at Oranienburg Civil Registry Office: 2 a.m., 18 April 1940. The cause of death was listed as *Körperschwäche* – physical weakness. His body could not withstand Nazi brutality one hour longer.

He was a nobody in terms of world history, and the world to everyone who loved him.

No words survive to describe the day Mania received a cardboard box from Sachsenhausen, printed with the words *Handle with Care. Urn. Don't Throw Away*. The urn contained ashes. She was told they were her husband's. In reality, there was no such finesse; no respect for the dead. Prisoners in the concentration camp were ordered to shovel handfuls of cremated remains into the urns, all mingled together. The urn represented the horrific finality of death. Mania began widowhood unable to bury her husband with proper rites and observances, although she did, remarkably, manage to arrange a memorial for him at a Berlin cemetery.

In an extraordinary act of love, Mania took the decision to spare her daughters the knowledge of their father's death. She couldn't mother them in person, wash their clothes, help with homework, dry their tears, hold them close, but she could love them from a distance, and through the power of this love protect them from the shock of bereavement. Her girls were left with hope, and it was sorely needed.

Rabbi Dr Schonfeld had less filtered news sources. He knew the Jewish school in Shefford was a precious haven from ever-worsening persecution in Europe, and that it would help the pupils 'weather the storm in the difficult years that may lie ahead.'[27]

What of all those trapped in Europe? Would neighbours and strangers rally round like the community in Shefford. How could any Jew find safety?

6

What Is Going to Happen to Us Next?

The world's been turned upside down.
– ANNE FRANK, DIARY ENTRY, 25 MAY 1944[1]

One woman in wartime Britain – one out of many, no doubt – learned to knit in the dark. She became so used to power cuts and blackout rules that she could sit in an underground bomb shelter, no lights, feeling her way with the work. She came to know all the stitches by heart. She felt the tension of the yarn and trusted in her skills. In the dark she crafted new clothes from precious wool.[2]

While generals watched pieces moved over maps and economists calculated financial costs, innocent civilians were forced to adapt their everyday activities. Strategic decisions taken by men at a military and political level impacted millions of people in monumental ways, and in a myriad of small, ordinary details. Even something so small as how to get hold of knitting wool.

Wool was a feature of war whether acknowledged in military histories or not. Generals wore wool, as did the troops they commanded. Socks, sweaters, leggings and vests weren't conjured out of thin air, although it may have seemed like that to knitters scrabbling to find supplies when stocks ran out.

The thrift of pre-war years was nothing compared to wartime making do. Household magazines in every country still able to print such luxuries crammed their pages with tips on how to make your own clothes, how to make all clothes last longer, and how to make something from nothing. Threads and yarns became so scarce it was hard to choose between mending a tear or sewing a button back on. The collective strategizing was a common connection in all countries affected by war. Jewish people suffered additional layers of deprivation and persecution, making their efforts all the more vital.

There was Jock Heidenstein in sleepy Shefford, who tried to tame the sag and stretch of her beloved red sweater with rows of clumsy stitches up the sides and on the cuffs. Jock's school had a mending room where volunteers wrangled an ancient sewing machine into action to repair torn clothes or darn socks. Jock clearly didn't turn to experts when repairing her jumper. Rather like the woman knitting in the dark, she was feeling her way without parents to guide her.

During the war there was knitting on buses, in bunkers, at the fireside or perched on rubble. During meetings, lunch breaks, bomb raids and concerts. Knitting for pleasure, for warmth or for a meal's worth of food. Knitting in groups by comfortable volunteers 'doing their bit' for the war effort; knitting in solitude and secret by those fearful of persecution.

In Amsterdam there was German Jewish teenager Anne Frank hiding in a secret annexe with her family, documenting their covert life in diary notebooks, including details of how she knitted a white sweater with wool smuggled in by non-Jewish friends. Not pretty, but warm, she said, and that was the main thing.[3] The Frank family had no chance to reach England like the Heidenstein girls. They hoped to be safe enough in the Netherlands. Relocating to Amsterdam could, at one time, have been an option for Chaim Heidenstein, since he had strong contacts there thanks to the rag trade. If the Heidensteins had moved, pre-war, to a Dutch sanctuary, it likely wouldn't have remained safe for long, as the Franks so tragically discovered.

In 1941, before Nazi roundups and deportations meant the Franks had to live their lives in silence and secrets, padding about their hiding place in woollen socks without shoes, Anne and her sister were photographed together. Anne, aged twelve, is seen in a patterned white cardigan, and Margo, fifteen, in a plain ribbed sweater. Usually parents with limited means like their children to have too-big knitwear, so they can 'grow into it.' The Frank sisters soon grew into their clothes . . . and out of them. One day Anne ruefully stood with her arms outstretched, and the sleeves of her red sweater were a long way from covering her thin wrists. She tried to smile at how absurd she looked. When Anne's father, Otto – the family's sole survivor – was consulted during a project to re-create the way the annexe hiding place had looked during wartime, he remembered his daughters knitting. White yarn, needles and unfinished knitting were added to one of the reconstructed bedroom scenes, in reference to Anne's knitting project. By April 1944, Anne had also acquired a red sweater, which she wore with a black skirt and tattered knee socks.[4]

On 7 October 1942, Anne wrote out a fantasy shopping list, imagining a spree in Switzerland. Among the multitude of coveted items were thick stockings, four sweaters and very precisely noted requirements for '3 skeins of white wool (underwear, cap), 2 skeins of blue wool (sweater, skirt), 3 skeins of variegated wool (cap, scarf).'[5] It wasn't so very different from Jock Heidenstein in England, writing to sister Stella's foster family in April 1942 to request a new suit and 'one or two blouses,' to be transformed from the old taffeta dress brought with her from Berlin. 'But I mustn't plan too much,' Jock added with a cold dose of reality.[6] Clothes were both practical and a form of daydreaming escapism.

One of Anne's favourite Dutch magazines, *Libelle*, captioned a knitting pattern from 1 September 1939 with the words, 'For these troubled times . . . the garment will undoubtedly do good service in the coming months.' This was even before the terrible hardships of occupation, and the roundups of resisters and Jews. Even so, the sentiment was sound: in times of scarcity everything was to be used; nothing wasted. This was particularly true for refugees, and families impoverished by Nazi persecution, perhaps hiding, like the Franks, with limited means. The prospect of sparse shop stocks or empty shelves made everyone appreciate the clothes they still had.

'One cannot lightly turn last years' jumper into this year's floor-cloth – not without exploring every possibility of giving it a new lease of life,' wrote English knitting experts in 1942.[7]

Wartime housewives were enthusiastically advised to re-sole worn socks with fragments from another pair, to reinforce the gussets of long johns with old knitted vests and to turn old socks into mittens. With oddments of wool a woman could knit toe covers for inside shoes, make a short-waisted short-sleeved sweater or, at the very least, rustle up a dishcloth. Old sweaters became baby layettes, or children's chest warmers.

Even if not knitting entirely in the dark, lights were sometimes a luxury due to coal shortages and sporadic electricity. A single length of burning cotton thread floating on a film of oil in a glass of water might be the only glow in a room with blacked-out windows. Knitting and mending might have seemed thankless tasks, but their importance was recognised. In April 1940, *Deutsche Hauswirtschaft* noted, 'The tedious, hidden, detailed work is harder, but also much more important because it preserves one and human life.' They made no comment on the fact that the economies of occupied territories were crippled by German rapacity, leading to even greater shortages and hardships for civilians.

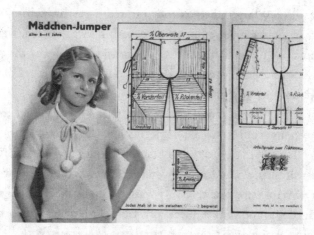

Pattern for a girl's jumper from the 1930s German knitting & crochet pattern book
Strick-und Häkel Lehrbuch.
Lucy Adlington personal archive

Experienced knitters knew how to unravel woollens no longer fit for service, how to soak the wool, dry it, wind it and knit it up again. Those new to knitting learned from others, or from trying to follow well-meaning diagrams in 'how-to' books. An army of housewives with homemade pinafores as uniforms took up their darning mushrooms to create lattice lines of mending on holes at elbows and toes, until sometimes the darns outgrew the garment. When that happened it was time to turn to magazines for advice on transformations.

The woollens were very much needed. Stella Heidenstein wrote to her parents in the winter of 1939–40 to say, 'The weather here is very bad. Most of the pipes are frozen and it is terrible without any water.' Her mother wrote, 'Dear child, here it is very cold. Take care of yourself. You should dress warmly.'[8]

Both Jock's sweater repairs and the immense thrift of the Frank family in hiding in Amsterdam were the highly admirable aspects of wartime ingenuity. On a vaster scale, the Nazis corrupted the concept of recycling, much as they tainted everything. The Nazi strategy of a circular economy, where nothing was wasted, was to have hideous implications for humans considered part of the process. All Jews in Nazi-controlled territories were at risk of being dragged into the recycling mechanism.

German children from Nazi youth groups were rallied to do house-to-house collections of scraps, including food tins, bones and textiles. These were tipped out of buckets and barrows into sorting yards. In Breslau, Anita Lasker's sister Renate was one of the workers at a recycling site. She certainly wasn't fired by Nazi ideology as she dodged rats and yanked pieces of usable cloth out of the reeking mountains. Anita didn't envy her the dirty, dangerous work.

'Got a rag?' asked *Deutche Hauswirtschaft* in July 1940. 'Without realising it the housewife receives a not inconsiderable part of the rags she passed on in a completely new form.'

In terms of consumables, the Nazis needed everything to be used until useless, then transformed into something with purpose again. So far so good. However, since even the most resourceful system could only recycle goods so many times before they were beyond recovery, the Nazis needed to top up the supply. Which meant plunder from conquered people and legalised robbery of Jews.

To acquire Jewish property, it had to become illegal for Jewish people to own even their own belongings. Jews arrested by the Gestapo could take very little with them, if anything. Special authorisation was needed to collect belongings left behind. When Anne Frank's hiding place in Amsterdam was discovered in August 1944, she was arrested with her family and bundled into the back of a police truck, carrying only a few possessions. Office workers who'd helped shelter the Franks collected her diary notebooks and handfuls of papers, at great risk to themselves. Everything else in the annexe was lugged out by the rapacious Puls removal company, to be sorted and sent to new owners in Germany, at great profit to the plunderers. Perhaps Anne's red sweater went onto Germany with the rest of the Frank belongings, to be worn by another teenage girl full of hopes and dreams. Perhaps Anne wore it to her onward destination. Either way, her fate had already been decided. Jews in Nazi-controlled territories were treated like rags: useful up to a point, particularly if repurposed.

However war impacted people's lives, they had to feel their way day to day, like the woman knitting in the dark. There were slow shifts and sudden calamities. Endless uncertainties and swift, fateful decisions. How could anyone know what was the right thing to do when safety was precarious and threats often unseen?

Working with young people during the war, psychologist Anna Freud observed, 'The war acquires comparatively little significance for children so long as it only threatens their lives, disturbs their material comfort or cuts their food rations. It becomes enormously significant the moment it breaks up family life.'[9]

Jock Heidenstein knew all about the breakup of family life. Even so, she knew she was lucky to have been evacuated to safety in the English countryside. Her little sister, Stella, was in London when the first bombs of the Blitz started – wave after ominous wave of German bombers and German bombs. 'She beefed it out,' in the words of her pal Sidney Cohen.[10]

Occasionally Stella's foster family, the Adlers, left their home in Hackney to stay with relatives outside the city. It was too difficult to sustain this split life. They decided to take their chances, first in a dug-out Anderson shelter in the garden, then, when they saw how easily these could be crushed under debris, in the public shelter at nearby Victoria Park. When they emerged after the all-clear sirens sounded, they would see London burning. 'Like a sunset in the east and the sun still setting in the west,' recalled Stella's best friend, Bernard Diamond.

Through all of this, Stella's foster 'auntie' Debbie Adler remained invincible. 'One of those people that had no fear,' said Bernard with admiration.[11]

Psychologists studying the effects of displacement on young children during the war had expected to find that although undoubtedly traumatised by the devastation of bombardment, the children who kept close family bonds – even during such violent destruction – were less emotionally damaged than those who were safe but separated.[12] But that's not what they found.

Staying together as a family was more often a luxury than a choice. Obviously the Heidenstein girls had been separated, whereas Jock's cousin Eva Fink was with her family when violence caught them, in the village of Wojnilow, near Lviv. It was June 1941. The cynical alliance between Russia and Germany had been broken as soon as the Nazis felt bold enough to wage war against them. Operation Barbarossa saw Germans pummelling Russian territory from the air and crossing newly established Russian borders with a seemingly unstoppable onslaught of machines and men. The invasion was to cause maximum devastation to land and life. Jews were particular targets, with special killing squads rounding up Jews wherever they were found for death in a holocaust of bullets. The Fink family had stayed together, with nowhere to go and nowhere to hide. There was Eva – aged fourteen, the same as Jock – and Eva's three brothers and her parents. Neighbours they'd lived alongside for years decided not to wait for Germans to reach the village. They needed no orders from Nazi murder squads. They unleashed antisemitism that had festered for years and turned on the Finks with appalling, gratuitous violence.

These words are hard to write, hard to read and hard to believe: Eva's family were beheaded with knives – her parents and her little brothers, aged ten and eight. The murderers then used their heads as footballs in the street.

Eva herself escaped with nothing but the clothes she wore. Her mother sensed danger and told her to run, just to get out – to *go*. Eva wept as she ran, feeling like a hunted animal.[13] Presumably the men of Woljnilow then cleaned off their knives and the women in their lives carried on knitting as though the Fink family had never existed.

Jock's fate could have been the same as Eva's if it hadn't been for the Kindertransport – that valiant initiative in the face of complacent governments who dismissed desperate refugees with a shrug: *We've no room.*

Eva Fink had no photographs of her home to remind her of loved ones' faces. No letters to treasure. No warm red sweater. She had to fight to survive every year of the war, untethered from home, carrying memories of family and nothing else.

Memories kept the soul's heart beating. No matter how dire her knitting wool supply, Jock Heidenstein never unravelled her little red sweater. She didn't soak out the kinks and memories. She didn't knit it up again into something new. When it was hopelessly outgrown she tucked it away, a reminder of childhood and home in Berlin. During the war she knitted like many others, for warmth, for gifts, for occupation. Over in occupied Poland were girls who would quite literally have to knit to save their lives. Among them, a girl whose fate would be tied to a red sweater too – Regina Feldman.

Like Jock Heidenstein in Berlin, or cellist Anita Lasker in Breslau, Regina Feldman thought of her home as a safe place. Regina was named Riva at her birth in 1925, affectionately known as Rivka to friends and family. In 1943 her name changed from Riva to Regina for very significant reasons, not long after her fingers had been clicking needles as she knitted a red sweater in the most unbelievable circumstances.

Regina knitted a lot of stitches during the war years, sometimes in the dark, and sometimes in bright light, but always with a shadowed heart.

Back in 1939, the year that Jock Heidenstein reached England and Anita Lasker got trapped in Breslau, Regina's life revolved around a house and smallholding on a road out of the Polish village of Siedliszcze, east of the city of Lublin, and not far from forest landscapes. Every spring the chestnut tree along the road to Regina's house burst out in new foliage. Bees made honey from the white acacia blossoms outside the house and tadpoles wiggled in the little stream at the end of the garden. By autumn, chestnuts had fallen and grown frogs had mated. With winter snow came sleigh rides and log fires.

War was just a concept to Regina. Not so for her parents. They'd lived through the upheaval and damage of the Great War. They knew just how vulnerable their home might be with Germans to the west and Russians to the east. Like the Heidensteins and the Laskers, Regina's family were Jewish. They could never be certain of safety. That said, the Feldman family were happily integrated with village life, Jewish or Christian. Her father, Josef, traded in construction materials, especially lumber, and had many business connections in the area. Her mother, Golda, was very well educated and, like many women, part of the domestic side of the community, linked through children, elder care and charitable networks. She also helped manage the business when Josef was away on trips.

As a girl Regina's life revolved around family, with her parents; siblings Theodor, Paul and Friedl; grandparents. Also, a wonderful menagerie of animals, and school, where Regina wore a jaunty sailor suit uniform, and friends, including best friend, Zelda Metz, who was like another sister. Amongst all the fun and all the studying Regina learned how to knit. Nothing significant about that. Not yet.

At first war was just caution and uncertainty, alien to her happy life. Then came planes strafing harvest crops and the sound of cannon fire. Then came soldiers, first Russians, then Germans. Then came refugees, desperate to find some corner of sanctuary.

Regina's safe world unravelled. It was, in the words of one wartime article on make-do-and-mend, 'The end of the old and beginning of the new.'[14]

The Feldman family thought they could stay safe if they kept a low profile and supported each other. There wasn't the slightest possibility of getting the Feldman children out of Europe, like Jock and her sisters had been rescued by the Kindertransport. Unlike people in the village of Woljnilow, who turned so viciously on Eva Fink's family, Christians in Regina's community chose to help the Feldmans when they could, despite the risk of punishment from occupying Germans.

From mid-May 1941, Jews of Siedliszcze were ousted from their home into a portion of buildings that had been cordoned off into a ghetto. Even though they were supposed to treat the Jews as dirty undesirables, the Poles allocated to the Feldman's home never lost sight of common humanity. They let Regina and her siblings sneak into the garden to help themselves to fruit and vegetables they'd planted in more optimistic times. They even suggested Regina and her sister, Friedl, could help clean the house, which meant the girls could gather some much-needed clothes and bedding to make their new one-room home more bearable.[15]

In the ghetto Regina went from a happy, safe, nourishing life to immediate, ever-intensifying poverty. Whenever Germans entered a Polish settlement they quickly demanded levies of gold from the local Jewish council. It was never a one-off demand. Decree after decree hounded the Jews. Each time they did their best to make payment, then there'd be a lull. A sense that perhaps the worst was over, and some kind of life could be eked out with whatever possessions remained. Better to pay up than to be beaten or shot – as if it were an either-or situation. Eventually violence against Jews would escalate once again. New orders were posted for more levies. Not just gold, but furs, whatever pelts had been hoarded to make winter in the ghetto a little warmer. Not just furs, but wool. A quota of wool per family that had to be fulfilled, no excuses or explanations. Empty hands meant emptied homes – people dragged away and just bloodstained debris in their wake.

Knitted blankets, socks, scarves and baby frocks – these were now offered up like a tribute to rapacity. Skeins of wool set aside for future knitting projects had to be handed over. Stray balls of wool were rounded up; oddments pulled from bags and stashes. It's strange to think of all this wool jumbled together at the collecting point, representing so many unmade sweaters or undarned socks. Off to German homes it went, so German housewives – but not German Jews like Mania Heidenstein – could cast on new stitches and knit new woollens.

'They cannot destroy us economically thanks to the ingenious measures of the Führer!' declared a magazine article on Winter Aid in December 1939, in defiance of future Allied strategies.[16] Ingenious measures indeed: raping a conquered nation's resources down to the last ball of wool. Remembering back to the 'Purely Aryan Enterprise' boasts of German yarn manufacturer Quelle, did any knitter feel a sudden revulsion that she might be using *Jewish* wool?[17] Of course not. Gold furs and yarns were no longer considered contaminated by 'Jewishness' once they'd been separated from their owners and given over to so-called Aryans.

'Extraordinarily few of the pathetic collection buried in every knitter's rag-bag drawer need finally be given up for lost,' was the buoyant message to wartime knitters in England.[18]

That was all very well for those like Jock Heidenstein, one of the few to be offered sanctuary. What hope was there for girls such as Regina Feldman?

A future friend of Jock Heidenstein, saved at the last minute from the Netherlands and brought to England where he'd eventually cross paths with Jock, summed up the question all Jews had to ask themselves: 'What is going to happen to us next?'[19] The ones who could best answer that question were the Nazi organizers at their desks dictating letters, calculating profits, synchronising transport links and issuing orders.

Regina could only live day to day.

She spent just over a year in the Siedliszcze ghetto. No school. No freedom. Hard labour sunrise to sunset. But the family were together at least, united during adversity. There were still friends, some old – Zelda – and some new: Hella Felenbaum. Hella had been evacuated from Lublin with her family. The Felenbaums survived by selling off, piece by piece, any clothes or jewellery they'd managed to salvage from home. Piece by piece all the Jews of Siedliszcze lost any sense of stability too, until one miserable day in October 1942 saw them juddering in horse-drawn carts out of the town to a labour camp staining the landscape around an old mill – Staw-Nowosiulki. It would need more than woollens to warm them that winter.

Barefoot and barely dressed, Regina, Hella and other young people of Staw were put to work ploughing fields and dredging waterways, with empty stomachs, feverish blood and a soundscape cracking with gunshots. Two months later they were told they could go home. If true, and the Germans were full of false promises, it could hardly be a joyful return. Regina's big brother, Max, had suffered a heart attack while clearing the rubble of the synagogue in Siedliszcze, and died because Jews weren't allowed to break curfew even to seek urgent medical care. Regina's sister Friedl wasn't in good health either – none of them were that winter. Max at least had been given a proper burial in the Jewish cemetery. Cold corpses lay still on the frozen ground at Staw.

But the remaining core of Feldmans were still together.

Until they weren't.

Families that had held on to each other for so long would soon have their attachments unravelled; their loving connections deliberately snipped.

On 19 December 1942 it was confirmed that the Feldmans would leave Staw the next day, although the talk now was of going to another labour camp, not back home at all. Men were separated from women and children for the journey. Regina squeezed onto a cart, close to her mother, sister and little brother, Paul. There were eight hundred of them being taken through the still, cold calm of a snowy day, escorted by Germans on horseback.

'Don't throw away gold and valuables,' threatened their captors. 'Keep them with you!'

Why would they throw away what few precious items they'd managed to hide from locals attempting to extort trinkets along the route? It wasn't as if any of them owned much after successive waves of robbery, after every item down to knitting wool had been taken. True, Regina's mother kept quiet about the wedding ring stitched inside the lining of her jacket pocket. She didn't know what would happen to them next, but she meant to be as well prepared as possible.

As it happened, anyone who did attempt to get rid of valuables was shot on the spot.

The convoy of wagons came to a crossroads. One way, the town of Wlodawa – somewhere familiar. Another way, into the forest, towards a place called Sobibor.

What next?

Regina waited in the cold at the crossroads. For Jews in Europe, every path, road and railway led to unknown destinations; a patterning of dislocation, concentration and . . . disappearance.

PART TWO

Unravelled

Dressed in as Many Layers as Possible

Hope was an elixir that kept us going.
— ANITA LASKER-WALLFISCH[1]

Occupied Europe in 1939–45 was a great time to run a removal firm. Or to own a truck, a car, cart, trolley, pram or hand barrow. It seemed like the whole world and their wardrobe were on the move, needing anything with wheels to help shift stuff. What couldn't be transported had to be lugged by hand or worn, whatever the weather.

Housing was at a premium when German invaders took over a new country, or once Allied bombs destroyed buildings in Germany. The Nazis' solution to the housing shortage was brutal and pragmatic, a combination of racist ideology and economic rationalization. They decided that Jews must move. From estates, fancy villas, proud town houses, smart apartments or even run-down tenement blocks in the wrong part of town: Jews were *out*.

The Lasker family in Breslau had enjoyed spacious rooms in a nice city apartment until the Nazis decreed it was no longer their home. Edith Lasker got busy selling furniture and all expendable items. What could they take? Only essentials, although this did include Edith's sewing machine and Anita's cello. The Gestapo sealed the apartment until new tenants were found.

The front door had closed on that part of the Lasker's life forever.

Their new living arrangements involved flat-sharing and ill-humoured relatives. Even so, they knew they were lucky to have somewhere to live. Anita could still study. Still enjoy music lessons. Still celebrate birthdays and small victories. The Laskers were among the final 25 percent of Jews living in Breslau. The rest had left Germany, including big sister, Marianne.

In September 1941, Adolf Hitler let his underlings know that the Third Reich was to be cleansed of Jews as quickly as possible. He approved the release of locomotives and rolling stock for removals. Heinrich Himmler, amongst others, was tasked with implementing the decision. Gradually the terrible news of imminent deportations trickled down to those who'd be worst affected – the Jews who were to be dispersed. As winter weather began to bite in November 1941, there were systematic transports from Anita's hometown, one thousand, or even two thousand people a day. It was only a matter of time before Anita's family was targeted.

At 6.30 a.m. on Wednesday, 8 April 1942, the first post arrived at the Laskers' new lodgings. Edith and Alfons received a letter giving notice that they were required to report to the police station at 9 a.m. the next day. After that it was said they'd be going to somewhere unspecified, to work. The night was spent packing and setting things straight so their daughters could manage without them. Anita and Renate went with them, hoping their parents would get a last-minute miracle; that there'd been a mistake. It was all so awful, and so unnecessary. Their father was a lawyer, their mother a musician – what possible labour could they be expected to do away from their home and children? The following Monday their parents had left on a train traveling eastwards.[2]

Anita and Renate had work, at least. The sort of work the Nazis valued, which meant a reprieve from relocation. Renate had been metaphorically tangled in a landscape of junk, compelled to endure long shifts at a recycling site sorting through squeezed-out toothpaste tubes and old tins. Everything to be used, nothing wasted – except her youth and talents. From here both girls were forced to labour in a paper factory. Renate was set to making serviettes, while Anita's job was considered a reserved occupation. She was part of the toilet paper production process.

She boasted to her sister that she could stick labels on about five thousand rolls a day, joking, 'I have attained a dexterity at doing this which I'll probably never be able to reach on the cello.'[3]

Irrepressible, the girls stole food ration cards which had somehow ended up at the factory for pulping.

Next to go on a journey into the unknown were Anita's aunt and uncle – leaving more room and calm in the flat they shared – then Anita's grandmother. It became increasingly difficult for the girls to work their long, long shifts and fend for themselves in food queues, so they conceded the need for support. Their move to the Jewish orphanage did not require a removal van: they took only clothes, essentials, and portable memories. The orphanage dated to 1880, founded at a time when the Jewish community in Breslau had the means and freedom to establish charitable institutions. The philanthropists who initiated the orphanage lived in an age of integration, imperfect but manageable. Unfortunately Anita and Renate came to it in an era when families and communities were being deliberately dismantled.

They never knew the exact date when they became actual orphans, rather than strays without parents. Their father was able to send some notes from Izbica ghetto in occupied Poland, then even these fragments of communication ceased.

The Lasker girls refused to act like waifs. They were feeling absurdly defiant despite their situation. With more courage than wisdom they began a daring scheme to upcycle paper in ways the Nazis would not approve. They started forging documents.

Many years later, Eric Williams, a British RAF navigator who famously tunnelled out of a prisoner-of-war camp in occupied Poland under cover of a wooden vaulting horse, was astonished to learn that it was cellist Anita Lasker-Wallfisch who had helped make fake passes for POWs such as himself, as well as French forced labourers in the paper factory, so that they stood a chance of passing police scrutiny while on the run during an escape bid. He'd always assumed his pass came from MI9, meaning British Military Intelligence. Anita, somewhat amused, made it clear that his forged papers had been crafted by daring teenage girls, typing away on an old machine, and recycling German paper in ways well beyond its intended purpose.

Even naïve Jewish girls could tell that the orphanage couldn't be a haven forever, not while life in Breslau was subject to sudden, frightening shifts. They decided to escape. They didn't have to tunnel out of a prison camp, snip wire or wear elaborate disguises. Posing as French girls and armed with home-forged papers, Anita and Renate simply packed a suitcase each and headed for Breslau main station. Since October 1941, all Jewish emigration from the Reich had been banned, making it perversely illegal for Jews to attempt to find safety. That didn't mean Anita and her sister couldn't try. They intended to take a train as ordinary passengers heading for Paris, where no one would know them as Jews. What to do when they got there . . . that was a problem for the future.

It was a future that never came to pass. They made it to the station all right. Renate boarded first, to find space for their luggage in the compartment. Anita was on the platform with dear friends Ruth and Werner Krumme, who'd insisted on coming to see the girls off. Any wartime parting was painful, given the seemingly infinite possibilities of calamity. Even with the optimism of a sixteen-year-old, Anita would appreciate how abruptly connections could be severed. Werner wasn't Jewish, but his wife was. In the Nazi worldview Werner was tethered to someone who had no right to exist.

Arresting the Krummes was just a bonus for the Gestapo, who appeared on the platform minutes before the Paris train was due to depart. They were there for the Lasker girls. Anita was caught first. Sweetly oblivious, her sister came to the train door and was arrested next. Their suitcases set off for Paris without them.

There was something of a glitch in transport. The black van never turned up to take them away. Police and dogs made a walking escort instead. Between being marched out of the station and on towards the Gestapo headquarters and the prospect of a torturous interrogation, Anita reached into her stocking top. How useful hosiery could be for tucking away small items such as a handkerchief . . . or a tiny vial of cyanide.

At the corner of Garten Strasse and Schweidnitzer Strasse – Anita's memory of the location was very particular – she and Renate took their secret stash of poison, poured the powder into their mouths and waited for the brief agony before death.

Anita was a little surprised not to smell cyanide's telltale scent of bitter almonds. It was sweeter than expected. She was equally surprised not to die. As she later found out, her friend had secretly substituted icing sugar for poison, otherwise it would all have been over. No story, no survival, no post-war life as a renowned cellist, no marriage, no meeting with Eric Williams, no red angora sweater on display in the Imperial War Museum, London.

'Our relief at still being alive was enormous,' she later wrote.

She wasn't done with life yet, not by a long way.

Unfortunately, the Gestapo wasn't done with her either. Prison loomed.

No more coffee and cake in the merry atmosphere of the Lasker apartment. No more family meals in the Feldman house. So many missing people, their places all too quickly taken by others, their rooms filled with strangers.

Knitting patterns for children starting a new school year, from
Deutsche Moden-Zeitung No. 10, 1939.
Lucy Adlington personal archive

At the Jewish Secondary School in Shefford, England, Jock Heidenstein was lodged with local people, far from her childhood home in Berlin. Her walk to school now took her along a busy road with English shops and pubs.

In modern Berlin, walking the route from Jock Heidenstein's pre-war home to her school – Linienstrasse to Auguststrasse – you are likely to pass through a pleasant square called Koppenplatz, named after a former mayor. At one end of the park, sometimes scented by rosebushes, is a disturbing scene. You face a bare wooden table. The sort of table that would stand in the centre of a kitchen, covered in baking pans, or children's homework, a sewing project or visa applications. There are two chairs. One is pushed under the table. The other is tipped up on the ground, as if knocked over in haste. The instinct is to reach down and set the chair right, but you can't. It is cast bronze, like the whole tableau. It can never be righted again.

The sculpture is the work of Karl Biedermann, put in place in 1996 to memorialise the Jewish residents deported from the neighbourhood. It is titled *Abandoned Spaces*. These spaces were not abandoned on a whim, or even by choice. Violence and bureaucracy enabled the relocations. No known photographs survive of the removals, the midnight flits, the arrests. But neighbours knew – how could they not know? – both the Jews who held their breath waiting for the knock to be on their front door, and the so-called Aryans grateful for their own safety. They heard police vans pull up, boots on the stairs, ringing of doorbells and pounding of doors.

Many arrests came at night, when the Gestapo preferred to do business so 'ordinary' citizens could try to pretend nothing grim was happening, but it was impossible not to notice the disappearance of entire families. In daylight the house clearance lorries came, with familiar business names painted on the sides. The sort of firms you'd book for moving house in happier times. When Jews vacated their homes, the vans were more like carrion crows, feasting on carcasses of abandoned rooms. The goods being hefted by removal men – furniture, bedding, crockery, clocks – none of it officially belonged to the Jews who'd bought it and used it. From 17 September 1941 a decree from Reichsmarschall Hermann Goering conceded only everyday needs to Jews in Germany: a right to clothing, food and living quarters. By late 1941 their use of living quarters was highly precarious. Valuable items were creamed off by officials and the rest deposited in warehouses ready to be sold at brazenly public auctions. Want a new sewing machine? Get to the auction house! Need a new bed? Place a bid! From egg cups to candelabras – all the clutter of cleared-out houses was up for sale.

Jock was spared all this reality. She had gleanings of goings-on back home in the letters her mother sent. The worst news was filtered out. Mania absorbed the truth so Jock wouldn't have to worry so much.

In Berlin the Gestapo called Hannah Karminski, director of the Jewish Advisory Board for Housing, into a meeting. She left with a pale face, unusually shaken for such a resolute woman known for having 'nerves of steel.'[4] Karminski had been one of the valiant team who'd supported the Kindertransport initiative, responsible for taking Jock Heidenstein and her sisters to safety in England. Now she faced a new task – clear hundreds more houses of Jews. Where could they go? No new houses were empty to receive them, even if Jews had been allowed to live in them.

In one of her precious messages, Jock's mother, Mania, was able to let her daughters in England know that she was leaving the family home on Linienstrasse. When Jock said goodbye to Berlin, had she really thought it would be forever? That she'd never see the rooms of her German childhood again? Fortunately there were still friends and family in Berlin to help her mother pack away memories, and to transport what was needed to a new, sublet home on Chorinerstrasse.

'I am very happy with the apartment,' Mania wrote to middle daughter, Rita, before sending 'countless kisses from your parents who love you.'

Mania also told her daughter to 'play a lot and forget the past.'[5]

Jock Heidenstein's past was rapidly being dismantled and dispersed. What happened to all the things she'd left behind because they wouldn't fit in the one suitcase permitted on the Kindertransports – the outgrown clothes, school books, childhood knick-knacks? Perhaps Mania was able to take all these, along with little David's teddy bear and toy building blocks. Perhaps she still hoped her children could all be reunited. Perhaps she knew, in her heart of hearts, that they were more likely to be scattered further.

Jock already had an uncle in Palestine, as well as uncles, aunts and cousins in occupied Poland. Miraculously one aunt, Chaim's sister Rosa Roifer, somehow evaded police scrutiny to escape Berlin and find passage to the US. She went to visit her sister-in-law Mania about a week before she left. Her journey coincided with the Japanese bombing of Pearl Harbour, on 7 December 1941. Mania said her final goodbyes. Then – the last letter.

In Berlin the post came three times daily. There was always the fear of bad news, or a summons. Mania was sustained by Red Cross messages from England. Twenty-five words of connection with the daughters she'd had to give up. Early in 1942 she sent her final Red Cross note to England. Jock remembered the news – 'that my Mother was expecting to be deported, with my brothers Michael and David, to Poland.'[6]

Poland. Her parents' home country. But this was not to be a visit to Mania's birthplace, Dobromil, or a catch-up with Chaim's brother Leo in Krakow, or relatives in towns and shtetls across the country. Deportees were not told the name of their next destination, or what they'd encounter at the end of the line.

———

In Berlin it was hard for locals to keep track of who was where, so many Jews were ousted from their proper addresses. There were all the men taken off to concentration camps, of course. Then the fit, young people able to pick up and emigrate. Then entire families pushed into trucks – gone. Even hospitals were emptied, including the Jewish hospital where the Heidenstein babies had been born.

It wasn't simply a question of moving somewhere smaller. From October 1941, Berlin Jews received notifications of impending deportation not just from their homes, but out of the country. Along with instructions to report at a nearby assembly point there was a questionnaire attached, going into great details about whatever scant property the deportee had held on to.

Jock's mother had to manage little David and toddler Michael as she filled in her Declaration of Assets – the *Vermögenserklärung*. What was even left to declare? She had no bank shares, no gold, no land. No carpets, tapestries or artworks. She was just a mother with two small children to care for and a maximum allowance of fifty kilograms of luggage. She had to sign her name to the statement *Keinerlei vermögenswerte verschwigen* – no assets concealed.

Not everyone had time to pack, even if they had the means to move their belongings. Sometimes there was a knock on the door, a cascade of commands, and a frantic harrying out of the house onto the pavement and into incarceration. Those who were prepared knew it was best to layer up in as many clothes as possible, to leave space in rucksacks and suitcases for other things. They had to dress as warmly as possible against the winter weather too. The first timetable of transports left Berlin in the winter months.

In November 1941, Jock Heidenstein wrote letters at her billet in the little town of Shefford. First to her sisters, Stella and Rita, then to her auntie Lotte in London.

'How do you like this weather?' she enquired of Stella, in laboriously joined up pencil lines that sloped down her economy notepaper from left to right. 'I like it very much but I wish I had a winter dress with long sleeves to wear and a pair of gloves. I am always as cold as ice.'[7]

Snow in Shefford meant trudging to school along slushy pavements, but at least there was a school to go to. Once at school, fuel was found to keep the stove warm in the main hall and there was always the cold anarchy of a snowball fight at break time to enliven things. Happily Jock's wish for a winter dress was granted. In January 1942, she wrote to give thanks for a parcel from Stella's foster mother, Debbie Adler, with a lovely selection of nice, new clothes, including a dress good enough for special occasions. Thanks to Debbie's generosity Jock could be warm inside and out. She was cared for.

Between the writing of Jock's two letters – November to January – thousands of Berlin Jews, already frozen out of society, were put on unheated trains eastward.

The tragedy was that, when called to report for deportation from Berlin, Jock's mother no longer had any way of communicating her own love and support. On the way to school Jock passed the Railway Steamer pub, reference to an era of more innocent train journeys. A train – a real railway steamer – would take her mother further and further away from her. Mania couldn't even let her daughters know where she was going. There was no chance to write, no way of sending a letter, and no knowledge of the destination.

The muster point for Jews in the Mitte district of Berlin was at a former Jewish Old People's Home on Grosshamburgerstrasse, walking distance from Jock's old home. It fronted an ancient Jewish cemetery now tangled with ivy and other creeping plants. Tall chestnut trees reached to the third-floor windows, not yet budding or bringing out new leaves that winter. Here Jock's mother and brothers joined hundreds of others, twenty or thirty to a room, all buffeted by overloaded baggage. They were three individuals out of about twenty-two thousand Jews brought to this transit centre.

Men at desks with shirts, swastika badges, ties and typewriters took Mania's Declaration of Assets. Just accountant types. Just doing their jobs. From Adolf Eichmann down to the lowliest secretary, they didn't consider themselves bad people; wouldn't call themselves perpetrators. They kept lists of names and addresses, ticking off each person once they'd been processed. All Jews had to swear they had no assets concealed.

Mania also had to put her signature to the statement, 'I, the undersigned, am the enemy of the German Reich.'

What had she done to be considered an enemy, except to exist as a Jew?

There are now no absolutely verifiable details of the next stage of Mania's journey. She first took one of the many trains listed as *Mit Unbekanntem ziel Ostwärts* – an unknown destination in the east. Following Jock's mother means balancing the bureaucratic euphemisms of Gestapo documents, and the ghosts of rumours passed down by survivors.

One cold winter's day, perhaps while Jock sat at her lessons in Shefford, Mania and Jock's little brothers were driven by truck to a freight yard in Berlin.

It might have been Grunewald, with its picturesque station building boasting a huge blue-faced clock with golden hands, and a roof that would eventually undulate a little from age. Now the stone wings carved above the door sprout from a train wheel, back then it boasted a Nazi swastika.

It might have been the Moabit yard on Putlitzstrasse, a grim landscape of abandoned factories and scrubby sidings where tracks 69, 81 and 82 were specifically used for loading Jewish 'freight' onto rolling stock of the Deutches Reichsbahn. Four decades after the war a memorial was erected to Jews deported from Moabit. It is a discordant metal sculpture on Putlitz bridge. One fragment of the poetic inscription reads, 'The ramp – tracks – steps and stairs had to go – this last way.'[8]

Surviving records show that Jock's Aunt Tauba, known in the family as Toni, left from Moabit on her 'last way.' Born in Przemsyl, like Jock's father Chaim, Tauba was fifty-five years old when she climbed into a cold cattle wagon along with over seventeen hundred other people. The majority of this 'freight' were women, the ones unable to leave Germany and not yet trapped in camps. There were also eighty-five children and teenagers. Her route took her along tracks not far from Anita Lasker's home town of Breslau, then on to the Lower Silesia region of occupied Poland and a place she'd likely never heard of.[9]

Aside from Nazi paperwork concerning her deportation, the only personal fragment of Aunt Tauba to survive is a note sent to Jock's little sister, Stella, in which she writes, 'I cried with joy that you are doing so well.'

However many miles Jock's mother travelled, east was the only direction. She didn't go directly to the end of the line. First Mania, David and Michael were unloaded into a transit ghetto, a place where Jews were corralled to suffer, work and wait. It's impossible now to specify which one. Some Berliners were initially transported to Minsk ghetto, unspeakably grim, although a hotbed of rebellion against German rule. Out of an estimated seven thousand Jews deported to Minsk from Germany only thirty survived.

Of Mania's neighbours, many went on trains to Piaski ghetto, just as horrific, and only a stopping-off point for far worse places, similar to Izbica ghetto, which was the last dwelling place of Anita Lasker's parents.

Then there was Riga, in occupied Latvia. Jock's father, Chaim, was never to know that some of his relatives in Poland were forced into the Rumbula forest near Riga, told to undress, then shot. A holocaust of bullets was unleashed on eastern Europe wherever the Nazis passed through. The trees of Rumbula also bore mute witness to the murder of some of Debbie Adler's relatives, the Londoner who'd taken Stella into her home and heart.[10]

Lodz ghetto in occupied Poland became the new home for many of the dispirited, bewildered German Jews clambering down from cattle wagons, such as shopkeeper Martha Jakobowitz, pictured sweeping broken glass into a bucket after her store was vandalised during Kristallnacht in 1938. Martha left Berlin before Mania Heidenstein, on the first November transport of 1941, passing through pretty Grunewald station for a new life in the city of Lodz.[11]

By the time Mania Heidenstein left Berlin, men such as Hitler, Himmler and Eichmann knew the eventual outcome of deportations east, even if the details were constantly being refined. But in this Europe of change, movement and motion, some journeys were towards life. It is in Lodz that we meet Chana Jochewet Zumerkorn, owner of a rather fabulous red sweater. Life and love would become embodied in Chana's stylish jumper of ribbed scarlet wool.

Lodz was a city that knew all about textiles, knitted and woven. It was comparable to Manchester or Bradford in England. In Lodz, weaver's cottages with high, sloping roofs were overshadowed by ornate nineteenth-century mills and intimidating blocks of grey industrial textile factories. Inside even the ugliest buildings the most beautiful fabrics were created.

Lodz was a city of machines and yarns, with fortunes to be made, and poverty to be endured. It was said half the population worked in textiles. Jews had financed and built many of the factories; Jews laboured in them. Chana Zumerkorn's father, David, was a small trader, working with her grandfather as a shoemaker.

Chana, her sister, Nechama, and her brother, Josef, were Lodzers born and bred. Josef was the oldest, born in 1918, the last year of the Great War. Chana was a year and half younger, only nineteen years old when the German army invaded Poland; Nechama was younger still.

All their lives would be changed forever by war.

The German army's triumphant entry into Lodz on 9 September 1939 was a spectacle of horses, armoured vehicles, motorbikes and marching. One boy watching the parade remembers the conquerors were so swollen with success they were singing '*Wir gehen gegen England* – We are marching against England!'[12]

England responded to the invasion with a declaration of war. Safe in England, Jock Heidenstein could only read about the collapse of Polish defences and occupation of her parents' homeland. Jews in Poland faced the choice of being persecuted at home, or escaping into unknown dangers. One of Jock's friends had experience of dressing to travel as a Jew in Europe, when you could only carry so much and there was never a guarantee of where you'd end up, or how you could warm yourself. Jock came to know Zahava Kanarek after the war. Zahava undertook her journey from occupied Holland 'dressed in as many layers as possible.'[13]

In Lodz, Chana Zumerkorn's brother, Josef, tried to persuade his family to leave the city, wearing and carrying whatever they could. At twenty-one, Josef chafed at the curfew imposed on Jews by their new German overlords, the escalating restrictions and deadly attacks on Jewish men in particular. By November that year he'd already been beaten, robbed and forced naked into the freezing waters of a lake at a holiday resort. That cold night bullets had been a mercy for those swiftly dying of exposure.

Josef made it back home to his family on that occasion, shivering and barely dressed. He was quite certain that 'the chances of remaining alive in Lodz were infinitesimal.'[14] Chana faced the choice of taking her chances in Russia, away from German brutality, or staying to endure the occupation.

Like Mania and Chaim Heidenstein, Chana Zumerkorn's parents – Dvora Gitla and David – had lived through the Great War. They knew it would be hard, but life had always been hard. They believed they could endure whatever happened. David was firmly set against leaving, telling his children, 'As bad as it is here, you have a roof over your head, you have a bed.'

The debate was pointless. One Polish soldier broken by defeat told Josef, 'If you can flee to the east, go. Save your lives.'

By east, he meant Russia. These words stuck with Josef as the German invaders forced him and his friends to fill in the defence trenches outside his home, dug when they thought there was a chance of holding off invasion. Even more so when he was seized on the street by Germans, compelled to clean an apartment stolen from a Jewish doctor, then beaten until he could barely move. At one point he suffered the humiliation of having to wash German vehicles with his own clothes. Josef, like many youths, had had enough. He'd leave until things got better.

Chana and Nechama travelled with Josef on the tram towards the train station. The uncertainty of journeying during wartime was as painful as the parting. The November weather was grim. Travellers going into the unknown definitely did want to dress in as many layers as possible, but poor Josef had few clothes left to wear after his recent ordeal of being stripped and forced at gunpoint into icy water. In a loving impulse, right there on the tram, Chana – as cold as anyone that winter, and owning little herself - pulled off the red sweater she was wearing and passed it to her brother, telling him, 'I'm sure you will need this.'[15]

Chana's red sweater would become a lifesaver and a red talisman of hope.

In the years of Nazi occupation of Lodz, Chana's family would need all the hope they could get.

What Lovely Things We Made in the Ghetto

We existed on what we had.
– JOSEF ZUMERKORN[1]

Josef Zumerkorn was gone. Chana's red sweater was folded in his rucksack ready to wear when needed. Chana and her sister, Nechama, decided to stay in Lodz. Once Josef was on his way the sisters had to hurry home before the German-imposed curfew of 5 p.m.

However tempting it might have been to set off on adventures with their brother, trusting to fate and taking only what they could wear or carry, things were different for girls. The dark reality was that in peace or war, predators sniffed out women for harassment and assault. Josef's female friends had to get inventive, acquiring escorts if they decided to quit Lodz. They pestered young men to marry them there and then, as a strategy in their bid for escape. It was a terrible perversion of the usual patterns of romantic courtship, and a sign of how desperate women were to get away. Very soon on his travels Josef got stopped and asked to provide husband status for a persuasive stranger. He had to refuse.

Besides the vulnerability of their sex, there were family expectations for girls like Chana: that they'd stay and look after their parents and grandparents. Traditionally, girls' lives were bound more to domestic roles, first as daughters, then as wives and mothers. It was hard to leave this pattern of life, and hard for many families to let their children go.

In Germany it very quickly became apparent that those who could escape the country were usually unaccompanied children, courageous young adults and men at risk of being rounded up. This left high numbers of elderly people and the women who took care of them, along with babies and toddlers. Deciding whether to stay or go was agonising. What would the Heidensteins have done, if they were in Lodz rather than Poland? There would have been no Kindertransport trains to take Jock, Rita and Stella to England and safety. Would they have tried to reach Russia?

Lola Weintraub, daughter of a Lodz merchant – a rag dealer like Chaim Heidenstein – wanted to leave Lodz. She was a year younger than Chana. Her widowed mother found the courage to tell her, 'If you want to go, I won't keep you,' and she began buying warm sweaters for Lola to take with her when the time came.[2] As it happened, Lola couldn't bear to leave her mother and sisters. Family ties weren't easily broken, and there was a sense of strength from staying together.

Chana Zumerkorn's parents were only middle aged and still very capable. All their lives they'd fought to maintain a loving, observant home, precariously lifted above destitution. A very poignant family portrait from 1920 still exists, showing Dvora and David dressed in their best clothes for the camera. The styles are up to date for the years just after the Great War. Dvora's hair is neatly sculptured and her dress has a sailor collar and piping. David is equally well groomed with a well-tailored wool suit and striped waistcoat. Josef, two years old in the photograph, has a beautifully stitched coat with six fat buttons and a flamboyant big-bowed cravat. He holds a wooden hoop, the sort used for bowling along the cobbles for fun.

In this picture, Dvora, David and Josef all look at the camera with formal dignity. Chana, just a year old, has clearly seen something just beyond the photographer. She looks as if she has the beginnings of a smile. Matching Josef's hoop, she has a ball to hold. It's about as big as her head, but perhaps keeps her from fidgeting as the group are immortalised in the camera flash. For all baby Chana wears a crisp white bow and flounced white dress, her footwear gives nuance to the portrait. The soles of her boots are thick, practical and worn; the nails on the heels are clearly visible. Looking closely, it's clear Dvora's polished shoes are firmly sensible too, as are Josef's lace-up boots.

Dvora and David Zumerkorn with their children Chana and Josef, Lodz 1920.
Yad Vashem/Holocaust Remembrance Center

Remembering his childhood years in Lodz, Chana's brother Josef, said, 'You can't grasp the poverty.'[3]

Money might be in short supply, but love and loyalty in the family were not. Dvora Gitla, their mother, was a housewife; their father, David, was a shoemaker.[4] They earned just enough to rent two large rooms of a tenement house in the Old Marketplace of Lodz – *Stary Rynek* in Polish – site of the original village settlement that had grown into the industrial city. It was a very Jewish area, with a small synagogue in the building where the Zumerkorns lived and Jewish neighbours all around. A well-rooted community that knew how to pull together in adversity.

In her early years, after the tumult of the Great War, Chana would have come down worn wooden steps from her home and into the square, a squalid chaos of stalls, carts and horses. Village women dressed in red woollen coats crouched by their wares, and town traders presided over miniature mountains of haberdashery, fabrics, stockings and lace.[5] From tailored suits to aprons, socks and skirts, Lodzers knew how to make things that people wanted to buy.

This rough, gritty market was closed for good by the time Chana reached her teenage years, leaving the square a little desolate but with a clear view of a nearby park and the busy thoroughfare of Zgierska Street. The square was a good place to meet friends – 'tons of friends,' Josef boasted – whether dragging their heels on the long walk to school, or for rare trips to the theatre, cinema and dances. Money might be tight, but culture wasn't unobtainable for those with an appetite for it. Josef was friendly with the vendors at local news kiosks who'd let him have papers that had been read and returned. In this way the whole family could follow local politics as well as read about the growing menace of Nazism in Europe.

Throughout Chana's teen years there was certainly talk of war, but the daily challenge of subsistence living pushed a lot of that to one side, even when one of her father's cousins turned up in

October 1938 telling ominous stories of how he'd been ejected from Germany just for being Jewish.

That was just normal, they thought; the usual antisemitism that had Josef occasionally stoned by Polish boys on his way to school, or Poles on the street hissing, *Hitler will get you.*

It wouldn't be Hitler personally, of course. After the invasion and occupation there were hundreds of German officials and hangers-on who were only too happy to subdue Lodz and to extort as much pleasure and profit from the occupation as possible. Any Pole was a target, but Jews – one third of the population – were singled out for particular persecution.

Josef Zumerkorn saw that his best chance of staying alive was leaving the city. He avoided getting strafed by German Messerschmitt planes on the routes out of town and embarked on a tumultuous journey with Chana's red sweater as both protection and memento.

Chana stayed behind to face the first harsh winter of the war. If she missed the warmth of her red sweater, she missed her brother more.

As Josef's worldview expanded, Chana's shrank. Jews became prisoners in their own city. Aggressive laws from the German occupiers came thick and fast. It was bad for all Poles, and worse again for Jews.

Chana's daily life became a battle between Nazi repression and Jewish resilience. Bakeries in the neighbourhood ran out of flour, so she had to stand in line for bread distribution, in fear of some Pole saying, 'There's a Jew.' That fear was compounded when it became compulsory for all Jews in Lodz to wear a 'Jewish Yellow' band on their right arm, soon after replaced by a yellow Star of David. Lodz Jews were the first in the Third Reich to be marked this way. Now antisemites could clearly see who their targets were. Prosperous mill owners were hounded from their homes and paraded in chains in a clanking tour of humiliation around other Polish towns.[6]

From 18 October 1939, Jews were forbidden to trade in leather or textile goods. All this, in an economy built around textiles. The ban was devastating news for Chana's father and grandfather, diligent shoemakers all their lives. Non-Jews no longer felt obliged to pay Jews for services anyway, so they somehow had to find Jewish customers to sell off stock in secret. As each winter passed, supplies of basics such as leather, wool and cloth dwindled until it took quite an investment just to buy a needle threaded with a length of cotton from a street pedlar. Eventually shoe leather became so scarce one Lodzer said hide scraps were 'like diamonds, worth more to me than all of my possessions combined.'[7] In Polish winters no one could afford to be without shoes or boots, yet Jewish footwear was reduced to holes and patches held together with string and optimism.

It wasn't just the usual shortages of a wartime economy. As Mania Heidenstein had already discovered, under German rule there was no such thing as Jewish property. Everything and anything could be appropriated, from factory goods, furs and silks, down to rags, scraps and offcuts. As well as Jewish belongings, the very names of their streets were stolen, replaced with German choices. Chana's home in Stary Rynek became Alt Markt. From April 1940 the city was named Litzmannstadt, not Lodz.

The poorest working-class areas of Lodz were designated as a Jewish ghetto. Any Jew outside the ghetto zone – rich or poor – was given notice to move. Dragging sledges or anything on wheels through blizzards and along icy streets, families salvaged what they could from their own homes to find a house, a room, a corner in the ghetto.

Chana's home was right at the edge of the new ghetto boundary, and inside the ghetto zone. Signs at the ghetto perimeter read *Wohngebeit der Juden betreten verboten* – 'Jewish residential area, entry forbidden.' From the former marketplace Chana had a view of a park she could no longer walk in and a street she could no longer reach. Tangled forests of barbed wire were strung along the main road beside the marketplace, so that non-Jews could still use the tram route that bisected the ghetto area. Just along from Chana's building was one of three wooden bridges arching across Aryan-only roads. Jews with yellow stars and worn boots had to climb up and down the stairs of these bridges to reach the other side of the road. Passengers in the trams could gawp at the creatures clustered on the ghetto streets, as if they were occupants of the world's most gruesome human zoo.

Ghettos in occupied Poland were a means of corralling and controlling Jews until the Nazis had finalised long-term plans. They were also a dumping ground for Jewish people deported from Germany and other territories under German rule. Trains from Berlin certainly made their way through snow, rain and starlight to bring their helpless passengers to the city. It may well be that Jock's mother, Mania, was offloaded in Lodz, along with little David and Michael Heidenstein.

Jews from Western Europe were relatively affluent compared to impoverished Jews of the ghetto. One young ghetto resident said, 'We gazed in awe at the newcomers in their well-tailored suits and well-padded coats.'[8]

Even by 1942, Berliners might still be wearing smart suits and warm clothes, with suitcases of spare garments. That would all change. The ghetto was already beyond capacity. Western Jews were hustled into a disused school building with nowhere to sleep but the bare floor. From here they'd have to learn to survive day by day.

If Mania did make it to Lodz after her departure from Berlin, she too would have learned how to survive in this landscape of cold deprivation. How to barter fancy outfits and elegant shoes for big boots and woollen shawls. How to wear thick woolly mittens when peeling potatoes. How to eat the peelings when there were no clothes left to barter for food.

In the ghetto, as one man noticed, 'Almost everyone clutches some clothing or a pair of shoes in their hands. They are either selling or have just bought.'[9]

The ghetto Bank for Purchase of Valuable Objects and Clothing made enormous profits once Jews from Western Europe reluctantly slunk in to exchange their precious wardrobes for ghetto money. This paper scrip was worthless outside the ghetto, but essential for a bare minimum of food inside. The income from the items went straight to the Germans, of course, at exchange rates to favour them too. It was the same when a ban on Jews owning fur coats came into play in December 1940. Despite the freezing weather, thousands of fur coats and collars were handed over so that non-Jewish Germans could be warm.

The restrictions on Lodz Jews were grim, and the situation only worsened as months of oppression turned into years. In these demeaning circumstances the people of the ghetto nevertheless worked a kind of magic to try to survive, even if they couldn't thrive.

Chana, the girl who gave up her sweater out of love, not duress, played her part in this magic.

Looking for fragments of Chana Zumerkorn in the ghetto is like seeking out scraps of red in a mountain of multi-coloured rags. It is mainly thanks to bureaucracy that we can now trace her at all. The lives of so many Lodz Jews are given a kind of immortality in printed forms, scrawled signatures, spreadsheets and notices bashed out on hardy typewriters.

Among all the records salvaged from Lodz archives are glimpses of the Zumerkorn family. A census of permanent residents of Lodz in 1931 lists the parents and three children – David, Dworja Gitla, Josef, Chana and Nechama. Just ten years later, in the 1941 listings of Lodz ghetto inhabitants, the Zumerkorns are still living at

Stary Rynek 2, but Josef's name is absent.[10] At this time Josef was darting from one chance of safety to another, battered by Germans, Poles and Russians in whichever town he came to. He found work in a knitting factory, then for the Max Factor cosmetics company in Warsaw, next on a farm near Bialystok in northeast Poland and finally across the border into Russia. There were brief, shining moments of kindness from strangers along the way that lit Josef's soul. And there was the constant warm connection of Chana's red sweater.

As for Chana, her life is more elusive and definitely more constrained. We find her again on 25 September 1941, when she applies for an identification card. Without an ID there could be no work. Without work, no food. No life. Her face is captured in a grey passport-style portrait attached to the application form, with head tilted but eyes straight to the camera. Thick hair is coiled at the nape of her neck. She's grown into a young woman not far from her twenty-second birthday. Her image is proof that she existed, but it says nothing of her hopes, her experiences, her quirks or character.

The ghetto bureaucracy proliferated because the Germans recognised opportunities to exploit a captive workforce, by stealing their businesses, and by bullying and starving them into forced labour. Organisation of the ghetto workforce was facilitated by a council of Jewish men headed by Chaim Mordechai Rumkowski, a charismatic, ambitious, abusive and even ruthless man. Rumkowski impressed upon the ghetto population that they should work to stay alive.

Since Lodz was a town of textile talents, the first workshops to be opened in the ghetto were small tailoring factories, sprinkled around the ghetto in unheated buildings with wide windows. These expanded to include an impressive array of establishments tasked with producing items including coats, hats, bedding, woollens and footwear, slippers, uniforms, underwear and toys.

The creations were brilliant, given the working conditions and limited resources. Like characters in a fairy tale, the nimble-fingered Jews of Lodz seemed to turn straw into gold, or at least transform debris into profit for the German overlords. At a literal level, Lodzers turned straw into shoes – giant platforms of plaited straw that went over military boots so that soldiers could manage the deep snows of winter campaigns. Workers in the straw shoe factory had to plait fifteen metres of straw every day or sew at least three pairs of shoes. Then the demand increased to six pairs daily. Anyone who objected would be sacked. They didn't dare object. Work was life, after all.

Chana's work was exacting enough, but far easier than straw plaiting. She earned her daily bread at a knitting workshop run by Abram Goldfarb at 19 Bazarna Street. It was only ten minutes away, but what an ordeal those ten minutes would be in deep winter. To reach the workshop Chana had to cross one of the high wooden bridges over the Jew-free tram route – so many steps for a hungry, tired walker! – then pass by Bazarna Square. Bazarna Square was a site of public executions. Under German rule, Jews could be hung for breaking any one of the hundreds of rulings, from attempting to escape the ghetto, to trading dresses or stealing yarn. Punishments for theft were grotesquely ironic given the Nazi predilection for robbery.

We can't now know whether Chana knitted the neat rib fabric of the sweater she gave to Josef. We do know that her ID application lists her as *Strumpfarbeiterin*, or stocking maker. The yarns she handled at work would be shiny cotton lisle and twisted wool. The legs that would wear this hosiery would be German. Aryan only.

Thanks to the efforts and talents of workers in Lodz factories, the Reich acquired a multitude of assets, with ghetto officials – both German and Jewish – creaming off the best for themselves. In return, the army of exhausted labourers got soup and bread. As one anonymous diarist in the ghetto noted with bitterness, 'We work hard and help them win the war.'[11]

Chana Zumerkorn was one of many thousands of Jewish labourers in Lodz who knitted her way from one meal to the next, no doubt helping support her family too. Her sister, Nechama, also made hosiery. At a knitting machine – undoubtedly appropriated from its original owner – a specialist could watch yarn get looped into socks and stockings at a rate of over five thousand stitches a minute, all the while checking that the wool didn't split or the needle snap.

Wehrmacht soldiers would trudge through snow on the Eastern Front in their new uniforms with protective straw over-boots. Those who had woven the straw with shredded, bleeding fingers had toes pinched by frostbite. German civilians could strut in new fashions, seduce in new lingerie, roll on new stockings, spread new lace tablecloths out for the evening meal and sleep under new bedding. The stitchers and knitters of Lodz were sometimes reduced to burning their furniture for fuel. This contrast is stark in photos of ghetto existence. German soldiers are bulky with long overcoats that strain over the many warm layers; Lodzers have frazzled knitwear, coats stripped of fur collars and cropped short, by order of the ghetto administration. They hunch against the cold in patterned shawls and blanket squares. There were literally millions of items knitted in Lodz . . . for people considered more worthy of warmth.[12]

One German soldier wrote home in praise of his recently received pair of 'brand-new hand-knitted woollen gloves, worked like mittens but with the index finger free to shoot and work the machine gun.' He was very pleased with this practicality, having 'always got cold hands when shooting.' He didn't acknowledge the labour or existence of the person who knitted these gloves. Or for the victims on the receiving end of his gun.[13]

Germans were snug; their victims shivered. 'Each winter seemed worse than the last,' wrote a girl working in the ghetto administration.[14] Given the vital need for clothing to warm stressed and starving bodies, and the lack of such clothing for Jews in wartime, Chana's gift of a woolly jumper to her brother is all the more significant. It goes beyond practicality. In a world of oppression and theft, her selflessness transforms an ordinary object – the red sweater – into something extra special, even spiritual. Her gift ensured her life would remain entwined with Josef's. As he travelled deep into Russian territory, he stayed connected through the jumper. His body was warmed by it, and it also covered his suffering heart.

Chana's generosity in gifting the sweater wasn't unique among the Jews of Lodz ghetto. We don't know if she made it herself, but there were others who committed time, talent, energy and precious yarn into crafting woollens for friends and family. It took ingenuity to acquire knitting yarn, even for homeworkers who had stocks allocated for this outsourced labour, let alone for workshop knitters under the scrutiny of bosses who had to account for every gram.

A hand-knitting class for girls in Lodz ghetto, March 1944, taught by
Mrs P. Bronowska.
Ross Henryk/Art Gallery of Ontario

Work created community in spite of harsh conditions and meagre rations. Tens of thousands of deft fingers transformed scraps into wonders. Although forced into the labour, the workers themselves found ways to resist Nazi degradation, whether by singing over their work, or by running lotteries in the factory to raise money for Jewish hospitals or dressing as smartly as possible despite shrunken flesh, aching bones and dilapidated wardrobes. Life surged regardless. Through their industry they showed the world what they were capable of, even if the world would not acknowledge the source. Artisans even created stylish Art Deco–style albums of images to showcase Lodz's commercial capabilities to German capitalists and profiteers.

Turning the pages of these albums, the viewer peers into a world that was once colour, though it is now black and white. Tailoring, lingerie, knitting . . . perhaps somewhere in the shots of workers bent over machines, yarns and fabric there is a sighting of Chana. Could she be the woman in a knitted top with puffed sleeves? The girl in a short-sleeved stripey jumper? We wouldn't know. Those who'd recognise her face are long gone.

A photographic parade of finished products shows the range of creativity of stitchers and knitters like Chana. German businessmen exploiting the Lodz ghetto browsed the album in the 1940s equivalent of scrolling on a shopping app. There'd be plenty to admire, from ladies sweaters with ribs, stripes or honeycomb designs to baby frocks, or socks of every shade and length. Did Chana knit any of the items recorded? How could we know? She was one of many thousands, of which only a few feature in the albums.

There is inevitably a shadow side to the albums, for all the pride in the production. The faces of women modelling available fashions are often in darkness to hide any hint of Jewishness or individuality. There are no yellow stars on the clothes they wear and all signs of malnutrition are hidden. The fates of all those involved in the machinery, making or modelling of Lodz enterprises were shadowed by darker Nazi plans.

Among the reams of administrative documents salvaged from Lodz ghetto is a rather querulous letter noting that a supplier to a yarn spinning department has fallen behind 'due to overstraining my workforce and my means of transport.'[15] The ghetto workforce were subsisting on starvation rations and suffering the diseases of poverty and prolonged stress. It's no wonder their punishing schedules were 'overstraining' them. As for 'means of transport,' rolling stock on railways to and from Lodz were overloaded not only with manufactured goods, but also with human cargo. The ghetto was being depleted.

In September 1942, Chana Zumerkorn received notification that she and her parents were to be relocated to another work camp. Her sister Nechama was spared. Many letters were written to ghetto officials, begging for exemption from relocation, citing one heartbreaking reason after another: too ill, too broken, too much needed for caring responsibility of other ill, broken relatives. Most were denied. The Germans imposed horrifically high quotas. Chaim Rumkowski scrambled to fill them. Children, invalids, pensioners – these were considered surplus mouths in a ghetto that existed for maximum productivity. Why then was Chana selected, when she was a stocking worker? More importantly, where was she being sent? The answer to both questions: unknown.

Ignoring the summons was not a good option, even though there were people who hid in bunkers, in wardrobes, in piles of rags. The problem for those going 'underground' was getting food. This was impossible without an ID card or a job. They couldn't live off crumbs and fresh air, and there was always a possibility that the new camp in the country would be healthier.

As ever, strong boots and warm clothing were priorities for

travel. These could be acquired by bartering kitchen utensils and other household goods. Some stitched bags and knapsacks to pack essentials. For the most impoverished it was simply a question of wearing everything they owned – becoming walking wardrobes. One girl, Barbara Stimler, survived her time in Lodz ghetto by knitting lace tablecloths. When transports out of the ghetto began she took to wearing two pairs of stockings whatever the weather, thinking it best to be prepared. There were even some people who slept fully dressed in case the Gestapo came to fetch them in the night.

Lodz documents mark 22 September 1942 as the date Chana changed her address. The Zumerkorns closed the door on their two-room apartment for the last time. They were joined by Chana's elderly grandparents. Farewells had already been made . . . or were now too late. Perhaps they hoped to meet up with friends and relatives who'd gone before them, because there'd already been many, many transports out of Lodz.

They crossed the old marketplace and walked with their luggage to the muster point as ordered. From here there was rapid transit to Radegast station. Here, Chana Zumerkorn waited for a train.

Some months before Chana's departure, an anonymous young woman in the ghetto wrote an entry in her diary: 'What lovely things we made in the ghetto! We take rags and make them into rugs, uniforms, everything a person needs.'[16]

Where did the rags come from? Where was Chana going?

The answer to both these questions are all tangled up with clothes, and an appalling secret.

9

Nobody Must Know

The railways are of particular importance in this vast country.
— BAEDEKER'S GUIDE TO THE GENERAL
GOVERNMENT, 1943

As Chana Zumerkorn stood with her parents and their baggage at Radegast train station, to the north of Lodz ghetto, she knew only that she was going to "work outside the ghetto," or so went the phrase being passed around by officials. It didn't sound so bad considering the claustrophobia of ghetto confines. Chana hadn't been beyond the ghetto boundaries since barbed wire was first unrolled and stapled to wooden stakes along her street, back in spring 1940. The ghetto was so cut off from the rest of the world she'd only get gleanings of news, passed mouth to ear in secret. It was very different from pre-war years, when her brother Josef had hovered around the news kiosks waiting for cast-off papers.

This isolation was deliberate. The Nazis knew how to keep secrets; how to hide the truth behind exuberant propaganda films, slippery language and fresh-faced lies.

In 1943 Baedecker's — the popular tourist publication for destinations in Europe and beyond — published a new edition on the General Government: the occupied areas of Poland under the aegis of the Reich. Or, to be more precise, they published a detailed colonial overview of conquered territory for German travellers wanting to see how Eastern Europeans were being civilised through Nazi administration.

The text of the publication is small and dense. There's so much to pack in for the tourist eager to explore! Rustic views soon to be improved by German agricultural techniques. Quaint peasants, continually benefiting from German work ethics. Cities and towns enjoying the introduction of excellent German culture. Yet even between the tiny typewritten lines there are absences. What's missing is more chilling than what is described.

Why does the Baedecker editor note that by 1943 some cities in the General Government are 'free of Jews'?

Baedecker's refers to Lodz by the German name of Litzmannstadt. It gives a population tally of 484,000 Germans, Poles and Ukrainians. No mention of Jews. The city is praised as one of Europe's most important textile centres, 'thanks to German energy.' Still no mention of Jews. Chana Zumerkorn's long hours knitting socks and stockings count for nothing, along with all the other thousands of Jewish labourers. The guide gives details of must-see ancient Christian monasteries and new Christian churches, as if synagogues had never existed. There are fold-out maps of city centres with curiously blank spaces, as if ghetto areas were invisible to the Aryan eye.

On visiting Lodz photo reporter Liselotte Purper declared with enthusiasm, 'Germans, myself included, feel right at home here. One no longer sees any Jews.'

Another reporter, Erika Groth-Schmachtenberger, praised the 'astounding energy' of the German administration for cleansing the city of 'foreign, parasitic elements.'[1]

In Baedecker's, tourists new to Litzmannstadt/Lodz are informed about the 'generous redesign program' in operation 'based on modern urban planning and socio-hygienic principles.'[2] Chana's journey out of the ghetto was all part of such ruthless planning and principles. In her short life – just twenty-two years old when ordered to muster for the train at Radegast station – she'd had no opportunity to browse a Baedecker guide, or to visit any of the countries they described, such as Great Britain, India, Italy or Egypt. Josef – without the benefit of any Baedecker book – was only in Russia because it was marginally safer than occupied Poland. Now Chana was leaving everything she'd ever known behind. Would anyone watch her go? Would there be anything left of her when she was gone?

German snapshots didn't directly lie about life in Lodz but they didn't come close to telling the truth either. Any time their camera lens pointed towards Jews it was from a perspective of superiority. Ghetto survivor Arnold Mostowicz summed up these photos best: 'Although they were real they did not show the truth.'[3]

Walter Genewein, dedicated Nazi and chief ghetto accountant, took hundreds of colour slides of the ghetto. They only surfaced in 1987, in a Viennese used-book shop. His compositions centred Aryan extraction of profit in the most orderly way possible. Chana might well be visible in the pages of Genewein's album, in busy streets or workshop scenes, contributing to the profits in Genewein's accounting ledgers. If so, she would not be named. We'd never know. Genewein's shots of Jewish life and labour are viewed through a lens of judgement, as if Jews were intrinsically untidy, for all their temporary economic value.

The modern viewer brings a different perspective, knowing each image is a precious memorialisation. In one of Genewein's pictures the camera lingers on a group of young schoolboys who are waiting for their soup ration from the ghetto kitchen. They are a rag-tag bunch. Thin, impatient, squinting at the camera from under motley flat caps. Just right of centre is a boy in a red striped sweater, marred by the splotch of a yellow fabric star. The camera captures him for a second. When that moment is gone the boy is gone too, moving into the next minute of his life.

He had a name. He had a family once, and memories, and an exquisite awareness of immediate hunger, clamour and the feel of wool on this thin body. The camera couldn't capture that. Just the flash of red remains – a soft connection with the red of the sweater that Chana gifted Josef.[4]

Other cameras were carried in the ghetto, but not so openly. Jewish photographers Mendel Grossman and Henryk Ross secretly

Children in Lodz ghetto photographed by Walter Genewein. The boy in the red striped sweater stands in the centre, wearing white breeches.
United States Holocaust Memorial Museum, courtesy of Robert Abrams

photographed Jews from Germany and elsewhere being deported from the ghetto in 1942. Surviving images show lines of people in a snowy street, bulging with luggage, from homemade backpacks to string bags.

Grossman had his coat specially adapted so he could snap thousands of pictures without police being any the wiser. As a Jew, he wasn't supposed to be recording the reality of life and death in the ghetto. These were secrets only the Nazis could know. The images that now survive immortalise the resilience of Jews in Lodz. They show scenes that were all too familiar to Chana Zumerkorn – women in fringed shawls selling scraps in streets white with snow; in patched overalls hauling a cart of floury bread loaves; in cardigans and aprons saying heartbreaking farewells between diamond-shaped gaps of the wire fence of the deportation muster point.

Just taking the photos was an act of resistance. For both Jewish photographers their official job was to take propaganda photos of ghetto industry, including the albums showcasing the work of stocking knitters like Chana. In addition Grossman and Ross were tasked with producing photographs for identification papers. They devised an ingenious method of posing multiple people at once, instead of using separate shots for each individual. The resulting print could then be cut to passport-size. This way they could pilfer spare camera film for his own projects.

Did Chana Zumerkorn take her place on the stacked benches and hold still for Grossman or Ross when she needed a photo for her ID application – the same photo that survives in Lodz archives to this day? It would be nice to think that she features in one of the joyful portraits Ross took, which give a fantastically vivid sense of vibrancy in ghetto life, alongside the misery. There are young people stealing a kiss, children enjoying birthday parties and well-dressed groups defying oppression. In reality, Chana most likely never crossed paths with these more privileged Jews in the ghetto. Hers was a world of scarcity and endurance.

Kisses, birthdays and pretty frocks last forever in Ross's happier images; they soon slipped into the past with the proliferation of deportation orders.

When Chana's turn came on 22 September 1942, there may have been a photographer at the station. Maybe the German Walter

Genewein, choosing to focus on subdued scenes of passengers and bundles by a static train. Maybe Mendel Grossman or Henryk Ross, capturing the agony of departure through stealthy shots of gaunt faces and clasped hands.

There are no surviving images of what happened when passengers eventually descended from the train.

But there were sometimes witnesses.

Twelve-year-old Zofia Szałek was set to watching cows, but she was a curious child. While the cattle munched and ruminated she sought out the strange place in the forest. An estate fenced off with long horizonal planks of wood. Beyond the fence was an abandoned mansion house, about a century old, built in a neo-Gothic style overlooking the river Ner. A palace, it was called locally. A palace it might have seemed to any farmers and villagers unused to tap water, bathrooms or electricity. Incomers considered the nearby town of Chelmno primitive, but it was a neat enough community of fields, orchards, streets and houses. The palace grounds had run-down outbuildings, neglected gardens and a church still used for Sunday services. It was some fifty miles from Lodz.

In 1941 the palace gained new occupants and a new, mysterious purpose. In the tussle for control of Poland, Russian invaders in the east had lost out to German colonisers from the west. Now men in green-grey uniforms were everywhere. They commandeered whatever took their fancy. They filled the streets with trucks, and jails or graves with those who objected. They took over the riverside estate and hired local Poles to make the place habitable. They named it Kulmhof.

For a while Zofia's mother had a job in the palace, cleaning and cooking for the German occupiers. Then the fence went up. The palace was closed off from prying eyes. Unknown workers arrived in sealed black vans. They were never allowed beyond the fence.

Locals speculated – was this to be another ghetto, like the one they'd heard of at Lodz? A place where Polish Jews would be corralled and kept for labour? Chelmno Christians knew about Nazi policies of discrimination against Jews. Some were indifferent. Some sympathised. No one dared object openly.

Men in uniforms weren't the only new arrivals in the area. On trains and in wagons German settlers appeared, aiming to farm and raise families. As if by magic, there were empty farms and homes waiting for them. The farms had tools in the sheds and animals in the fields. The homes had curtains at the windows, food in the cupboards and crockery on the shelves. There were even vases of fresh flowers arranged to welcome the settlers. This was all the work of the Nazi Women's Labour Service. Young recruits were proud of the fact that they could freshen up a whole house in just a few hours, once the original Polish householders had been hustled off the property with a few bundles of belongings. The Poles were not permitted to take away the best stuff, of course. Not any pans, clothes or coffee grinders that could be washed and tidied, ready for use by the new owners.[5]

Germans based at the Chelmno palace were also homed nearby. Zofia's mother made a bit of money cleaning for them, with Zofia to help, when the girl wasn't out minding cattle . . . or spying into the palace estate. The men in uniforms tolerated Zofia. She was Catholic, after all, not Jewish. Just a little local girl. They thought her harmless. Indulged her, even. She peered through the fence and hid in bushes to watch whatever the Germans did in the woods around the palace. A child could creep in places adults wouldn't suspect.

By early December 1941, the palace was a very busy place. Outbuildings and servants' spaces were converted into workshops. Zofia spied tailors, shoemakers and embroiderers, stitching endlessly for the Germans at the palace. There was even a wool combing area, although she didn't at first understand why.

The main building was not to be a luxury country home for some Nazi bigwig; not a hunting lodge even, for German occupiers who fancied themselves a good shot against deer and boars. The once grand mansion rooms were devoid of finery and stripped of all furnishings. In place of artworks and antiques, they became filled with a strange, limp treasure.

Used clothes.

This textile hoard was collected and sorted by harried workers who tugged at garments to divide them into piles: best quality, wearable, rags. Zofia watched as garments came flying from upper windows of the palace – empty sleeves and trouser legs flapping as they fell, thrown by nameless, faceless workers. Down on the ground, in the palace yard, clothes were heaped into a tangled textile mountain. Sometimes little trinkets fell from pockets. Mostly all the pockets had been emptied; valuables had been torn from hiding places in seams, hems and shoulder pads. When it rained, the clothes rotted. Up shuffled shackled workers, stuffing clothing into blanket bundles.

Eventually an enormous tent went up in the palace yard, big enough to hold a circus.[6] There was more sorting, more bundle stuffing. Clothes were disinfected in a van filled with devilish clouds of sulphurous smoke. The nicest garments were selected by Germans who worked at the palace. Others were distributed to German settlers. A chauffeur called Tonni was known to be just your man if you wanted to buy a nice frock on the sly, no questions asked. Vans took heavy loads on the road to the town of Lodz, some twenty miles away, where the clothes would take on new lives and find new wearers.

On one occasion Zofia approached a Jewish boy called Moniek who worked sorting the mountains of clothes. Her mother had died and she needed a pair of knitted black stockings to go into mourning. Not a problem. Stockings were sourced and gifted. Zofia never mentioned how long she wore them; whether they were snagged or darned or faded over time. She never knew what became of Moniek.

Endless clothes – but where were the people?

'Nobody must know,' said one of the German staff who paid Zofia to clean for him.

They knew.

Anyone could see the trucks of people driving towards the palace grounds. Locals somehow knew they were Jews and Roma. Zofia even watched transports of children drive to the palace. One day, roaming, she came across a groaning man in a ditch watched by a man in uniform. She backed away and ran home. Curiosity got the better of her. Returning to the estate, she came to understand where all the piles of clothes came from: she witnessed naked people being beaten into vans then gassed to death. Decades later she remembered the scenes: 'Here they used to undress. There was an enormous pile of these clothes.'[7]

From December 1941 onwards the palace and grounds were used as a site to finesse details of industrial scale murder, utilising adapted vans to gas people en masse. At first they were mainly victims from the local area. Later the palace was a killing site for transports brought from the city of Lodz and elsewhere. Young Zofia had inadvertently stumbled across a prototype for the hideous superstructures of later extermination camps such as Treblinka, Sobibor, Majdanek and Auschwitz. The atrocities at Chelmno were a step along the path to the Nazi 'Final Solution' – eradication of all Jews alongside other people considered 'unworthy of life.'

It's one thing to read of genocidal policies; far harder to hold in mind what this meant for millions of ordinary individuals. People we've never met, and can never know. For a moment we can pause and think of a girl who gave away her warm red sweater, because a beloved brother needed it more. A girl who lived all her life in a tiny apartment in an old market place. Who worked, laughed, cried, dreamed. Whose life was everything to her, but nothing to her murderers.

Twenty-two-year-old Chana Zumerkorn, along with her parents, her grandparents and endless others, saw the sky for the last time at Chelmno. She felt autumnal air on her skin as her clothes were shed. She breathed her last in agony. She was buried without ritual, without mourners, without a grave marker. Because men with rotten hearts wished it.

Years after the war, Zofia Szałek, still living in the Chelmno area, was asked what she'd witnessed at the palace killing site. She said it had looked like 'the end of the world.'[8]

'Nobody must know.'

Easy for Zofia's German employer to say, yet for all the secrecy there were always clues.

When the man came home from work his boots stank from standing in grave pits. It took a lot of soaking to get the filth from the leather. Zofia rubbed them with soap the German gave her. The Germans never had any shortage of soap, it seemed, or whatever was needed. She noticed that at the end of the working day the man's uniform buttons had been torn away, leaving loose threads. She understood this was the work of frantic fingers, as victims fought for their lives.

The secrecy around the killings wasn't from a feeling of shame. Heinrich Himmler – one of the main Nazi architects of genocide in Europe – notoriously boasted that the eradication of Jewish life was 'a glorious chapter that has not and will not be spoken of.'[9]

Secrecy was imperative to ensure that Jews elsewhere in Europe could be tricked into believing their docility under Nazi rule would be rewarded with life. If the truth about the extermination centres was widely known it would be far harder to suppress Jewish revolts. There was also the matter of maintaining a façade of charitable benevolence back in Germany, so that non-Jewish Germans could continue in a complacent belief that goods doled out by welfare organisations were voluntary contributions by generous donors.

The Nazi regime worked tirelessly to render Germany 'Jew-free.' It was hardly good propaganda to let citizens know that they were wearing warm clothes taken from trembling Jewish bodies moments before death. The crimes inside the wooden fence at Chelmno were too horrific to be scrutinised by civilians back in Germany, by German families who came to settle in Poland after the Nazi invasion, or by ethnic Germans already living there.

Local Poles – Jewish or Gentile – didn't see the killing, but they smelled the burning of the bodies, and the smoky bonfires of belongings considered without worth – letters, mementos and photographs carried by victims on their final journey to the palace in the forest. Local Catholics went to worship in the mansion's church on Sunday, even though it was the space where victims undressed and folded their clothes for the last time. Sights and smells were evidence of the horror. And then there were the screams.

'I had to cover my ears,' Zofia remembered.

Nobody must know. This was the mantra of the German Zofia cleaned for. In contrast, prisoners trapped in Chelmno were anxious that the *whole world* should know of the atrocities they witnessed and endured. Izaak Zydelman was one of the last prisoners alive in the palace workshops before a liquidation operation on 7 April 1943. He was part of a group of Jewish tailors forced to sew for German officers and he kept a covert notebook of testimony, defying the secrecy. Izaak wrote, 'I wish I were a bird. I would fly far to the good world and tell them about everything that is happening.'[10]

More like rabbits than birds, there were escape attempts from the camp. Zofia's own home was searched by Germans hunting for Jewish escapees. Most escapes ended with discovery and death: witnesses were a threat to the secrecy.[11]

The crimes were impossible to hide, and clothes acted as evidence.

Farmer Rozalia Peham was married to a German police officer working at the Chelmno camp. She admitted that her husband gave her gifts in wartime, including a smart suit. She explained, 'My husband said that he had bought it from one of his colleagues, who had been in Italy and sent it to him.'

It was a nice story. Did Rozalia believe it? Unlikely. She'd already had jewellery as loot, and when pressured during post-war testimony she eventually conceded, 'I saw piles of clothes in front of the palace in Chelmno . . . I received leather for shoes from Chelmno.' Perhaps it comforted her to spin fictions. The truth was not so easily suppressed.[12]

One fundamental reason for secrecy about the killing site at Chelmno was so that transports from Lodz ghetto could continue without fear or fuss. Right until the bitter end Hans Biebow, German head of the ghetto, told remaining ghetto residents, 'I assure you we shall look after you. Pack your things and assemble to be transported.'[13] To sustain the lie, evidence of extermination had to be hidden.

Personal effects of the victims in Chelmno were burned on site, in a deep hole near three apple trees. The clothes, as young Zofia had already witnessed, were too valuable to be destroyed. Bundles of clothing were transported back to the ghetto to be sorted there. An entry in the Chronicle of Lodz Ghetto, 21 July 1942, notes, 'Since the end of May the ghetto has been receiving enormous quantities of clothing.'[14]

Those tugging at the mass of garments felt growing horror as they recognised some of the clothing as worn by friends who'd gone to 'work outside the ghetto.'

One of the most extraordinary photographs taken by Mendel Grossman in Lodz ghetto features the Church of the Holy Virgin, just along the road from Chana Zumerkorn's home in the old marketplace. The church was deconsecrated when the ghetto was sealed and the synagogues burned. Below gothic vaults and stone-eyed statues Jews excavated mounds of plunder bundles. The church was also a repository for mattresses and bedding stolen from Jewish communities in the Lodz area. In Grossman's photograph the whole space is ethereal, with dim shafts of sunlight and floating white feathers. The feathers flew up as eiderdowns and mattresses were torn open. Once fumigated they would be stuffed and stitched into new covers for new owners – Germans. Chana would have known the church as the White Factory, named for the perpetual soft coating of down.

Every last bit of value was extracted from the clothing harvested at Chelmno camp. For knitwear and underwear that couldn't be salvaged, a grisly looking machine was fetched from Lodz. It was a contraption of grinding cogs and sharp teeth. A *Reisswolf*, or shredder – called the Wolf, for short. Like a monster from a fairy tale, the steam-powered Wolf tore into woollen clothing, shredding sweaters and socks into a mass of fibres, muting them to greys and browns, with perhaps a flash of red. These fibres could be recycled into new yarns and new fabrics. Silk was spun into thread used to embroider flashy insignia on German uniforms. Cotton could become shirts, blouses and frocks. Wool would be knitted into socks, mittens and sweaters.

The textile industry of every country practised salvage and thrift, including turning old rags into new cloth, but the Wolf of Chelmno was symbolic of the grotesque extremity of Nazi recyling: to repurpose plunder into profit and to reduce victims to meaningless fragments – to almost nothing.[15]

At the final dismantling of the Chelmno operation, every effort was taken to destroy evidence. With the mansion buildings blown up, the bodies deep in pits and refuse piled onto bonfires, it seemed that the secret would be kept. The site was abandoned. A forester came to plant juniper, pine and birch seeds over the burial pits and waste holes. Saplings grew into trees. Tree roots grew into the tainted ground.

And yet, for those who go looking, there are still traces of evidence, whether burned, buried or shredded. Post-war archaeologists visited the Chelmno site, sifting soil and rubble for clothing fibres, bones and buttons – whatever could be found. Across the palace estate they recovered tiny mementos of lost lives. Fabric scraps, zips, press-studs . . . cuff links, thimbles, a needle case, a measuring tape. The testimonies of fragments and fibres is at once mute and eloquent.

Chana Zumerkorn was one of 150,000 people murdered at the palace in the woods, a life reduced to names on documents and a dim ID photograph. But the Wolf's sharp teeth never tore into her red sweater. Wherever the surges of hardship took him, Chana's brother, Josef, held on to that sweater.

Elsewhere in occupied Poland, threads of knitting wool bound together other survivors destined for camps that were just innocent names on the Baedecker tourist maps. Among them, the remote village of Sobibor.

Who Can Knit?

*You see the men and you can't believe these men do so
many evil things.*
– MIRIAM KAHANOV, DAUGHTER OF HELLA
WEISS-FELENBAUM[1]

One day in 1983, a seventy-one-year-old German named Karl
Frenzel walked into the court building in Frankfurt-am-
Main. Just an ordinary-looking man in an ordinary suit.

The first time Hella Felenbaum saw Frenzel was in December
1942. He wore a Nazi uniform then; she was eighteen years old, and
with her mother and her friend Regina Feldman at a place called
Sobibor. The last time Hella saw Frenzel he was firing a machine
gun at her and she was running for her life, without her mother.

She never expected or wanted to see him again. Yet here she
was. Face-to-face with him on German soil.

Hella had refused to attend Frenzel's first war crimes trial in
1965–66, submitting a written testimony instead. After conviction
and a life sentence, Frenzel had been released on a technicality in
1982 then rearrested and put on trial again. This time Hella – by
then married and a mother herself – agreed to go to Germany to
bear witness against Frenzel if her daughter Miriam would accom-
pany her. Four decades had passed. After all she endured at the

hands of the Nazis, Hella could barely cope with using German products in her house, let alone face the idea of being in Germany. She couldn't even bear to return to Poland, her homeland.

'Don't go there,' Hella told her grandson Eran, when he spoke of a 'roots' visit to learn more about her life before and during the war. 'The land in Poland is full of the blood of Jews. Wherever you are treading you are treading in Jewish blood.'[2]

SS Staff Sergeant Karl Frenzel was responsible for more than a little bloodshed. A member of the Nazi Party since 1930, he'd graduated from murdering disabled people as part of the Nazi T4 'Euthanasia' program, to mass murder of Jewish people at a secret facility in occupied Poland: Sobibor. Like Chelmno, the prototype based in a palace in the woods where Chana Zumerkorn met her fate, Sobibor was built solely for the purpose of extermination. It was horrifically successful. Frenzel was present during its construction, and its dismantling, working with a dedicated core of German officials and supported by trained thugs of different nationalities. He was responsible for key elements of Sobibor administration, under deputy commander Gustav Wagner and the camp commandant.

That day in court in 1983, Hella and Miriam were talking with Judge Kremer when Frenzel walked in. An ordinary-looking man in a suit. Miriam shudders at the memory still, aware of all her mother had been through. Frenzel himself claimed to have been traumatised by his experiences of Sobibor.

'For us it was also a very bad time,' Frenzel told Thomas Blatt, a Jewish Sobibor survivor. 'I'm sorry that I was in this mess then.'[3]

This mess, as Frenzel called it, was the murder of an estimated quarter of a million Jews in Sobibor; murder that he had ably facilitated over many months. Hella would have been one of the victims at Sobibor if it hadn't been for luck, daring and knitting skills.

It was the same for her friend Regina, born Riva Feldman,[4] the girl from Siedliszcze who'd travelled in the same convoy of carts with eight hundred Polish Jews from Staw labour camp; whose cart had poised at a crossroads in the wintry woods. The line of wagons had taken Regina, Hella and all the others along the road to Sobibor.

Like Hella, Regina had lined up on Sobibor's sandy soil in December 1942, as Karl Frenzel and other SS men shouted their orders. At that time she couldn't have the faintest concept of coming face-to-face with Frenzel at the courthouse forty years later, for the 1983 trial. When she stepped off the plane it was the first time Regina had set foot in Germany since 1949. It had taken a lot of persuading, and the support of her son Andrew, before she'd join the list of witnesses for the prosecution. Regina was only just seventeen when she first laid eyes on Frenzel. Back then he was a healthy young man with reddish hair, blue eyes and pale skin. In 1983 he was stooped with a cane. She had no trouble recognising him, despite his age and civilian clothing.

When Regina had interacted with Frenzel during the war he'd been godlike to those forced to serve him, with power of life and death – mostly death. In her 1963 written testimony, Regina said Frenzel 'behaved like a beast.' She accused Frenzel's superior, Gustav Wagner, of 'blatant brutality.'[5]

Beast . . . brute . . . this implied the perpetrators were unthinking animals, yet in 1983 Frenzel sat in the dock, very much human, a man in a suit, unflinching as Regina described the monstruous violence he had inflicted on her and countless others.

God . . . beast . . . monster. However tempting it might be to categorise Frenzel as something other than human – an evil aberration – we can't push him away as an anomaly, or a race apart. For all he embodies horror because of his murderous actions, he was as flesh and blood as those he persecuted. He was a man whose collars needed scrubbing, whose shirts needed ironing, whose socks needed darning.

Regina and her friend Hella knew this. In Sobibor they washed his shirts. They knitted his socks.

It's unlikely Frenzel ever knew their names, or if he did, it was only to demand some labour from them, or to call them for punishment. What was it to him that he helped organise the murder of their parents, their siblings, their friends, their neighbours? When Regina's son and Hella's daughter came to Frenzel's trial in 1983, they were children without grandparents thanks to Frenzel and others like him: men who swapped suits for uniforms, then thought they could put a suit on again and get away with their murders.

Regina and Hella had been robbed of their parents and grandparents, but in one precious sense they carried their mothers with them, thanks to an intergenerational connection. It was their mothers who taught them to knit, and knitting saved their lives.

'We knew there was a camp called Sobibor and something was going on there,' Regina later recalled.[6] That was as much as they did know about their destination in the woods.

In European folklore and fairy tales the forest can represent a place of danger and discovery. Young heroines in the stories are admonished *Don't step off the path*, because straying from well-trodden routes can lead the unwary wanderer into the arms or jaws of savage beasts. The suave gentleman who offers flowers and flattery could be a wolf in disguise.

Sobibor, deep in a forest of birch and pine, was saturated with deception, much like Chelmno, where Chana Zumerkorn of Lodz had been murdered. Sobibor's fences were woven with leafy branches to hide all secrets.

From spring to autumn, flowers bloomed in window boxes and carefully tended garden plots. The soil grew lush vegetables. Snowy-white geese ran around the well yard. One surviving photograph shows grinning German officers cuddling little piglets. Other snapshots show men in uniform relaxing in the sunshine in front of pretty white buildings with cotton gingham curtains at the windows.[7] Among these men was Karl Frenzel's superior, Gustav Wagner. Both Frenzel and Wagner would be civil-seeming monsters in a fairy story.

Sobibor was no fairy tale. No matter how unbelievable, every moment was real.

When Hella first arrived at Sobibor camp, she described the experience as dreamlike. It was all so surreal, right from the very first sounds of Strauss waltzes wafting into the dark night. She was travelling in that convoy of horse-drawn wagons, loaded with eight hundred Polish Jews. The roads were so bad the wheels got bogged down in mud. It was December 1942. Deep winter. Sobibor had been in operation since April that year. Regina was on one of the wagons with her surviving family. Also in the group of unwilling travellers were Regina's cousin, sixteen-year-old Zelda Kelberman, along with other girls from the labour camp at Staw. One of these was Esther Terner, just two years older than Regina.

'We wanted to get it over with,' Esther had to admit, because the journey was so long and hard – a whole day just to travel twenty kilometres.[8] Freezing and gnarled with hunger, the people in the convoy of carts came to a gateway with a gaudy sentry box, fences laced with greenery and two tall, striped flag poles. One pole flew the SS runes, the other flew a swastika. Across the gate in bold white lettering – *SS Sonderkommando*. Special Command Unit. None of the new arrivals had any idea what that meant.

The yard within was lit as bright as daytime.

Men and boys were hustled to one side, women and girls to another. Regina's brother Paul went with her father, Josef. She stood with her mother, Golda, and her sister, Friedl. Aside from the clothes they stood up in – and Regina was still huddled in the coat she'd been wearing since first being forced from home – they were practically destitute. All they had was each other.

A tall, good-looking German stood on a podium flanked by other well-turned-out officers. This was Gustav Wagner, although Regina did not know that yet.

He called out, 'Who can knit?'

What a preposterous request. Here they were, transplanted in a strange place in the middle of the forest, and he asked about knitting?

Who can knit?

It wasn't just the unexpected nature of the request – the question itself was rather absurd. Why ask a group of girls and women who could knit? Chances are, they all could. Even Hella, who'd grown up in a comfortable middle-class home with an academic mother and enough money to buy whatever clothes were needed, even she could knit. Her mother had taught her, the same as mothers across Europe taught their daughters. It was considered a fundamental part of a girl's education, so obvious a skill it was taken for granted.

Yet here was a German, blowing breath clouds in the cold night air, asking who could knit.

The first girl selected by Wagner – a German-speaking Pole named Mira – stepped forward and began asking others, *Can you knit?*

Golda urged Regina to step forward. '*You* can knit.'

Regina was reluctant. Golda insisted, pushing her out of the crowd, urging Friedl to do the same. When the time came, Friedl decided she wouldn't leave her mother. Regina stood there alone. Mira picked out a few more, including Regina's cousin Zelda, as well as Hella Felenbaum, two sisters and a few others. At first Esther Terner was passed over, but she spoke up saying that was her skill, and so was added to the group. There were twelve in total, mostly girls Regina knew from her hometown, or from the labour camp at Staw.

The knitters went one way. Their friends and families went another.

Regina was told the others would go to work somewhere else.

The twelve girls were disinfected, like livestock during a contagion, then led to an empty wooden hut, just four walls, a roof and a floor. It was obviously a new building, with the scent of freshly cut wood. There was another smell in the air, harder to place.

The girls were too numb to cry, too shocked to sleep. Food was delivered by a Jewish man. Just bread and weak coffee substitute. They were all thinking it was to be their last meal. The rest of the night hours were freezing. They had no beds, just one blanket each and the warmth of companionship. In the morning they were taken to another barrack building. Inside there were piles and piles of shoes, each pair tied together with shoelaces or string. The girls were told to pick some.

'Here,' said a German to Regina, as solicitous as a salesman in a shoe shop, 'these will probably fit you.'

He held out a pair.

Regina knew those shoes well. They were one of the pairs her father had laboured over so lovingly each evening back at home, making sure they were beautifully polished and well turned out for the next day. They were her sister Friedl's. Regina was overwhelmed at the sight of them. If Friedl's shoes were here, where was Friedl? Where were all the other people who'd once walked in these mounds of footwear, whose distinctive treads and foot spreads had worn the soles and shaped the uppers?

From then on, the girls knitted, like heroines of a dark fairy tale, forced to fulfil an impossible task, such as spinning straw into gold. In this instance, they were knitting yarn into life. Mittens, stockings, gloves, sweaters, caps – a multitude of woollens were magicked from their needles. With a stove installed in the barracks their fingers would at least be warm enough to ply the knitting needles. They were allowed washing water and soap to ensure the yarn was kept clean, and kept apart from the rest of the camp to avoid lice infestations. Wooden bunks were hastily constructed, wide enough for three girls to a bed. The hut was officially known as the *Strickstube* – Knitting Room.

Much of the work was for the German army, vital woollens to help them through another desperate winter of fighting. The girls also knitted for Sobibor personnel. A rare photograph that only came to light in 2020 shows Sobibor guards lined up in winter, bulky with wool coats, gloves and scarves; heads swathed in knitted balaclava helmets. Their boots are undoubtedly lined with thick woollen socks.[9]

Regina, Hella, Esther and the others had a quota of one knee-high sock per day. 'They had to be big and long and warm,' Regina

Sobibor guards in winter gear.
United States Holocaust Memorial Museum collection, gift of
Bildungswerk Stanislaw-Hantz

was told.[10] The typical German army sock was knee-high, grey and ribbed, with bands of white or red contrasting wool at the top to show the size. One band for small, two for medium, three for large.

Socks are perhaps on the lowest level of the clothing pecking order – not quite underwear, not quite special. Too ordinary to pay much attention to. Too common to think of preserving. Very easy to lose under the bed, or in the wash. Even so, a few army socks survive from this era, collected and traded by militaria enthusiasts. However humble, like knitted sweaters, socks should never be underestimated. They are fundamental to survival in harsh climates.

Knitting one sock a day might not seem like much. Chana Zumerkorn, back in the Lodz ghetto, would be able to produce a complete long sock every hour on a knitting machine. By hand, it's a different story. The girls sitting around the Knitting Room stove had to transform roughly five ounces of 4-ply wool into a pair of socks every two days. With concentrated effort each sock could take about seven to nine hours, depending on the style of the sock and the thickness of the yarn.[11] This wouldn't include the time it took to wind the wool, or to wash, dry and shape the sock. In everyday life a knitter might work on a sock for half an hour in the evening when other tasks were done. At this rate a pair could take weeks. Regina didn't have weeks. She had one day.

There was no question of missing this target. Somehow they sensed their lives depended on pleasing the well-groomed SS who ordered the quota. The girls sometimes knitted into the night, after lights out, illuminated by the embers of the dying fire. They knitted from memory, without patterns – an impressive feat for even experienced knitters. Their work was functional, not creative. Every day socks were collected from the twelve girls, like some kind of tribute.

In return they got food and warmer clothes, so Regina no longer needed to sleep in her coat, just on it.

Shoes, yarn, clothes . . . how was Sobibor so well-stocked in the middle of such scarcity? The answer was disturbing, as Regina discovered when she picked out warmer garments. She found her sister Friedl's things. If Friedl wasn't wearing them, and she was nowhere to be seen in the small camp, it didn't bode well for her.

'I had to take my sister's clothes,' Regina remembered with sorrow. 'They wouldn't fit me, but I had to take them.'

These clothes were the only tangible connection with her sister. Friedl's cast-offs were a tiny fraction of all the goods gathered in Sobibor's sorting sheds. Every time a transport arrived there were more and more belongings to deal with. More goods for the Germans to steal and redistribute, yarn included. Trains replaced wagons as the tally of deportations increased.

Locomotives came by day and by night, slowly coming to a halt outside an unprepossessing station building with the simple black and white sign SOBIBOR. The trains were met by men of the *Bahnhofkommando* – Station Squad – looking smart in dark-blue overalls and caps embroidered with the letter B inside a yellow triangle.

From the east, trains brought the broken-down human debris of Jewish ghetto existence. People reduced to destitution through antisemitic despoilation. Poles and Russians who'd endured enough already knew nothing good could be at the end of the line. They usually had patched and padded clothes, few valuables and meagre food supplies, much like Regina and her family.

From the west, trains delivered Jews who'd certainly known hardship, but who still came from communities with the resources to look after the poorest members. It is incredibly touching that Jews being forcibly deported from Westerbork camp in the Netherlands, for example, were sent on their way with warm clothes and blankets, generously collected and redistributed by the

Displaced Person's Aid Bureau in Amsterdam. Among the donations to internees at Westerbork were 600 sweaters, 700 pairs of
knitted stockings, 725 mittens, 500 earmuffs and 1000 blankets.
In an appeal for garments doners were implored to give good quality
items: 'Do not send worthless cast-offs, but only what you yourself
would use.'[12] Social worker Gertrude van Tijn-Cohn was director
of the Displaced Persons Aid Bureau and head of this Dutch initiative. She instructed staff 'to treat everyone seeking your help with
goodwill,' countering the dehumanisation of the Nazis.[13] This selflessness explains why Sobibor 'welcomed' so many new arrivals very
well-equipped for winter in what they assumed would be a labour
camp.

From Paris, Amsterdam and many other cities, towns and
villages they came, usually via transit camps, some dressed in city
clothes with styled hair, cosmetics, expensive luggage and heeled
shoes. For a while in 1943 there were actual passenger trains from
the Netherlands carrying people who, in their innocence, expected
porter service on arrival.[14] These arrivals were reassured to be given
paper receipts for their luggage, and to be told they would be reunited with their suitcases later. Their valuables were to be handed
over to a security kiosk for safekeeping, along with purses and hand
luggage. All very civilised. All pure deception.

Nothing was returned to the rightful owners. Everything was
hauled into the sorting sheds and tipped onto tables like a macabre rummage sale or flea market. Jewish workers hurried to divide
the booty into piles – shoes, coats, woollens . . . underwear, books,
hairbrushes, toys. Every little ordinary, precious object people had
taken the trouble to pack or carry with them. All the while men
such as Gustav Wagner and Karl Frenzel sauntered between the tables, eyeing the best pieces for themselves, making sure – on threat
of a whipping or worse – that nothing valuable slipped their grasp.

The amounts of plunder were staggering, as Regina would discover when she was put on sorting duty herself. The shifts for labouring inmates were sometimes as long as fourteen to eighteen hours a day. There could be a hundred Sobibor prisoners sorting at any one time. Once the SS had picked out whatever took their fancy, the goods were sorted by quality – new, good, not good. There was such a surplus, the 'not good' items were burned. Valuables went into wooden boxes which would be delivered under guard to Berlin. The rest were stacked into piles of about ten or a dozen items, tied with string and stored until there was enough to make up a full trainload. Given the number of transports, each with about a thousand people, that didn't take long. Jewish workers struggled to lift and carry the heavy bundles, particularly when SS were bullying them into running faster, faster, faster, an Alsatian dog let off the leash to harry them. One day three men collapsed under the weight of a bundle. They were all shot dead.[15]

Soon after Regina found Friedl's clothes, she made an even more disturbing discovery. While pulling, folding and packing garments she came across a jacket that was only too familiar. It was her mother's. The winter jacket Golda had been wearing when she pushed Regina forward on that first fateful night in Sobibor when Wagner asked, 'Who can knit?'

Regina told her friends and showed them the jacket. They didn't believe her. How could she even possibly recognise it, out of so many hundreds and hundreds of jackets? Regina was certain. She recognised the name of the tailor, stitched inside. More than that, she knew the secret Golda's jacket carried. Out of sight of the SS Regina tore the lining of the jacket's breast pocket. There it was, where her mother had sewn it for safe-keeping – Golda's wedding ring.

Regina had a choice. Drop the ring into the box of valuables, to be sent back to Berlin and melted into gold ingots. Or . . . steal it back from the Germans. She certainly didn't want to give it up. The ring was the only fragment left of her parents' marriage. It was a shining remembrancer of all their happy days in the tree-shaded house at Siedliszcze. This ring had been on her mother's fingers as Golda turned the pages of books, as she'd helped her children with fiddly buttons, as she'd taught Regina to hold knitting needles. To give it over to the Nazis seemed criminal. To keep it was courting death. Thirty years after the event Regina was still able to recount the murder of a hungry boy in Sobibor who'd dared to take a tin of sardines for himself. SS Corporal Hubert Gomerski shot him just outside the table where she worked. She saw the boy's feet as he lay dead on the ground.[16] Regina also knew that for men like Karl Frenzel and Gustav Wagner – recipients of her knitted labour – violence was as ordinary and everyday as putting on socks in the morning. At Frenzel's trial, Regina described the SS man murdering a young Dutch boy nicknamed Caruso because of his beautiful singing voice.

'As God exists, as I am sitting here, he bashed the boy to death,' she told the court.[17]

There in the sorting shed she made her mind up. Since she couldn't safely keep the ring herself, she'd ensure the Nazis would never have the chance to wear it or profit from it. With utmost secrecy, she used her shoe to wear a gap in the loose wooden floorboards then dropped the ring into the sandy soil beneath. There it could lie, a small memento of her mother. Proof that Golda had once been warm and breathing.[18]

As for the clothes in Sobibor's sorting shed – including most of the garments Regina's family had been wearing when they first climbed down from wagons into the camp – these many, many tons of textiles were to be stripped of all evidence that Jewish stars or Jewish names had ever been stitched onto them. Next they were hauled to a labour centre called the Old Airfield near Lublin. Here women inmates disinfected garments, re-sorted and sent them on to new wearers.

One surviving inventory from a Lublin warehouse included four chests of needles, thirteen chests of sewing threads, twenty chests of wool and twenty-seven chests of yarn.[19] Just consider how many needles it would take to fill a chest. Picture all the different colours on reels of thread. Imagine the feel of wool and yarn textures. Some would have been looted from tailoring and dressmaking workshops, some from haberdasheries. Some from the luggage of optimistic deportees, packing for a future that included clothes mending and sock knitting. They had assumed their journeys had return tickets, not a terminal destination.

Back in Sobibor, the small group of girls selected to knit did not have the luxury of diving into a chest of yarn to pick out wool for socks. The Lublin goods were destined for German citizens – housewives who'd grumble about the war if there were absolutely no goods available for their needs. Regina and the knitters had to turn to another source, one that was also replenished each time the shriek of a locomotive whistle signalled new arrivals. They had to recycle woollens.

Onto a wooden table went sweaters, cardigans, bed jackets and blankets . . . anything that could be pulled apart. They had to make old wool new again. Stripes and patterns were awkward to undo and knit up again. Plain colours were best. Helping the knitting commando was a little girl called Irene, daughter of one of the workers. She was about twelve years old, with dextrous fingers. Irene teased apart the woollens until they were nothing more than a pile of crinkly yarn. This then had to be washed, often in cold water from the well, which was a horrible job in winter weather. Dried and rewound, it would be knitted up again. The only trace of the person who'd once worn the woollens was in the yarn of the new garments.

So wird verschiedenfarbige Wolle gefärbt:

Die Wolle einer alten, hellen und dunkelfarbigen Strickerei oder Häkelei auftrennen und über ein Brett wickeln.

Die zwei mehrfarbigen Wollen vom Brett herunternehmen, abbinden und mit kochender Farblauge färben.

Die gefärbte Wolle über eine Leine hängen, trocknen lassen und dann auf Knäule wickeln.

Die zu einer Farbe zusammengefärbte Wolle kann man nun zu neuen Strickereien oder Häkeleien gut verarbeiten.

Old woollens unravelled, boiled in lye and used to make new knitted garments,
'*Aus Bunten Restern*' (*From Colourful Leftovers*) magazine.
Lucy Adlington personal archive

Irene's young brother was a very skilled knitter. He joined the girls as they transformed old into new.

It would have been red sweaters worn by girls such as Jock Heidenstein and her sisters that were unravelled, if these lucky girls hadn't been saved on the Kindertransport. It could have been the red sweater worn by Anne Frank if she wasn't still safely in hiding in Amsterdam at that time; then if her deportation train hadn't been sent to Auschwitz instead of Sobibor. It could have been Chana Zumerkorn's red sweater if she hadn't gifted it so spontaneously to her brother.

The wool Regina unravelled in Sobibor represented the everyday experiences of thousands of Jewish people, who could never have dreamed that their homemade or shop-bought sweaters would end up having so much more value than their own lives.

Heads down the girls knitted, from before dawn until long after dusk. No matter how subservient they looked, they had not given in, they had not given up. Friends drawn together around the fire, they shared stories of home, memories of loved ones and songs learned in happier times. And they planned.

When the day's work was finally done it was time to clamber into the bunks to try to sleep. Although she hadn't been able to keep her mother's wedding ring, Regina still had a watch given to her as a fourteenth-birthday present, in what seemed a different life. She wrapped it deep within her coat and used it as a pillow. On a nearby bunk Esther Terner used her boots as a pillow. They were made of a lovely soft leather and she resisted wearing them in Sobibor, choosing an old pair from the store instead. Regina's father, Josef, with his pre-war penchant for clean footwear, would have been proud of her. Esther's friends were more credulous and wanted to know why on earth she wouldn't wear such nice boots.

Esther announced with defiance, 'With these boots I'm going to escape from Sobibor.'[20]

She wouldn't be going alone.

An Irresistible Urge to Flee

'Our life in Sobibor was only counted by the moments.'
– REGINA ZIELINSKI NÉE FELDMAN[1]

Escape?

A girl could dream.

In Sobibor dreams were a kind of escapism, as long as the night-mares could be kept at bay.

Regina Feldman had a dream that she was back in the intoxi-cating beauty of her garden back home, revelling in the peace and shade of the apple tree, but she was tired and ill. Painfully worn out and ground down. In the dream her mother came to her, reassuring her that help would come the very next day. Esther Terner had a dream that she was free, and her mother was telling her she would survive if she took shelter in a barn on a farm she recognized.

This was spring 1943. It's a remarkable testament to the knit-ting girls that they'd managed to endure a whole winter in Sobibor, given the shocks they'd suffered as well as the horror of existing in such a hellscape. As ever, life found ways to sustain the spirits, through a thirst for revenge, the lure of hope and through mutual support.

Frankly, Regina needed whatever support she could get. The knitting commando was disbanded, leaving the girls free to join the main women's barracks and make new friends, including some young Dutch women salvaged from the Westerbork transports. However, her new work squad involved hard labour on meagre rations. She was transferred to the Laundry Squad.

Even out in the real world, few housewives owned a washing machine in 1943, unless it was a brave contraption on legs heated with a gas ring, with a paddle in the tub operated by turning a handle. There were industrial scale steam laundries in operation, but why would the SS need machines when they had endless Jewish labour?

The laundry was all done by hand. This was no mean feat when every drop of water had to be drawn from the well in heavy buckets. Fuel had to be collected to heat the water, since many garments needed to be boiled to kill off lice. The process was backbreaking. Stained garments were scrubbed with disinfectant soap on a washboard, then added to the main wash to be pounded with a posh stick. Soapy laundry was dragged out with tongs, the tub emptied and several successive rinses carried out. Wet laundry was dumped into a baby's pram to be taken out for drying. Then there was the starching and ironing, using metal box irons filled with chunks of coal. God forbid a too-hot iron would burn an SS man's shirt, or a too-cool iron would leave unsightly creases. Sobibor staff had standards to uphold! Their clean clothes singled them out as superior – heroic even.

Regina's friend Hella Felenbaum also slaved in the laundry block. Malnourished since 1939, Hella was tiny, by far the smallest worker in the laundry. She struggled to manage the heftiest tasks. Kindness kept her going: Ada Lichtman – formerly a kindergarten teacher, widowed when her husband was shot – ensured Hella was given lighter jobs, and an inmate carpenter constructed, in stealth, a kind of wooden stepstool so Hella wouldn't look too short and puny when SS came round to check on worker capability.[2]

The labour might have been bearable if it wasn't for the daily torment of Sobibor's SS men. Fear of violence was absolutely justified. Rapes of Jewish women by SS men were not unknown. Beatings were as common as breathing. Men such as SS Staff Sergeant Karl Frenzel dressed the part of civilised humans but the stains on their consciences could not be scrubbed clean like shirt collars. When Frenzel told Dutch inmate Max van Dam to paint his portrait, the artist was faced with a dilemma: how to create an acceptably flattering physical likeness that also expressed the soul of such a person.[3]

The girls working in the laundry knew all about men trying to wash away evidence. On one memorable occasion a grimy SS Corporal Hubert Gomerski stormed into the washroom after some brutal action. The girls assumed he must have been hunting partisans. He shouted at them all to stand to attention and look away, then flung his entire uniform including his underwear into a rinsing tub. He tried and failed to clean everything himself, eventually leaving the astonished women to deal with the mess. His clothes were thick with blood outside and faeces inside: evidence of violence, but also of his own involuntary terror at some point. So much for being heroic.[4]

Kurt Frenzel's uniform no doubt needed special attention after his customary brutality when receiving each new transport. Hella saw for herself how Frenzel killed a young child by breaking their skull on the wagon side. This was the same Frenzel who sat in court four decades later and dared to claim he'd always been fair.

'I never punished unless they had done something wrong,' Frenzel whined after his trial for war crimes. He was speaking to survivor Toivi Blatt who, as a boy, had been his shoeshine in Sobibor.[5]

Toivi and the laundry girls knew otherwise. Frenzel used his polished boots to kick a teenager who'd dared wear a headscarf in bitter cold weather – hardly a crime, unless, like the Nazis, you consider existing as a Jew a criminal act.

In early spring, Regina fell afoul of SS Staff-Sergeant Wagner's appetite for blood. Her so-called transgression was pausing while water heated for the wash. She was already feeling wretched due to an untreated ear infection. There were no medical facilities for Jews in Sobibor. Dragged before Wagner, Regina was told to bend down and lift up her skirt. The whip Wagner used had metal inside the leather. Every lash raised blisters. The tip of the whip coiled round her body. Twenty-five lashes were the normal count, and prisoners were expected to keep an accurate tally. If they missed a number or passed out from the pain, the punishment started over.

Regina was tiny, but tough. She also had the absolute support of every Jewish inmate watching.

'But somehow we held out,' Regina commented afterwards.[6]

It's no wonder she was tired and dejected the night she dreamt of being home in the garden. *I'll send help tomorrow*, her mother said in the dream.

Miraculously, the dream came true.

It was Frenzel who inadvertently transported Regina 'from heaven to hell,' as she later described it. It was all because of his need for nice shirts.[7] He wanted a seamstress. Regina wasn't very experienced but she said she could do collars and cuffs. Frenzel seemed satisfied and told her to clean herself up, since she'd be sewing in the German quarters. Frenzel had been in charge of the original knitting squad, and knew she did good work.

The greatest perk aside from avoiding backbreaking laundry labour? She got to sit down.

The SS at Sobibor were all about perks. Anything to make their lives sweeter, the tedium of the posting more bearable or their status more swollen.

Sewing shirts was the least of it – a task women through history had to provide for males in the family until ready-to-wear clothing made manufactured shirts more affordable. There was gold galore in the camp thanks to all the booty stolen from Jews. SS men made inmates craft bespoke jewellery etched with twirling initials. Similarly, Regina found herself stitching similar vanity pieces for an SS man who wanted his initials *F.R.* on his handkerchiefs. SS Captain Franz Reichleitner became commandant in Sobibor when the original commandant, Franz Stangl, was transferred to Treblinka extermination camp to continue his horrifically efficient work there.

Stangl had set lofty sartorial standards in Sobibor, strutting about the camp in a highly distinctive tailored ensemble. He claimed his clothes suffered wear and tear – 'it was so hot,' he complained. 'Not everyone was as sensitive.'[8] He had a white linen three-piece suit made up locally. Quite an apparition for Jews spilling out of cattle wagons at Sobibor camp station stop.

The officers had a cosy coterie which could include wives. Reichleitner, for example, was married to a friend of Stangl's wife, Teresa. Strictly speaking none of them were supposed to profit from appropriated Jewish goods. On the sly it was a different matter. Wagner often asked inmate Ada Lichtman to make up bundles of nice things to be gifted to German visitors to the camp. The 'gifts' were, more often than not, to treat the SS men themselves. In Regina's new sewing detail was a skilled seamstress who had to transform silk from parachutes into shirts and underwear for the Nazis.

To help ease the trauma of committing daily atrocities, the SS men had generous leave to spend time recuperating with their families. They didn't go home empty-handed. Esther, Ada and Regina saw the SS leaving camp with bulging suitcases.

'I am going on holiday and I need several things. Put a parcel together for me,' Gustav Wagner would say.[9]

The same seamstress who made luxury silk shirts from parachutes had managed to smuggle her baby into the camp. With the help of the other women in her barracks she kept it alive. Wagner only found out two weeks later. Eager to continue enjoying his silk tribute he gave the mother the chance to live – if she let the baby die. The seamstress spat in Wagner's face. He shot them both there and then. Baby first.

Wagner also liked taking dolls home as gifts for his children. So did Frenzel. The girls in the sewing room had to make the dolls new clothes. The dolls had been taken from Jewish children arriving at Sobibor.

'If I could just kill one, for what had happened, I would feel better,' said Esther Terner, attempting to express how the girls felt existing in the same space as such killers. 'But you have to keep your mouth shut, and just pretend you don't see, you don't hear, no emotions.'[10]

There was a great deal the SS at Sobibor wanted to keep hidden, behind their fences woven with branches and their deceptive language of 'processing' and 'special treatment.' As at the Chelmno camp, the ethos was *Nobody must know*. But Regina wanted to know: what had happened to her family after they were separated on arrival? Where were Josef, Golda, Friedl and Theodor?

It was through knitting that she found out.

It's so satisfying to watch someone knit. Needles click, yarn turns to loops and fabric grows, inch by inch. For centuries hand-knitting has been associated with women and domesticity, despite the fact that men also knitted. The female knitter became almost a stereotype – harmless, occupied, perhaps a little fluffy. Appearances can be deceptive. Knitting is a most excellent cover for listening, watching and bearing witness.

Requiring special goods to be made on the sly meant the SS inadvertently gave the makers opportunities to observe things which were meant to remain secret. It was similar for inmates forced to clean German living quarters, and for all those sorting luggage in the sheds.

Having the chance to enter German spaces wasn't without danger. On one occasion Regina's group had been told to knit Wagner a white sleeveless jumper. Was he mimicking Franz Stangl's white attire, perhaps? When it was done, someone had to brave Wagner's quarters to present it to him. Mira Shapiro, a woman who acted as a kind of chaperone for the younger girls, had this unfortunate task. She came back to the group pale and shaken. Wagner had told her to 'disappear quickly before he might do something to her.'[11]

There were so many disappearances in Sobibor. So many secrets. The worst one of all concerned Camp III.

Regina's work took her between Camps I and II. These were essentially reception and administration areas. Beyond that was a mystery shrouded in smoke and horror. The camp structure was arranged so that when trains disgorged their human contents, these people were carefully corralled into a seemingly safe space – a large fenced area. While still docile and bewildered, they were told to divide, men to one side, women to another.

Undress! They were told. *Hang your clothes on the pegs. Tie your shoes in pairs. Don't be afraid.*

After the undressing there were piles of neatly folded clothes in the yard. Each little heap represented a person. While they waited, some children played in the sandy soil of the yard. Tensions grew. Guards moved in to ensure even the sick or elderly undressed swiftly. They would be taken directly to the hospital. It all had to be done so quickly, before the new arrivals could act on their growing unease.

At what point did people realise the reality of the place? Usually not until they had moved beyond this yard and up a funnel of fences all woven with greenery. Not until long plaits of hair had been cropped off. Until they came to Camp III. Even here the illusion was maintained that all was well. One SS man would approach naked children to give them sweets. He patted them on the head and told them 'everything will be fine.'[12]

As soon as they left the undressing area, a squad of workers loaded the discarded clothes onto blankets then lugged them through a gate into the sorting sheds, where they were thrown pell mell onto tables. The yard was swept. Only one to two hours had passed.

'We were not allowed to witness anything,' Regina said, years later. They still heard screams from the sorting sheds. Camp III was a forbidden place. 'Whatever was going on there we were not supposed to know.'[13]

The spatial arrangement of Sobibor was deliberate, both to deceive new arrivals and to help the SS make a physical and psychological separation between their lives and their work. The camp's first commandant, Franz Stangl, freely conceded, 'At Sobibor one could avoid seeing almost all of it.'[14] The fences, gates and camouflage showed how much the Nazis needed to compartmentalize their guilt, their crimes.

Here is where Regina's red sweater enters the story. To be precise, a sweater she was compelled to make. It was not a sweater chosen with love, like Jock Heidenstein's, or a sweater gifted with love like Chana Zumerkorn's. In contrast, the red sweater Regina knitted was symbolic of how little Jewish life was valued by their persecutors. Regina was worth nothing beyond the services she provided under duress. However, knitting this sweater enabled Regina to bear witness to genocide, and to defy the perpetrator's rule *Nobody must know.*

In the summer of 1943, Regina and her cousin Zelda were given a particular knitting task. They were isolated in a separate barrack building and ordered to knit a sweater using dark red wool with navy stripes. It was salvaged wool, of course. They were not to tell anyone who they were knitting for. It might have been Frenzel,

Wagner, or any one of the SS perpetrators. They were absolutely not allowed to be visible.

With extreme caution they looked out of the barrack window. Now they saw what was on the other side of the fences; what happened after the clothes were shed. They saw a line of naked people waiting for their turn to be murdered.

'That was the gas chambers there,' Regina said softly, remembering the sight decades later.[15]

How do you process such information? How do you sit and knit, needles clicking, red yarn looping, trying to understand that men have deliberately planned a facility with the sole purpose of turning innocent people into corpses? Kalmen Wewryk, another Sobibor inmate, remembers Dutch women arriving from Westerbork transit camp one Friday, shouting, 'It's impossible! It's impossible!'[16]

It should have been impossible, yet the view Regina saw while knitting one red stitch after another was a process normalised step by step in a few short years.

Right from the first, when schemes were mooted to disenfranchise Jews in Germany, a majority should have resisted and said, *We don't support that*. When moves were made to terrorise Jews, all civilians, police and military personnel should all have said, *We won't do that*. Architect firms should have refused to draw up plans for gas chamber construction. SS men should have refused their transfer to extermination centres.

But they didn't.

They thought it wouldn't get so bad, perhaps. Or that somehow Jews deserved what they got. Or they claimed to be following orders, afraid of what might happen if they objected. Or – and this is the most likely – they allowed themselves to be desensitized to the process. They dehumanized the victims. They pulled up their warm socks and wore their new sweaters and told themselves they were on the right side of history.

Karl Frenzel would eventually concede that 'what happened to the Jews in those times was wrong.' This was only after many years in prison with time to reflect. Even then, he tried to shift the blame onto the victims, wondering why didn't they revolt sooner.[17] Yes, the man who'd supervised the reception of tens of thousands of new arrivals, deceiving them with speeches, Strauss waltzes, neatly weeded flower beds, leafy fences and luggage tickets; the man who smashed children with his bare hands and whipped workers into compliance, this man dared to wonder why hungry, frightened, disoriented people didn't fight back.

In one sense, Frenzel missed the point that every second spent breathing was a kind of revolt for Jews in Sobibor. Every row of red striped sweater Regina knitted was proof she was still alive, and still bearing witness. There were also many, many specific acts of defiance, both silent and violent.

Among Regina's group there was Esther, on mushroom picking duty for the SS, who took her foraged harvest into the cellar of the SS canteen, spotted a large pot of soup cooling and calmly spat in it. 'Don't ask me what else we did to that soup,' she recounted with great satisfaction. 'And they *ate* it.'[18]

Then there was Selma, working with Regina in the sorting shed, who was enraged that all the clothes of murdered Jews would be sent back to Germany. She kept a pair of scissors to slash the most beautiful garments so they weren't fit to be worn. This rage lifted her out of despair, as did pilfering food and clothing for her friends.[19]

Even the naked people at the gas chambers fought: one time Johann Niemann, who took so many snapshots of the jolly life of SS men in Sobibor, was seen around the camp with bandages – apparently he'd been attacked by a woman with a knife.[20] The woman is nameless to history – as are most of those who fought back at every stage of the genocide – but her defiance foreshadowed Niemann death and was a kind of prelude to another great act of resistance. An uprising. An extraordinary rebellion grown out of both hope and despair.

'I was seventeen years old and refused to die', said Regina's cousin Zelda.[21]

Zelda Kelberman's parents were murdered in Sobibor's Camp III before she arrived. Her brother met the same fate the day Zelda and Regina were selected for the Knitting Squad. Despair was a reasonable response to such bereavement. Zelda thought hope was a distraction. There was only a refusal to die. She said they'd all end up in the frying pan sooner or later. Esther Terner disagreed. She held on to hope and faith.

Hope kept people going. It kept them breathing, kept them working, kept them alive. There was always a chance of something better – right? Regina had already felt nurtured by dreaming of her mother's love. She was to receive another gift.

Having Jews kept alive to do jobs around the camp led to a clandestine network of information. One amazing day, Regina got a message from the mysterious Camp III. Ordinarily there was to be no connections whatsoever between Camps I and II, and Camp III. Very rarely there were hints of the activities there – rising smoke was one evil sign – and sometimes fragments of messages. One such fragment came to Regina. One of the workers in Camp III had been asking about anyone with the name Feldman. While doing repairs in the women's barracks, a Jewish electrician spread the word. Regina heard. She learned that her dear brother Theodor was alive!

It was incredible news. Her brother must have been equally delighted to know Regina was alive too. Under cover of working in the sorting shed, Regina met up with a man from Warsaw tasked with delivering food to workers in Camp III. He promised to put a note in with the food letting Theodor know Regina would be in position to watch when he came to collect it. In place at a discreet window, Regina waited.

Decades later Regina still resonated with wonder at the memory of what happened next. 'It really happened,' she remembered. 'I saw my brother. I'm sure he saw me.'

She said it was like having a little bit of home left.[22] Not much, but a little bit. Theodor looked changed, of course. He was burned by the sun, and certainly suffering from the terrible work he had to carry out. There were times in the years that followed when Regina doubted Theodor saw her. She wanted to believe he did. Hope is a powerful thing.

Hope can also paralyse: if there is hope in the heart, why take action to change things? It took the wreckage of some hopes to convince the inmates of Sobibor that an outrageous, impossible scenario was the only choice: revolt. Esther, one of those who was part of intensely secret meetings to plan revenge and escape, phrased it best: 'If you succeed it would be wonderful, if not you'll get a bullet in the back – it's better than going to the gas chambers.'[23]

Frenzel had wondered why inmates didn't rebel sooner, yet he was the one who crushed all attempts to escape Sobibor. When a group of Dutch prisoners working in the forest attempted to escape, they were either shot in the woods, or captured and brought back to camp to be executed in front of the others. One in ten of all inmates were selected to be shot with them. Frenzel and Niemann presided.

Regina said it was heartbreaking, 'All of us standing there and we couldn't help.'[24]

There were so few Jews alive in the camp – just the ones needed to maintain operations – they all felt like family, so these reprisals hit hard. For Regina, there was more sorrow to bear. On 27 June 1943, her mother Golda's birthday as it happened, Frenzel told the assembled inmates that all those working in Camp III had been shot attempting to escape. This included Regina's brother Theodor, so recently glimpsed from a window.

She'd heard noise in the night and wondered if it was the end of everything. In fact, there had been no escape attempt. No partisans storming the camp to liberate them. Just a dog, wandering in the minefield around the camp, setting off an explosion that then sparked the SS paranoia. For that Theodor was killed.

Perhaps the final confirmation of the apparent hopelessness of their situation came after the liquidation of another extermination centre in occupied Poland – Belzec. In June 1943, a transport of prisoners arrived from Belzec; all were executed. These were Jews who'd been spared the gas chambers long enough to work and serve the Nazis. Perhaps they too had hoped for escape, rescue or reprieve. In the pockets of their clothing were notes written in Yiddish. Last fragments of defiance.

> We are told we are on our way to work. It is a lie.
> Avenge us.
> You are the last. Everyone else is gone.[25]

These words were whispered around the camp. It was clear that death would be the finale if they stayed in Sobibor. Escape was the only option.

When that time came, there were bullets, there were dogs, there were exploding mines and death all around. Regina started to run, one single thought in her mind: 'I only remember an irresistible urge to flee Sobibor.'[26]

I Feel Good That I Fought

One day they told us not to ask many questions but to be ready.

– REGINA FELDMAN[1]

Escape!

'It was crazy even to think it,' said Regina's friend Esther, but the prisoners of Sobibor knew they had to try.

Small groups met in secret. Plans were concocted and discarded. A tunnel was begun, then abandoned. Over summer 1943, Regina, Zelda and others had been put to work in a new sub-camp of Sobibor, sorting and cleaning captured Russian guns. It was suggested they could smuggle grenades back to the main camp under their dresses, which could then be used to blow up German buildings. There was also talk of arson in the sorting sheds, to create a diversion. All of these schemes were so desperate as to be suicidal.

The catalyst for decisive action came when veteran inmates of the camp – led by Esther's cousin-by-marriage Leon Feldhendler – were joined by a group of hardened Russian prisoners of war. These men from the Red Army were on a transport from Minsk, an area known for savage resistance by Jewish fighters. They were led by a lieutenant named Alexander 'Sasha' Pechersky. This was September 1943. By October, enough trust had been established between old inmates and new arrivals to agree that they would work together. Regina wasn't in on the plans, but when Pechersky's Russians arrived she felt a ray of hope. Even though it seemed the world had forgotten them, isolated as they were in the middle of the forest, she had a feeling something was going to happen.

At first, escape seemed inconceivable. The odds against it were stupendous, not least because the SS retaliated viciously against any perceived slight to their authority, let alone more obvious rebellion. Regina was still injured from being whipped by Frenzel. She also still grieved the execution of her brother Theodor. Esther had already seen how a trainload of people had tried to resist selection: quicklime was thrown into the train wagons, causing agonising death.

Far from turning her away from the idea of escape, such atrocities only made the desire for revenge burn hotter. Willpower alone wouldn't be enough to set them free. Even if a few of them could make it past the wire fence, the guards with machine guns and a fifty-foot-wide perimeter seeded with mines, they knew there would be terrible reprisals against all the other innocents left in the camp. Who wanted that on their conscience? Feldhendler and Pechersky came up with a brilliant, outrageous solution to this issue. They decided that there wouldn't just be a small, select group of escapees. They would all make the attempt. The whole camp. Six hundred of them at once.

How to achieve this?

By exploiting the SS love of perks and treats. The same greed that had men like Frenzel and Wagner commissioning silk shirts, warm sweaters and monogrammed handkerchiefs would be their undoing – or so the planners hoped.

As it happened, clothing had already featured in one successful escape from Sobibor, much to Frenzel's fury. A male inmate managed to hide a wounded inmate among the giant bales of plundered clothes being packed into a train for Germany.[2]

The Jews in Sobibor knew so much about their persecutors, due to existing alongside them and serving their needs. It was a forced, repugnant intimacy, but it gave them the gift of knowledge. As Esther later said, 'We knew every corner, every inch in the camp.'[3] They also knew the foibles of each SS man. The essence of the plan was to lure German officers to the camp's tailoring and shoemaking workshops where they could be dealt with one by one and their weapons stolen. This would even the odds against them slightly. Details of the plan were finessed. A date was set. Deferred. Set again: On 14 October they would put the plan in motion.

For all they felt a fierce need for revenge, women and girls were excluded from the initial action. Their efforts were put to managing inaction and anticipation. They had to temper their suspense with the reassurance that 'when the time comes you'll be told.'

On the evening of 13 October, they gathered in the barracks, tense and apprehensive. One girl was convinced they would all die, that the sun would rise and set without them, that the flowers would bloom and wilt and they'd just be dead. Fierce Esther Terner wouldn't succumb to defeatism, even though death was a likely outcome. She had been trusted with the truth by her cousin-through-marriage Leon Feldhendler.

'Girls, at least something is going to happen!' she declared.[4]

To calm their nerves one of them sang quietly in the dark.

'Be prepared,' Regina was told.

For what? They could only speculate.

Hella Felenbaum remembered, 'We were already doomed to die so we were willing to take our chances.'[5]

The word was, all inmates should wear extra pieces of clothing –

if they had any – for afternoon roll call the next day. Ready for action, Esther put on two sweaters, a coat and a headscarf, and she finally wore the lovely leather boots she'd been saving since she first got to Sobibor. All those months ago she'd vowed she'd escape in these boots. Today was the day she'd fulfil that promise, or so she hoped.

Regina did not have the benefit of the striped red sweater she'd knitted. That had long since been finished and given up to an SS man. She wasn't allowed to keep the product of her own labour. At least she still had her coat from home, the one she used as a pillow. She added a woolly scarf to her usual ensemble. She wore these on the morning of 14 October 1943, on her way to work in the German sewing room. She also filled a little bag with sugar cubes – gifts doled out by the SS she knitted for, as if she were a horse who liked treats.

Carrying bulky luggage was out of the question. They'd be lucky enough if the SS didn't get suspicious seeing them in layerings of winter clothing. Sasha Pechersky, one of the key organisers of the revolt, said he didn't believe in luck when he was offered a clean shirt to wear in the uprising. It was a gift from a woman who'd been put to minding Sobibor's rabbits, which were bred for food and furs. From the rabbit runs, this woman could see through the wooden fence to naked children, women and men being led up the tunnel of branches to Camp III and the gas chambers. She knew what was at stake. She had been an invaluable asset during planning stages, given the code name 'Luka.' Pechersky called her an 'inspiration.' Whether the smart blue shirt she gave Pechersky would bring luck remained to be seen.[6] He told Luka to change into men's clothes. A dress would be too cold for what lay ahead.

In contrast to the inmates' careful consideration of the clothing they'd escape in, the SS – complacent and oblivious – were eager to indulge their taste for impeccable appearance, and this would be their downfall.

Four p.m. Just two hours before sunset. Time for action. Time for violence. Weapons had already been stolen and stashed.

The men chosen to attack and eliminate SS officers had been forced to inhabit a world of death and brutality. That did not mean they found it easy to take on the task of killing. It had to be done, and without any Germans being alerted, or the whole uprising would be defeated in minutes. One by one the SS were to be invited into Jewish workshops.

Johann Niemann was lured with the offer of a superb new coat. *Come to the tailor's workshop and try it for yourself*, he was told. Up he rode on his white horse. Niemann was the man with a camera who photographed his SS cronies relaxing at Sobibor. His lens was never pointed at Camp III.

Some of Niemann's snapshots include indistinct figures of Jewish workers, and that's all they were to him. But they did fine tailoring! Esther saw him go into the tailor's room. His horse was led away as he stepped inside. He unbuckled the belt with his holster and service weapon. An axe felled him. His body was hidden in a cavity hollowed out among the clothes of murdered Jews. Sand was scattered on the floor. Ready for another victim.

Joseph Vallaster was offered some marvellous new boots in the shoemaker's workshop. Perfect timing! He was going home on leave in a few days and would look particularly fine. It would be good to relax after all his efforts ensuring operations in Camp III ran smoothly. And could the shoemakers run up some nice slippers for his wife while they were at it? *Sit here and see how well the boots fit*, he was told. An axe took him too. Pieces of old leather were spread across the bloodstains.

Siegfried Grätschus, commander of the auxiliary guards, loved getting his boots polished at the end of a shift. *Sit here while the shoeshine gets to work*, he was told. His corpse was buried in mountains of shoes taken from the feet of murdered Jews. Josef Wolf, one of the sorting shed supervisors, couldn't resist the temptation of a new leather coat. *Come over here, try it on*, he was told. His still-warm body went into one of the big bins used for sorting plundered garments. Rudolf Beckman, another supervisor in the sorting sheds, waved off his invitation to try on fine new clothes. He said he was too busy and headed for his office. How could he be eliminated now? Dutch woman Selma Wijnberg slipped a knife into her boyfriend Chaim's hand. Chaim Engel followed Beckman. Selma saw him reappear on the roll call square a short while later, looking shaken and bloodied.

But where was Karl Frenzel?

He'd been in the carpenter's workshop earlier, and raised the tension levels when he commented that the men were wearing good suits, and jokingly asked if they were going to a wedding. Gustav Wagner at least was out of the camp, on leave, no doubt enjoying doling out gifts made by Jewish prisoners in Sobibor, perhaps even wearing a red sweater.

Five p.m. Twilight. A light rain.

Regina's world focused to a few short minutes as she stood and waited in the sewing room. Other inmates assembled as if for roll call, when in fact they intended to march brazenly out of the main gate. Hella was there from the laundry room, with Esther, Ada, and Zelda. Many of them came with their work tools still in hand. Some prayed for liberation. Others prayed for at least a swift death. There was no time to wish each other luck, or even for stirring speeches from the uprising leaders.

A body was discovered. The alarm was sounded. Frenzel was alerted.

What's going on? called a guard as he drove into the camp. A swarm of prisoners beat him with their tools.

'Then we all cheered,' said Hella with satisfaction.[7]

Regina thought she heard Pechersky shout, *Everyone for themselves!*

Afterwards – mayhem.

Fifteen minutes. That's how long the uprising lasted, just a frantic fifteen minutes. Toivi Blatt, one-time shoeshine to the SS, taunted Karl Frenzel with this fact after Frenzel's trial.

In fifteen minutes a tide of fierce people surged at the camp perimeter. Even before electricians had disconnected power to the fence, prisoners were battling to get over it. Then with axes, knives and scissors they hacked at the metal. In one part of the camp the fence actually collapsed from the weight of bodies pressed against it. Hella took up a set of pliers and set to work with the help of her friend Abraham – success! They got free. She ran.

There was shooting from the towers. Just a few shots at first, until guards realised what was happening, then shooting everywhere. Machine guns, rifles, pistols – bullets tearing into flesh and bone. Esther joined a group of people clambering up a ladder behind the carpenter's shed. She jumped out of the camp and felt a bullet scrape her skull. Fuelled by the will to live, she ran.

Toivi Blatt was almost crushed as he reached the fence. He got snared by his coat and trapped there, an easy target. Quickly he slipped out of it. Ada Lichtman's coat also got snagged by the wire. She too shook it off and ran.

Regina didn't have far to go from the sewing room to a hole in the fence. Yes, she could have cowered in one of the huts, along with the other inmates too terrified to move, but she had scented freedom. She was desperate to escape. Through the chaos and bullets, she ran.

Explosions. One after the other mines seeded in the perimeter field were triggered. Pechersky and Feldhendler had planned for prisoners to throw things into the minefield to detonate as many mines as possible, but they couldn't clear them all, not with guards and SS firing all the time, mowing people down like a scythe in long grass. Frenzel played his part, firing at Jews until they were either killed or out of range.

Escapees stumbled over bodies of fallen comrades. They were blasted off their feet by exploding mines, and, if still alive and able, they dragged themselves upright and ran on.

'Nobody looked back,' said Regina. 'We were just running.'[8]

Her only aim was to get out of the camp and die breathing free air, or live to give testimony. If just one Jew made it out of Sobibor alive to bear witness, then the uprising would be a success.

At that time she wasn't to know that about three hundred prisoners succeeded in breaking out of the camp. It was an extraordinary achievement, against the worst possible odds.

They'd done it. They'd made it. Three hundred Jewish prisoners had liberated themselves. And now? Running. In any direction that led away from the bullets.

They scrambled over fallen trees and cut logs – pine, birch and alder. When parched, they paused to suck snow. As they ran, they left boot prints and speckles of blood from wounds.

None of them was physically strong after hard labour, abuse and starvation rations. Some were injured. All burned with the need to be free. But which way was freedom? Where was everyone?

The forest soon swallowed all three hundred. Regina found herself alone with her cousin Zelda and a man named Simon Rozomowitz. Hella's group was broken up until she was left with just two friends. Esther was with a larger group, which also made them a bigger target. Ada struggled on with her friends Ursula and Käthe.

They all knew Germans were in pursuit, with weapons and dogs. It wasn't safe to stop, even when clouds covered the moon and left them in darkness. Those who'd worn triple layers of clothing now found themselves too hot to run. Escapee Selma Wijnberg shed her second sweater and the outer pair of woollen trousers she'd worn for warmth. Later she'd regret the loss, but she kept her coat and shawl. Regina kept her coat at least, but the little bag with her stash of sugar cubes got snarled in a bush. She had to run on and leave it. Life was her absolute priority.

The Germans were determined to hunt down escapees, not only to salvage some sense of pride after the humiliation of a mass breakout, but also because Jews were still Jews, and still destined for extermination according to Nazi policy.

Among the local Poles were plenty who saw Jews as prey too. Some were plainly antisemitic and aligned with Nazi beliefs. Some were eager to profit from the four-hundred-zloty reward. Others hunted these human rabbits for their 'fur' – their clothes. This was one reason that escapees who'd had the opportunity to prepare packages of spare clothing for the uprising now let them fall, not only because carrying anything slowed down their flight, but also because owning too much made them a target for robbery. Sweaters and boots were particularly coveted that winter. In wartime even rags were valuable, so it's no surprise that Jews on the run would be seen as easy victims.

Regina's group were ambushed in the forest by locals demanding all their money. 'One even wanted my boots,' she remembered. She refused that absolutely, essentially telling them *Over my dead body*. Luckily, the robbers baulked at that fatal scenario.

'I thought, no, not this time of the year. I can't give him my boots, it will take my life.'

Warm, dry feet were more precious than money that winter. Regina's defiance paid off. She kept her boots.[9]

Toivi Blatt, Frenzel's shoeshine, covered many miles after his escape from Sobibor. After so much effort he was devastated to realise he'd lost his bearings and was still close to the camp. A farmer offered to hide him and two friends. Alarmingly, he was only after their clothes. After luring them inside he shot all three of them. Toivi somehow survived the bullet meant to kill him, and had to play dead as the murderer took his trousers.

Hella and her companions got hopelessly lost. They eventually threw their jackets down to be lighter. During their meanderings some of Hella's group were set upon and robbed by locals, with three of them murdered.

No matter how much they ran, somehow they still came back to the familiar DANGER – MINES signs that marked Sobibor territory. It was incredibly demoralising. At one point, hiding among the trees, Hella was certain she heard Karl Frenzel talking with a Polish man about the escape.

'We'll get them all,' Frenzel said.

The Pole knew Jews were nearby, but he chose not to betray them. The humanity of those who did not persecute Jews was in vital contrast to those who chose to hunt them. For the escapees from Sobibor, any fragment of hospitality was a miracle.

Regina eventually came to benefit from the most beautiful act of generosity. First, she had to find ways to survive in the forest.

Stillness in the forest.

In the world outside, unremitting war.

Among the trees around Sobibor, the crunch of feet on leaf litter, hoarse breaths, distant shouts.

Shelter was a pressing need for Sobibor's survivors, both to hide from the hunters and to rest a little. Food was equally essential. After three days of wandering Esther Terner arrived at a farm just as the farmer was leaving for Mass. Instead of eyeing up clothing, or thinking of the reward, this farmer calmly helped Esther clean her wounded skull, and he gave her his food. For this man, his Catholic faith meant he should help those in need. Eventually Esther reached the very same barn she'd dreamt her mother had told her to find. Here she found sanctuary. Selma Wijnberg also experienced incredible generosity when she and her boyfriend, Chaim Engel, were taken in by Poles and hidden in the loft of their haybarn. It was their haven for nine long months. To pass the time she knitted socks and a sweater, with yarn and needles provided by the hosts.

Like Esther, Regina felt as if her mother was watching over her. As she wandered with Simon and her cousin Zelda she began to recognise landmarks – places she knew from when her father had been in business and trading with locals. That still didn't make it easy to orientate. Like so many others, Regina and her companions realised they were back near Sobibor. They had to set off all over again. Desperately fatigued and starved for food they dared to knock on a few doors. Some stayed shut. Some opened, but only to tell the strangers to move on. Perhaps the caution was understandable. Germans in occupied Poland made it clear that they would execute Poles found harbouring Jews. It helped that Regina and the others didn't look like typical concentration camp prisoners: no shaved heads and distinctive striped uniforms. Essentially, they looked like 'normal' people, which made it easier for some locals not to treat them as victims.

Finally the trio saw a light in the night. A farm at the edge of the forest. They bartered Regina's watch for space in a barn and a simple meal of bread and milk. They had straw for a bed and, even more of a luxury, the farmer's wife brought them hot potato soup. It seemed a feast after the measly raw potatoes they'd managed to scavenge from cold fields. They weren't safe, by any means. In the morning they heard Germans using pitchforks to jab the straw piles. Miraculously, they weren't stabbed or discovered. It was after leaving this farm that Regina, Zelda and Simon were ambushed. Regina always wondered if the farmer had betrayed them after all. It didn't eradicate her faith that she could get help. By this point they were only a couple of miles from Wlodawa. Zelda decided she'd take her chances there.[10] Not long afterwards, Regina became separated from Simon. She was alone.

Yet not alone. 'Somebody was always there when I was in the tightest spot,' she later said.[11] She also knew she carried her mother's love and courage with her. Fortified with this belief, Regina decided to go home. It was the best decision she could have made. It would be life changing.

Meanwhile, Hella's shelter was deep in the woods. The abandoned forester's hut she'd found was as good as a palace to the exhausted escapees. An even greater treasure was the discovery of a sack of potatoes. Her group lit a fire and roasted them: a feast! It was too risky to stay in the hut, so they had to brace themselves to wander the freezing forest again, carrying old sacks as blankets. They scavenged cabbage leaves and, in desperation, asked strangers for bread and milk.

Tough as she was, Hella's upbringing had been in a town, so foraging was a new experience. She might well have starved if it hadn't been for a chance encounter with three bold Russian POWs who'd escaped from a labour camp with spades that they used to kill small animals and birds. One day they gifted Hella's group a piglet. As Jews this presented a dilemma. Pork wasn't kosher. Hella took the view that her life was at risk if she didn't eat. After the war she continued to enjoy bacon and fatty pork – known as *spek*. She reasoned, 'If God wanted me to survive he could have brought me kosher things. I'm alive today because I ate non-Kosher.'[12]

Survival was everything.

In spring they might have enjoyed the forest's abundance –

the beauty of willows, periwinkles, irises and orchid, as well as the nourishment of game and mushrooms. In the brutal winter of 1943 the glades, lakes and bogs became frozen, with no shoots, berries or duck eggs to eat. They had to take what they could get. Yet once the basics were provided – shelter and food – the survivors of Sobibor needed a reason to go on living. Each looked for a purpose as an antidote to despair.

When Hella broke through the camp fence at Sobibor she had aimed to cross the river Bug to join Russian partisans. She still remembered the words written on notes left by victims of Belzec camp – *Avenge us*. She intended to honour their plea. These words gave her the courage to battle on.

It wasn't hard to find partisans in the forest – or to be found by them. The big problem was how the partisans would react. Soldiers of the Polish Home Army were not immune to the corruption of antisemitism. Some acted on the race hatred, attacking Jews, despite having a common enemy in the Nazis. Women and girls wandering the forest were particularly vulnerable to sexual assault. Not all militant resistance groups welcomed or helped women due to stereotypes that portrayed them as weak, surplus to requirements or an encumbrance.

Hella took up with a Russian partisan group that had the good sense to value all contributions. It was common for women and girls to be allocated maintenance activities in partisan camps, including cooking and laundry, in addition to clothes making and mending. Partisans could not fight without food and warm clothing, both of which had to be stolen or scrounged. Knitwear was rare and precious. Surviving images of partisans portray hardy people layered in mismatched civilian clothes with woollen scarves and cobbled boots, anything to keep frostbite at bay.

As fighting in the forest intensified, Hella trained as a medic. Injuries from accidents or combat action had to be treated with rudimentary facilities. Those who recovered were carried by wagon from one encampment to another. Before long Hella herself was on this wagon, with a wounded foot. It didn't stop her. Nothing could now. As soon as she recovered she went back into the fray, this time taking up arms against the German occupiers.

'They gave me a gun and we terrorized them big time,' she later recalled, with great satisfaction.[13]

Hella initially learned how to fight from the Russians she met in the forest. Despite her small size – a girl who needed a wooden step to look taller while working in Sobibor – she had immense courage and ability. Put simply, the Russians respected her because she was a good soldier. It was obvious as soon as she was trained to use a weapon that she was very capable.

Eventually she was inducted into the Russian army and kitted out in a new uniform. By this point she had fought Germans right up to the Czech border. This diminutive, educated, middle-class daughter of a fabric merchant joined a regiment responsible for mining railways and bridges. She'd come a long way from the terrible December evening in Sobibor's reception area when Gustav Wagner had asked, 'Who can knit?'

Hella's life should have taken a very different course, but the horrific policies of the Third Reich derailed her pre-war plans and destroyed her family. She chose to fight back. Her uniform was soon pinned with medals as she fought battle after battle liberating Czechoslovakian territory from the fascists. These medals would one day be passed on to her daughters and grandchildren. They were a solid reminder of her fight against persecution.[14]

Hella was one of many women and girls who fought for their own freedom, and to free others. 'Fighting because she knows she has to fight,' was how Hella's daughter Miriam would later phrase

Hella 'Helka' Felenbaum-Weiss in uniform at the end of the war.
Photographer unknown/Ghetto Fighters' House Museum, Israel/Photo Archive

it.[15] Although men created boundaries around leadership positions, women all played their part and suffered equal hardship, whether operating as gun smugglers, couriers, medics or combatants, or in a multitude of other vital roles. Hella remembers being so cold her boots seemed to have grown onto her feet. She became used to drinking snow and washing in snow.

As for killing Germans, that was something she accepted as necessary in the war for peace. Reflecting on combat after the war Hella said, 'I feel good that I fought.'[16]

The forests of Europe were teeming with resistance; with Jews and non-Jews who rebelled against Nazi occupation. Survivors of the Sobibor uprising played their part in the struggle. But there was more than one way to resist. Regina Feldman's form of fighting was to live. To live and also keep alive the memories of her lost loved ones. To do this she chose the tactic of subterfuge and infiltration. Her journey would take her west into Germany, with no red sweater to warm her, even as train after train deported German Jews east to a place so vast it surpassed even the atrocities at Sobibor.

Auschwitz.

PART THREE

Remnants

The Train Seemed to Have No End

Somebody was helping and I'm still certain that it was my mother.

— REGINA FELDMAN[1]

Regina Feldman was waiting to take a train.

To reach this point and this station platform she had walked many, many miles. From the people she met on the way – the ones who could be trusted – she learned what had happened to family and friends left behind when the Feldman family was moved to Staw labour camp, then to Sobibor. It was bad news. All the Jews left in her hometown of Siedliszcze were felled by bullets or deprivation.

Still she kept going.

She was saturated with memories as she trudged or hitched the distance between Sobibor and her former home. Soon she was walking down the street where she'd once lived. The leaves had fallen from the chestnut trees along the road. The synagogue was destroyed, as was the Jewish cemetery. Otherwise there were still shops, and homes and businesses; people going about their lives as if there were no such place as Sobibor.

The Germans had a very similar attitude: pretend it had never happened.

Within five days of the Sobibor uprising, Heinrich Himmler cancelled Operation Reinhard – a policy dedicated to exterminating Jews in occupied Poland which included operation of the death camps Sobibor, Treblinka and Belzec. This was one of the most significant repercussions of the bravery of those who rebelled. A specialist in organising Jewish assets arrived at Sobibor from Treblinka, where there had already been a successful uprising. He came to oversee the packing up of the Jewish clothing that remained in the camp after the revolt. He also gathered the fragments of the Germans killed in the uprising – 'comrades,' he called them – to send them back to their families. Who knows what items were included. Monogrammed handkerchiefs? Hand-knitted woollens? Perhaps even the striped red sweater Regina had knitted for an SS man. This sweater was physical evidence that she had once existed in a place where Jews were brought to be wiped out of existence.

Any prisoners left alive in Sobibor, unable or unwilling to join the escape, were executed and their bodies destroyed. In contrast, the SS *comrades* had reverential burials, photographed for posterity.[2] Most of the camp buildings were dismantled. The site was ploughed over. Pine saplings were planted. As if it had never been. The soil tells a different story – tiny personal objects lying hidden until future archaeologists would find and preserve them. Spoons, combs, spectacles, rings. Perhaps even Golda Feldman's wedding ring, recovered by her daughter Regina, then re-covered in Sobibor's sandy soil.[3]

It would have broken Golda's heart to know that her daughter, Regina, suffered so much. She would also have been proud of Regina's resilience and ingenuity, and almost certainly relieved to know that pushing her youngest out of the crowd that first night in Sobibor in response to the call, *Who can knit?*, gave her the chance of life.

Those who are gone leave a legacy for people who knew them; those who remain carry this legacy.

Even when absent, our loved ones affect the ways we approach life and inhabit our worlds. In this sense, they do not vanish entirely until the last person who remembers them has also passed on. Regina certainly felt her mother was guiding her, and so she kept going, back to the house where she'd played as a child. Where she'd watched tadpoles in spring and enjoyed sleighing in winter. Where she'd learned to knit. Her steps were guided by memories. For her, the red sweater knitted in Sobibor did not hold any precious sentiment. The garment that did carry emotion was the wool coat she'd been wearing since her family was first evicted from their home.

As she approached Siedliszcze, she saw the once familiar landscape was distorted through ruin, erasure and change.

The house with the fruit trees and the tadpole stream was now home to the wife and children of a policeman, Christians from northern Poland. Despite the serious risk of repercussions from German occupiers, they were big-hearted enough to welcome Regina and to invite her to stay. She'd once been to school with their daughter. This humanity was an incredible contrast to Regina's experiences at the hands of antisemites, but she still didn't feel safe in Poland. It would take only one sour individual to recognise she was Jewish and turn her over to the authorities. However, there was something at once simple and superlative that this family could do for her. Since she couldn't exist without some kind of fake ID, Mrs Wojciszyn, the policeman's wife, let her use her daughter's birth certificate to obtain identity papers. This is how she became Regina, from her actual birth name Riva: Regina Wojciszyn.

Fortified with this new Christian identity, Regina saw an opportunity to escape her blood-soaked homeland. Through other wonderfully generous friends she obtained money, new clothes, a travelling bag, and a railway ticket to Lublin for starters. Her strategy was to alight the train before Lublin, where there would be mandatory checks of travel documents, which Regina couldn't pass. To her horror, the train didn't stop. She joined the crowd heading for the turnstiles. Just when she thought she'd be stopped and questioned, she saw a mother with small children and a lot of bulging baggage. Regina offered to help. The mother – a stranger – colluded with the tactic so that Regina could avoid inspection. Regina was forever grateful for such acts of solidarity.

'There was always somebody in front of me who helped me on the hard journey' she said.[4]

She acknowledged that without this help she wouldn't be alive to tell the tale.

Once in Lublin, Regina treated herself to the remarkable luxury of an apple and a donut, both very expensive in wartime, and she registered for work in Germany. She would hide in plain sight in the heart of the Nazi empire. On 2 November 1943, just two weeks after racing for her life across Sobibor's minefield, she was eating bread and jam on a train towards Berlin, where she'd change for another service to Frankfurt-am-Main, in hopes of finding work.

Regina's train pulled into Berlin during yet another air raid. The Allies were retaliating after attacks on Britain, aiming to humiliate Nazi leaders who'd once ridiculed the idea that Berlin would ever be in danger. Luckily, some of the most devastating raids took place after Regina's train had pulled out of Berlin. In this 'Battle of Berlin,' Lancaster bombers and Mosquitos devastated neighbourhoods around the Tiergarten and Charlottenburg. They wrecked much of Augsburgerstrasse, where Anita Lasker had been housed during her Berlin stint of cello lessons, and destroyed the KaDeWe department store where Anita had spent many happy hours browsing.

As for the Heidenstein's Berlin home on Linienstrasse, it was spared direct bomb damage. By the time Regina passed through Berlin, Mania Heidenstein, mother to sisters Jock, Rita and Stella, had long since taken a train journey out of the city, en route to her final destination.

Mania Heidenstein was waiting to board a train.

It was a very different experience from waiting to see her girls off on Kindertransport trains from Berlin.

The first railways, known as the Permanent Way, were devised to transport coal. From there they evolved to whisking passengers as well as freight along an ever-increasing network, at remarkable speed and gratifying punctuality (more or less) regulated by synchronised clocks. Travellers could enjoy the excitement of a day trip to the seaside by train, or a more glamorous sojourn between Paris and Istanbul on the Orient Express. They commuted on trains, sent parcels on trains and connected with friends, relatives and colleagues by train.

Then came the Third Reich.

Despite the wartime need for troop trains, hospital trains and goods trains, the Nazis dedicated railway lines, crews and rolling stock for the transportation of humans to slaughter. The parallel lines of metal rail tracks led to genocide.

Who did Mania stand with on the platform? What did she have left to carry, save her two little boys? Was she helped into the cattle wagon by fellow travellers? Did she find space to sit, or did they sway through the miles, clinging together? The most bitter stories are ones that were not told, that could not be shared or recorded. We will never know if she spoke with her companions, or if each traveller was wrapped in their own thoughts of what they were leaving, and what they were heading towards.

They were all now controlled by policies crafted in Berlin and spread across the Reich. Their watches might tick away minutes, but their time was now strictly in the hands of men many miles away, sitting behind desks with blotter pads and telephones, in offices with filing cabinets and clacking typewriters. Railway timetables had once been thick repositories of possibility – the journeys you could plan! The places you could go! Now the Nazis made the most monstrous use of time, to schedule deliveries of people into the concentration camp system.

However long the journey – and they could last days, with no food, water or fresh air – the destination was inevitable.

When Regina took a train westward, she was a daughter without a mother. Mania Heidenstein, travelling to her final destination in the east, was a mother without her daughters. During the war years, Jock, Rita and Stella boarded trains in England, with paper tickets of different colours, travelling between towns and villages in proper passenger compartments. The sort with scratchy upholstery, and net bags above the seats for luggage. With windows that could be lowered to let in fresh air. With porcelain lavatories and water for washing. They could stare at passing towns and fields. Wave to people if they wanted.

Mania held on to her boys in the dismal fug of a freight wagon. No seats, no windows and just a bucket as toilet for as many as a hundred people. She was in darkness until the doors of the wagon were unlocked and hauled open again. We don't know if she was met by daylight or spotlights.[5]

Mania was only forty, or thereabouts, when she arrived at Auschwitz-Birkenau. Not young, not old. She was with young children, which meant a straightforward choice for the men on the arrival ramp making selections: pregnant women, and those caring for babies, toddlers and young people under sixteen, they were all considered unfit for work, and unworthy of life. The names of pregnant women and those caring for babies, of toddlers and young people under sixteen weren't taken on arrival. They weren't going to be in the camp long enough to be registered.

There is, remarkably, a surviving series of photographs that show part of the people-processing in Birkenau. It's hard to view them in hindsight; to acknowledge that what we see as black-and-white images were full-colour, present-tense moments for the many hundreds involved. The photographs were taken in 1944, long after Mania's arrival. The photographer has a vantage point taking in the length of a train, with passengers disembarking, regrouping, then being organised into groups. At first, you notice the adults, tall and loaded with bags. You look again and see there are so many children! Babies bundled in crochet shawls. Toddlers clustered, in soft wool bonnets. Older children in knitted pixie hoods and slouchy socks. Teens trying to look as grown up as possible.

Ankunft eines Transportzuges – Arrivals of Jewish women and children from Hungary 1944, from the 'Auschwitz Album.'
Yad Vashem/Holocaust Remembrance Center

Among the many trainloads of human cargo delivered to Auschwitz-Birkenau were girls who'd grown up with Mania's daughter

Jock. Her school friends and neighbours from Berlin. The same smiling girls featured in the little photograph album gifted to Jock when she took the Kindertransport train towards England. Who wrote *In memory of* and *Forget-me-not* on the creamy pages. For some of these girls, their fates can be traced through fragments of bureaucracy and pages of testimony in Yad Vashem.

Helene Spitz Kiwowicz, who once went to school with Jock, was deported from Berlin on 9 December 1942 on transport number 24 and murdered in Auschwitz. Her father, Joachim, had already died in Dachau. Her mother, Bertha, was on the next transport, leaving 14 December, first to Riga, then following her daughter along the rail tracks to Auschwitz.

Helene 'Hella' Sternlicht, who shared the Heidenstein's address in Berlin, was arrested with her mother Dora, her sister Mimi, and brother Leo, on 3 March 1943. They left Berlin on a freight train the following day, transport number 34. They arrived in Auschwitz-Birkenau on 6 March. Their last day.

It could have been Jock standing dazed on the ramp at Birkenau; Jock walking along the well-trodden path with Helene, Hella and Mimi, with Mania, David and Michael.

As it was, Jock was at school in England, writing to urge her little sister, Stella, to do well in exams – 'and think what a pleasure it will be to our parents when they hear of it.'

On 9 March, three days after her former neighbours had been killed, Jock wrote again about her own upcoming exams, and about the value of having had 'a Jewish upbringing at home.'[6]

Although Jock inevitably worried for the well-being of her parents and brothers, in the lack of news from Europe there was always the hope of a reunion one day. That a place such as Auschwitz could exist was too outlandish for most people in England to believe. That people would be killed simply for being Jewish should also have been unbelievable. Too many people accepted this concept as normal, even desirable. If not, the mass murders could never have been carried out.

Under escort, the women, girls and babies not selected to work in one of the many Auschwitz enterprises formed columns. They walked from the train into the camp extension known as Birkenau. They went alongside wire fences to patches of green grass and steps underground. Children held the hand of whatever adult was nearest.

The steps led down to undressing rooms with benches to sit while unlacing shoes and unrolling stockings, and pegs to hang dresses, coats and bags. There were inmates of Birkenau on hand to help the smallest children undress. *For a shower*, they were told. All belongings would be collected after disinfection.

Mania would have seen signs explaining the process. She might even have been handed a piece of soap. For the last time she undid her boys' buttons and folded their clothes. Some women sensed danger. They nestled their babies under piles of clothes, in a futile attempt to protect them.[7]

Rudolf Höss, commandant of Auschwitz since 1940, was familiar with every aspect of the killing process in the Auschwitz-Birkenau gas chambers. He observed women in the undressing rooms and noted that some either suspected or outright knew what was going to happen next, 'even with the fear of death all over their faces.' His admiration for the mothers is obvious when he remembers them talking lovingly to their children on the very threshold of death.

What did he expect them to do? Fighting would only initiate outright violence, and women had long been socialised to avoid conflict to protect the vulnerable.

Helpless in every other respect, the mothers and carers gave love where they could, hiding the fatal truth from their little ones for as long as humanly possible. One mother in particular stuck in Höss's memory. Before entering the gas chamber she hissed at him, 'How can you murder these beautiful, darling children? Don't you have any heart?'[8]

The terrifying reality was Höss did have a heart – a heart that had the capacity to love his own children, but hardened towards those labelled 'subhuman.' Genocide was his job. He had no answer for the mother, either at the time, or when the war was over and he faced his own execution. On she went to the gas chamber. As did Mania.

Comforting children. Shielding their faces. Holding them high in the hope they could breathe cleaner air at the top of the chamber.

Mania's thoughts and emotions cannot be captured; they are not recorded. Perhaps terror flooded her. Perhaps she held on to the hope that her three beloved daughters would be safe and would continue to feel her love long after she was gone.

Eyewitnesses recalled that before the end, Jewish people would recite the Shema Yisrael prayer, a prayer which might also be familiar to children as part of their bedtime ritual.

> *Hear O Israel, the Lord is our God, the Lord is one. And as for you, you shall love the Lord your God with all your heart, with all your soul, and with all your strength.*

Processions of prams pushed from the train ramp to storage were a macabre testament to the murder of Jewish babies deported to Auschwitz. There could be hundreds, even thousands. The prams were cleaned, reconditioned, shipped back to Germany for babies born to non-Jewish mothers. Their wheels would continue to turn – some in Berlin perhaps, along the very pavements Mania had once promenaded her babies. Along streets Regina Feldman could only glimpse from the train during her journey to Frankfurt.

After a few hours, all that was left of Mania Heidenstein and her boys were wisps of ash. Their bodies would have been prised apart once the gas dispersed from the death chambers, then dragged to ever-hot ovens.

Her daughters in England had no pictures of her, to remember her face, or to conjure up their life together as a family in Berlin.

The only surviving photograph of David and Michael Heidenstein shows the two little boys seated together and hugging. It was taken on 10 August 1939, when they were two and four respectively. Michael – Meschi to his family – has a cotton shirt and shorts. David has rumpled socks and a white knitted sweater. He holds a tiny teddy bear.

'The boys are very precious, smart, and also cute,' Mania had written to England in the summer of 1940.[9]

Whatever they wore at their last undressing three hard years later, and whatever toys they still carried, all would be thrown into blanket bundles then hefted to the vast plunder warehouses not far from the Birkenau gas chambers. Here inmates had to sort the debris of human lives, just the same as at Chelmno, Sobibor and every other killing site. The work was overwhelming. 'It was next to impossible to remove the countless clothes,' commented one of the perpetrators, SS Unterscharführer Pery Broad, without any reflection on the tragic murder of those who'd only just shed these clothes.[10]

Those who processed the discarded clothes were used to compartmentalizing emotions; they couldn't have functioned otherwise. Even so, sorting and packing children's clothes caused incredible pain.

The Heidenstein clothes would be a few garments out of millions. Perhaps they were part of the bales taken by train to Berlin, on the return journey Mania, David and Michael never got to make. Perhaps they were buried among the mountains of other items that could not be sorted before the camp was evacuated and liberated, along with other poignant mementos – a red leather shoe with undone laces, socks with patterned tops, a cotton frock with a red collar.

Each remnant tells an unknown story, memorialising the children's lives and fates.

Have David and Michael's little shirts and shorts been resurrected from the mass by modern specialists, carefully working to conserve the textiles that lasted longer than their original owners?[11] If so, how would we even know? Mania, David and Michael are gone. Three out of an estimated one million Jews murdered in Auschwitz. Their names are remembered only by the few members of the family who survived Nazi persecution, and by those now reading these words.

May their memories be a blessing.

In a matter of hours the train Mania and her boys arrived on was emptied, cleaned and sent back out into the world again. Another train soon took its place.

Anita Lasker was waiting to board a train.

She was at Breslau station. The same departure point for her 1938 trip to Berlin for cello tuition. It was late November 1943. Her destination: Auschwitz.

According to the German authorities, her journey was undertaken 'voluntarily.' The 'black Maria' used to transport her to the main station in Breslau told a different story, as did the lock on the special prisoner transportation cells inside the train.

There was a certain amount of déjà vu about the experience, reminding Anita of how she came to be arrested while attempting to escape Germany by train from the same station. Back on that terrible day in September 1942, Anita and Renate had been hopeful of some kind of freedom in Paris. Instead the Gestapo arrested the two Lasker sisters, along with friends Ruth and Werner Krumme, who were on the platform to see the girls off.

From the station, Anita and Renate were driven over the old city moat with its tree-lined promenade and to the prison on Graupe Street. The girls had known plenty of anxiety living as Jews in a Jew-hating regime, but to hear the keys clanking as the lock was closed on their cell, that really hit home. Being young and naïve, they at first tried to bluff their way out, telling their captors they were just French girls. The Gestapo were patient. They'd known about the girls' resistance work for months. Eventually the sisters came clean. Yes, they were Jewish. Yes, they had attempted to save their lives by fleeing the country. Yes, they understood this was a criminal offence.

The Nazi 'justice' system was all so surreal. Devastating though being in prison was, Anita still found so many elements ridiculous to the point of hilarity. There was the guard who lectured her on why Hitler was such a great guy, and couldn't Anita just understand why the Jews had to be destroyed? There was the fact that her suitcase, left in the train compartment at Breslau station, had made its way unaccompanied to Paris, where it was tracked down and returned to the Graupe prison. Anita had to make a formal acknowledgement that nothing was missing before her luggage was confiscated and later raided by one of the prison guards. Anita later did a double take when she noticed the guard wearing a smart dress her mother, Edith, had made specially for Anita's cello playing. Irrepressible, Anita went to the prison governor to complain about the theft. In another surreal interchange, the governor ruefully pointed out that even though Anita's accusations were credible, the thief had the moral high ground because the thief wasn't Jewish.

The dress stolen from Anita was one of the few tangible connections to her mother remaining.

When the trial day came round – 5 June 1943 – the sisters had to change into civilian clothes. Renate selected a dress of beige angora wool embroidered by their mother. The familial connection might have given her courage, but it did nothing to humanise her in the eyes of Nazi lawgivers. At that time she wasn't to know that angora wool would play a significant part in Anita's survival in the coming years, thanks to a certain red angora sweater.

One of the most twisted ironies of Anita's time in jail was the fact that it was safer to be inside than out. As long as Anita and Renate were in prison, they weren't on their way to Auschwitz. Regina Feldman and her friends had been desperate to break through the wire of their incarceration in Sobibor; the Lasker girls were just as keen to remain behind bars. They had the warning set by their friend Ruth Krumme, and by another Breslau Jew they'd roomed with at the Jewish orphanage, nineteen-year-old Hanni-Rose Herzberg. Ruth and Hanni-Rose were both acquitted in the special court, then promptly re-arrested by the Gestapo and sent to their deaths in Auschwitz.[12]

A guilty verdict in court brought some relief, but also separation. Renate, being the eldest, took the brunt of the blame. She was sentenced to three and a half years in the grim Jauer women's penitentiary in Lower Silesia, crammed full of political prisoners and murderers. Whereas the prison labour doled out in the Graupe prison consisted of painting toy soldiers and sewing endless buttons onto cards, Renate, stripped of her angora dress and now clomping around in prison clogs, was handed a batch of stinking grey socks, told to unravel them and to tie all the resulting lengths of yarn together to knit up new socks. The Wehrmacht truly were experiencing dreadful shortages if they had to resort to these grotty tactics to keep soldier's feet from freezing.

Renate despaired. She just didn't have the skill to turn old socks into new, and she was in solitary confinement with no one to help. Happily her next allocated task was netting shopping bags in a rainbow of different colours. German housewives could queue at shops with empty shelves, carrying one of these prison-produced bags, never thinking about the Jewish fingers that had knotted them.

No matter how monotonous prison labour was, whether button sewing, sock knitting or bag making, it would seem almost idyllic compared to the next stage in the Lasker girls' journey. Despite being sticklers for the law, all certainties were void when it came to Jews. Genocide overruled the prison sentences. Renate left Jauer on one train. Anita saw a last view of Breslau through the barred windows of the black van taking her to the main station. From here she'd board another train going east.

All journeys to Auschwitz seemed both too long and too short.

'The train seemed to have no end,' said corset maker Sara Zyskind, remembering her own journey from the Lodz ghetto. It was the same route stocking maker Chana Zumerkorn would have taken if her life hadn't already been cut short in Chelmno.

Norway, the Channel Islands, France, Germany, Belgium, Latvia, Greece, Italy . . . These were just a few of the departure points for Jews and other persecuted people in territories controlled by the fascists. Railway lines cut through cityscapes, forests and farmland. Signals lifted or dropped, track points switched, crew shifts changed. Inside passenger carriages or freight wagons the human cargo could only endure and brace for arrival.

Renate Lasker feared the worst. In Jauer penitentiary she had gleaned information from a prisoner transferred out of Auschwitz: 'I learned for the first time what till then I had refused to believe: that every single horrible thing that had been whispered about Auschwitz was *true*.'[13]

Anita Lasker was about to discover that there could also be small miracles and rare beauty amidst the horror.

14

In Auschwitz They Stripped Us of Everything

I didn't exactly come with high hopes into Auschwitz.
— ANITA LASKER-WALLFISCH[1]

Busy fingers.

Smooth hands lifting telephones and snapping fingers for service. Manicured hands typing orders, nails flipping through card index files. Ink-stained hands signing off on orders, invoices, blueprint designs.

Gloved hands wielding batons and guns; leathered fingers curling round guard dog leashes.

Grazed, blistered, bruised, broken, cold-bitten hands quarry sand for cement, hammer fence posts into hard ground, drag weeds from swampy ditches, lay chimney bricks one on top of the other.

Auschwitz-Birkenau is built.

The archaeology of incarceration is still visible eight decades later, corroded, crumbled and rotted now, or shored up with modern replication. Hard fragments are testimony to past horror.

In late November 1943, Anita Lasker was delivered to the Auschwitz offloading platform. She was assaulted by clamour, visions of people in crow-black capes and a horrendous stench.

Ironically, being a convicted criminal meant she didn't have to run the risk of being selected for death as soon as she arrived. She went straight for processing and undressing in Auschwitz II – the camp extension called Birkenau. Birkenau was also the main women's camp. It was vast: barbed wire and barrack blocks as far as the eye could see. Efforts were under way to extend the camp, expecting even greater numbers of miserable inmates to be crammed in.

At the time of Anita's arrival there were 33,846 female prisoners in Birkenau, of which 8,487 were classed as too sick to work. The daily death toll was horrific – over 1,600 registered female inmates in November 1943 alone.[2] Anita had no idea of these statistics, of course. These were collated for the camp administration to assess, running their fingers down columns of numbers. To the SS the death tally was just logistics; just one more factor in their ledgers of profit and loss. Each corpse meant one death closer to their aim: to eradicate all Jews and all other 'undesirables.'

It was freezing when Anita arrived. She was commanded to undress. Cold fingers unbuttoned clothes. Cold fingers pulled at the pompoms on her red shoelaces. Fingers clenched as her head and body were shaved; as a number was inked on her left forearm. She became 69388. At the time, Anita had no idea that getting a tattoo meant she still had a slim chance of survival in the camp. She was considered fit for work, and that was the only reason any inmate was left alive. Most of the people swelling onto the train platform day and night went to their deaths without being registered.

Prisoners doing the processing of new arrivals were eager to hear whispered news from the outside world, and also to make connections.

How's the war going? they'd ask, eager to hear of Allied advances. *Where are you from? What did you do before?*

What had she done before?

'I used to play the cello,' she told them.

Instead of laughing in her face at the incongruity of this comment, the girl processing Anita was delighted. While everyone else was led away – destination unknown – Anita was pushed towards showers. Real showers, with real water.

A stylish woman in a camel-coloured coat appeared. There were more questions about Anita's training, then the most surreal revelation: 'We need a cello, we have an orchestra here.' [3]

Anita had been stripped of her clothes, her freedom and all sense of security, and yet out of the blue was an offer to continue playing.

There are fragments of Auschwitz-Birkenau that do not survive, unlike cement, wire or bone. Invisible things, seen or heard then gone into the realm of memory. There was kindness in the camp, between friends or even strangers. There were still occasionally dreams, or talk of impossible things such as satisfying meals, warm beds, even freedom.

And there was – almost unbelievably – music.

For the first few days, prisoner number 69388, Anita Lasker, found herself in a compound without a single blade of grass, in a barrack without a single nook of comfort. This was quarantine.

She was completely cut off from the outside world. Elsewhere people had different battles. Jock Heidenstein was deep in her studies at Shefford school in England, having no idea there was a place called Auschwitz, or that her family and friends had terminated journeys there. Regina Feldman was in Germany hoping to start a new life under an assumed identity, having escaped another extermination centre.

All Anita could do was wait, cold and bewildered. When the quarantine period was up an SS man came to call for her – 'Where's the cellist?' Already her life had a touch more value than the other women in quarantine. To be called a cellist was to have an identity. Anita was more than just a number.

She was taken to another building in the Birkenau extension camp. Block 12, the music block. Home of the women's orchestra. Where once she'd played chamber music every week with her family, taken lessons in Berlin, then believed all hope of even touching a cello was probably gone, now Anita had to let her fingers find the notes again as she auditioned for the orchestra director, violinist Alma Rosé, the woman in the camel-coloured coat.

Rosé had a superb musical pedigree, and had already known great success with a women's orchestra before the war. But she was Jewish. She'd arrived in Auschwitz in July 1943. By December she was in charge of the Birkenau orchestra, motivated as much by an aspiration for music as by a quest to salvage some lives from the gas chambers.

Thanks to Rosé's extraordinary talent and discipline, what might have been a farcical medley of folkish instruments – accordion, mandolin, violin – was crafted into an orchestra that could play whatever was requested of them, albeit with adaptations. There were about forty musicians, Jews and non-Jews, in addition to other women brought in to copy out new arrangements of music. Thanks to the camaraderie and support of her companion musicians, Anita had a far greater chance of surviving Auschwitz. For as long as she was required, at least.

While Anita auditioned for Alma Rosé, playing the slow movement of a concerto, she had focus. A distraction. When she had her eyes on pages of music she wasn't looking out of the windows of Block 12, to lines of people going past, lining up for the gas chambers. But there was no hiding from the fundamental purpose of the Auschwitz-Birkenau complex: to provide workers for the SS and to exterminate anyone considered surplus to requirements.

'We had a job to do,' Anita said.[4]

The buoyant tunes were terribly discordant in the context of this job.

Every day the musicians trudged through ice, rain or mud to set out chairs and metal music stands at the main route out of the camp. Each morning they played marches for all the poor souls being harried out to do hard labour. Each evening they played marches for returning workers, bringing back the corpses of those who didn't survive the ordeal. 'The music drives them, like the wind drives dead leaves,' wrote Auschwitz survivor Primo Levi of the marchers' torment.[5]

One violinist who joined Anita and the others at these brutal performances said, 'There was something infernal about the music we played.' She felt completely impotent in the middle of so much violence and injustice. Like Anita, she had to play on.[6]

Music was meant to harmonise the horrible operations at Auschwitz-Birkenau. To normalise them even. Another reason that Anita's fingers were kept so busy coaxing beautiful music from a cello was because the SS loved their perks, in Auschwitz as in Sobibor.

What better way to relax after a week of mass murder, than listening to selections from operettas, popular dance songs, classical medleys or sublime arias from *Madame Butterfly*? The SS could indulge in a supposed love of culture each Sunday when the orchestra played special concerts, or simply come to the music block to request their favourite music. One of Anita's companions in the orchestra was even picked to play music for Frau Kramer, wife of the man in charge of operations in Birkenau killing centre.

The women's orchestra was established in April 1943 by SS-Lagerführerin Maria Mandl, a professed music lover and brutal authoritarian. She gained entertainment and status from running the orchestra, and even stretched to respecting Alma Rosé, despite the fact the violinist was a Jew. She still didn't consider Alma or Anita or any of the others as equally human. The musicians only had value because of their function. In return, the musicians needed Mandl's patronage to stay in the sanctuary of the music block. It was a humiliating symbiosis for the prisoners.

Another bonus for Anita when she came to the music block was the chance to wash – a rarity for inmates – so that fingers playing the cello were scrubbed, with clipped nails. Because the SS were terrified of typhus contagion – the disease was rife in the camp – any prisoners who interacted with them had to be clean and lice-free. When the orchestra were on show for special occasions they were kitted out with white blouses and blue pleated skirts, stitched in Birkenau's small-scale sewing factories. They 'ironed' these uniforms by laying them out under their mattresses. They had to look nice when playing for the SS – all part of the illusion of Nazi culture.

It wasn't a very convincing façade. One of Anita's new companions said they all looked 'more like a troupe of ill-nourished orphans than an orchestra.'[7]

Equally at home beating inmates or tapping in time to a tune, Maria Mandl loved to be stylishly dressed and well groomed. She wasn't alone in this, which is why select inmates were pulled from the morass of the camp populace to serve the SS, who could then enjoy the services of hairdressers, masseuses, tailors, dressmakers . . . and knitters.

Some prisoners found work knitting sweaters at an industrial level, made to be sold for profit beyond the camp. The SS kept the profit, the prisoners kept alive for a while longer.[8] At least one knitting work squad was housed in the SS administration block – the Stabsgebäude – just outside the Auschwitz main camp. It was a beautiful white building which also served as billet for female guards, and roughly three hundred prisoners tasked with serving the SS. Most of them were put to administrative tasks, such as filing prisoner admittance details . . . and logging prisoner deaths. In the double-level basement of the building were kommandos of knitters and stitchers, including an extraordinary fashion salon where mainly Jewish inmates crafted exquisite fashions for elite Nazi women, both in Auschwitz and in Berlin.[9]

Many of the knitters and sewers were long-term survivors of Auschwitz: Slovakian girls and women who'd been on the first official transports of Jews into the camp, back in spring 1942. In those early days their mortality rate had been 80 percent. By winter 1943, when Anita Lasker reached the camp, the Slovakians who'd endured thus far knew how to get the least dangerous jobs. They also used their relative privilege to help others find comparatively safe work, whether flexing their skills in the camp orchestra or wielding their needles in the basements of the admin block. This network of support was in direct defiance of Nazi policies to set inmates against each other, fighting for every inch of bunk space or every mouthful of food.

'We had no scruples whatsoever to take the best stuff for ourselves,' said a Jewish girl called Jutta Pelz, remembering how she and her companions pilfered scraps of yarn to make things for themselves or as gifts. 'Entire suitcases with yarn, thread and other sewing tools were regularly delivered to our work place.'[10] In a creative act of sabotage Jutta deliberately darned SS socks in a rainbow of colours, pretending no grey yarn was left.

In addition to the official knitting squads, individual SS guards coerced inmates into knitting for them, in return for perks such as a ladle more soup, or a small carrot or potato. Perla Blass was one such knitter. Like Chana Zumerkorn, the stocking maker who'd gifted her brother a warm red sweater, Perla had experience of working with yarns in Lodz ghetto. Unlike Chana, she'd avoided deportations to the Chelmno extermination site in the forest, finding herself in Auschwitz instead. Perla's cold fingers made woollen mittens so that the guards' hands could be warm. Although Perla spoke very little about her Holocaust experiences, she did emphasise that the reason she survived to knit sweaters for her daughter, and a wide circle of acquaintances, was because knitting saved her life in the camp.[11]

The men and women responsible for everyday atrocities in Auschwitz, Sobibor and any other sites of atrocity were not mythical monsters. They were human beings who got exasperated pulling off dirty socks to see a hole in the heel or toe. Who were a little mortified that the inmates tasked with mending their socks darned the holes with kaleidoscope colours, not regulation grey. Who entirely disassociated themselves from prisoners without any kind of warmth.

'I longed for a pair of snug, warm socks,' was the wistful memory from one girl in Auschwitz, while the perpetrators who tormented her, who supported the system that deprived her, had good boots and dry feet.[12]

In the midst of so much suffering, the SS at Auschwitz-Birkenau wanted music, warmth and fashion. How could Anita reconcile working for such people? She was horrified that genocidal abusers were so ordinary; that you wouldn't guess what they were like if you just met them in the street. 'You don't have to be a monster to be able to descend to that sort of depth,' she said after the war.[13] For her, this was the most frightening element of the nightmare she was in.

All these privileged prisoners, with their busy fingers making music, mending socks, sewing clothes – was there any chance of fighting back? Of sabotage, even?

The inmate put in charge of the Auschwitz fashion salon, a young Jewish woman from Slovakia named Marta Fuchs, refused to permit even the slightest act of sabotage on the garments created. Not out of respect for the SS clients – Marta was a dedicated member of the Auschwitz underground and committed to doing what she could to steal from the Germans to help other inmates – but because of an unbreakable desire for artistic excellence. Marta understood that her dressmakers could survive better if they kept their standards and their humanity. In this she was remarkably similar to Anita's music director, Alma Rosé. Anita recognised that Alma Rosé had such enormously high standards because she wanted her musicians to escape into excellence. Their integrity could be a bulwark against the degradation of camp existence.

One of the Slovakian inmates brought out of Birkenau was twenty-seven-year-old Gabriela Braun, known as Ella. After months of hard labour and mistreatment, Ella was so weak, and so full of infection, she could barely lift her hands, let alone knit. However, her expertise was required. A loyal friend, who also had connections with Marta Fuchs of the fashion salon, had put in a word for Ella with the highest-ranking SS man in Auschwitz: Rudolf Höss, overall camp commandant.

Höss brought his family with him to Auschwitz. As the camp was built and expanded, his new home was decorated and filled with plunder. As the camp population grew, his home was serviced by prisoners. As inmates froze to death during roll call his greenhouses had extra fuel for the boilers so the plants would thrive. Babies born in Auschwitz were not usually permitted to live, and they certainly couldn't thrive. The little Höss children had every comfort possible, including the prettiest knitwear.

Sick, weak Ella Braun would ordinarily have been selected to go undress for the gas chamber. Instead she created snug cardigans and lacy baby layettes, at the request of Hedwig Höss, the commandant's wife; the same woman who established the fashion workshop under the aegis of Marta Fuchs. At the birth of her fifth child, Annagret – born at Auschwitz – Hedwig Höss would have been kitted out with everything a mother and baby might need, such as a fluffy bed jacket, carrying shawl, bonnets, cot covers, pram suits and bootees. It was also typical to use bits of leftover wool to knit doll's clothes. Something for Annagret's two older sisters, perhaps.

Looking back on her labour for Hedwig Höss Ella said, 'They were beautiful things, and she was so happy with my work.'[14]

Did appreciation for Jewish skills help the SS staff and families see them as human? Regina Feldman certainly hadn't found this to be true in Sobibor when she knitted socks and sweaters for the SS. At Auschwitz one of the inmate gardeners working at the Höss villa confided to Hedwig that he was the father of a child born in the women's camp. Hedwig sent the mother a pink baby jacket.[15] Generous? Hardly. The jacket would be the result either of theft or enslaved labour from a prisoner. More significantly, the baby and mother wouldn't likely have long to live thanks to the regime Hedwig supported and which her husband enabled through his dedicated administration of the camp complex.

Hedwig spoke for many of the SS at Auschwitz when she said

Patterns for girls' knitwear from
Deutsche Hauswirtschaft, November 1940.
Lucy Adlington personal archive

of the Jews, 'They must disappear from the face of the earth' and 'at the proper time the end of even the English Jews would come.'[16]

Baby clothes were a chance to showcase intricate stitches in lovely combinations, all with names evocative of natural beauty – moss, feather, honeycomb, spider, rosebuds lattice and bee's wing. The very words, like notes of music, lift the imagination out of the Auschwitz reality. During war, pretty baby things were a luxury for most civilians, and a dream from a vanished life for concentration camp inmates.

Ella's busy fingers turned this dream into wonderful knitwear. Thanks to the protection of her elite work, she began to get better.

'I don't even know how I did it,' she marvelled, 'this knitting for the commandant.'[17]

It literally saved her life, even as Anita avoided death by playing the cello. Anita was still sharply conscious that it might only be a matter of time before the luck ran out. The thought was always with her, 'We are still alive today but tomorrow we may be smoke.'[18]

At the same time Ella Braun was knitting for the commandant's family, an expert in England wrote, 'The best periods of knitting have always occurred when yarns have been scarce or expensive.'[19]

The reasoning was that thrift inspired genius when yarns were in short supply. Thrift was not an issue for elite SS. Rudolf and Hedwig Höss enjoyed stolen abundance, and wanted for nothing except morals and compassion. The real genius came from prisoners looking to conjure warmth from next to nothing.

For Auschwitz inmates, every tiny fragment was a precious treasure. They'd been stripped on arrival at the camp, not only of clothes, but also carefully stocked sewing kits and knitting needles.

'Nothing remained but naked existence,' said Dr Lucie Adelsburger, transported to Auschwitz along with Dr Erna Davidsohn, the very same woman who had escorted Jock Heidenstein on the Kindertransport from Berlin to England. The two doctors gleaned new clothes where they could: 'Each piece of clothing was an event.'[20] This could be a scrap of material, or some hand-knitted socks gifted by a friend.

In modern times, socks are still given as presents, perhaps as a novelty gift, or an unimaginative stocking filler. They are now cheap to buy and semi-disposable – more likely to be thrown away than darned. During the Second World War, socks were appreciated as a good addition to one's wardrobe. In a concentration camp, socks were prized as much as gold. That people owning next to nothing themselves would make the effort to acquire wool to knit gifts for others was a testament to their humanity.

'Buttons, thread, needles and safety pins were non-existent,' said one survivor. She swapped some of her bread ration to get wool.[21] The fact that food was the currency to buy warmth made the purchase even more valuable. Rations barely sustained human life, and hunger was a constant.

When musician Fania Fénelon was stuck with a hole in the calf of her stocking before a concert she was worried how she could mend it, aware that 'everything had to be bought and I hadn't any bread.'[22] Anita had to learn to repress hunger pangs in order to 'shop' with precious bread. This was on top of the usual exhaustion from practising eight hours a day, six days a week in addition to performances. In the music block friends did sometimes loan a needle and thread, but everyone had to wait their turn.

Generosity between prisoners shines out all the more brightly because of the darkness of the conditions they endured. There were so many instances of gift-giving that may seem small out of context but which are truly heroic given the circumstances. There was a German girl called Sophie who made gloves for another Jew she saw pushing wagons along railway sidings near her work kommando. In return he somehow rustled up oats and sugar for her birthday. The only reason Sophie could knit the gloves in the first place was because a girl in the SS mending room acquired yarn and needles for her.[23]

Other women used oddments of wool and contraband knitting needles to make woollens to smuggle out to the Polish resistance, who were operating beyond the camp confines. They crafted earmuffs, sweaters and gloves. Despite their own suffering these knitters had the courage to gift warmth and solidarity to others in need.

Such networks of support were crucial for survival. Anita herself recognised that although luck played its part in who lived and who died, the only way to endure long term was to have a surrogate family, 'to be with other people,' as she put it.[24] The girls and women of the orchestra were one such group of allies, supporting each other in every way possible.

Orchestra director Alma Rosé summed up the strategy: 'Survive together or die together. There was no halfway road.'[25]

This concept of community, of solidarity, was often referred to as being *tightly knit*. It was a term Anita used too, evoking that sense of being bound together into a whole, like woollen knitwear. Strange as it might seem to outsiders, the girls and women of the orchestra sometimes found themselves joyful, even playful, laughing and enjoying moments of fun. In turn they also bullied each other not to give into apathy or despair.

The conditions for musicians in Block 12 were bearable, even luxurious compared to the utter squalor of existence beyond their barrack building. However, undernourished bodies traumatised by living alongside a daily reminder of death were still at risk of exhaustion and serious illness. For all there was a stove in the music block, Anita knew she needed more than a blouse and skirt to stave off the bitter cold of winter in Auschwitz.

On arrival she'd had all the clothes stitched by her mother taken away. As one inmate deported from Lodz ghetto recalled, 'In Auschwitz they stripped us of everything.'[26] To add another vital layer of warmth, Anita the cellist went in search of a sweater. The one she found would become an iconic emblem of her will to survive in Auschwitz and beyond.

Battling for Survival by Sheer Instinct

I had not melted away into the grey mass of nameless,
indistinguishable people.
– ANITA LASKER-WALLFISCH[1]

I t was soft, it was bright, it was red.

Anita Lasker, the cellist from Breslau, found a sweater among the piles of plunder stripped from people deported to Auschwitz.

It could have come from a woman such as Jock Heidenstein's mother, Mania, bought in Berlin in happier times, before Jock and her sisters were sent away on a Kindertransport to England. It could have come from a girl like Chana Zumerkorn, knitted in the ghetto of Lodz. It could even have been from a girl like Anne Frank in Amsterdam, part of a wardrobe carefully hoarded during months of hiding and imprisonment, before her eventual deportation to Auschwitz.

As it is, we'll never know who first wore Anita's new sweater, or who knitted it. Who spun and dyed the wool. Who sold the balls of yarn.

It was pulled from a mountain of other woollens; one garment among millions.

Soft, bright, red – it must have stood out from the rest of the garments, much like the way red shoes draw the attention of modern visitors to the Auschwitz-Birkenau State Museum when they encounter a silent mound of slowly rotting shoes on display; some of the footwear found in the camp when it was liberated in January 1945.

Liberation was a fever dream for inmates such as Anita. She had to survive one day at a time, and that meant not freezing to death while playing the cello outside in winter.

There wasn't a lot of colour in Auschwitz, mostly shades of feverishness, blood and mud. Pallor, sickliness, faded textiles. Flame red at night, from the crematoria chimneys; ash grey when the wind blew the wrong way.

When new inmates were stripped of their own clothes and tossed a medley of mismatched garments to wear – women's uniforms having run out – there were startling splashes of emerald green, baby pink, or navy polka dots. In the women's orchestra there was the red of copyist Hilda's bag. Twenty-year-old Hilda, one of Anita's friends, crafted the cotton bag out of pillowcases. She used it to keep sheets of music safe.[2]

Belongings taken from deportees, including Anne Frank and Anita Lasker, were piled up and sorted in plunder warehouses, known in camp slang as 'Kanada,' because the country Canada was supposed to represent a land of plenty. In the thirty barracks full of booty in Birkenau, female inmates laboured wearing white headscarves. The smaller warehouses in the Auschwitz main camp saw flashes of colour – women and girls in red head coverings.

And there was the red of Anita's new sweater.

For Anita the colour red was already significant, thanks to the distinctive red laces with pompoms on the shoes she'd worn on arrival at Auschwitz. Her shoes, inevitably, had been taken by someone else – a guard, or a prominent prisoner, she never knew for sure.

However, the red laces brought about a miraculous reunion with her sister.

Renate Lasker arrived in Auschwitz some weeks after Anita. If it hadn't been for the red laces she might never have known Anita was in the camp. As it was, Renate recognised Anita's black shoes with red pompoms and asked about the girl who'd worn them. Anita was known as *the cellist*, so from there it was only a matter of finding her way to the music block for a reunion. Not only were they happier together, Anita gathered all her courage to ask SS-Lagerführerin Maria Mandl if Renate could be given the relatively privileged role of camp courier or messenger. Mandl, in a bizarre fit of generosity, agreed. Renate couldn't be said to thrive in Auschwitz – that was almost impossible for prisoners – but she did get stronger and get access to clothes that were slightly better quality than the usual mish-mash of tawdry remnants usually tossed to Jewish inmates.

It was easier for the SS to treat prisoners badly if they looked less than human. Most inmates were valued beneath rags in the SS worldview. It was hard not to internalize the contempt and degradation of their treatment in Auschwitz. Conversely, wearing semi-decent clothes might evoke slightly less contempt from the SS – as when the camp orchestra turned out in their white and navy uniforms. Having clothes even one step up from worn-out textile dregs also propped up a prisoner's sense of identity. As a cellist, Anita was incredibly lucky to have meaningful work and tolerance from the SS, if not respect.

She still wanted something warmer than what she had.

Female inmates were supposed to have one dress and one pair of shoes or clogs. The majority of Jewish prisoners were rarely issued underwear or stockings. Acquiring additional clothes could give warmth, dignity, comfort and individuality. As such, they were strictly off limits to prisoners. In theory. All plunder belonged to the Reich. As such, it was strictly off limits to SS too. In theory. In reality, staying alive was a great incentive for any inmate able to acquire extra layers. Greed was a great incentive for any SS staff wanting to acquire everyday treats or luxuries, from the commandant to the lowliest SS guards.

Commandant Höss stated that 'Any member of the SS who laid his hands on this Jewish property was punished with death on Himmler's orders.'

He did concede that an 'immense' amount of property was stolen by the SS and even railway men responsible for train transports. He also accused prisoners of stealing, grossly overlooking the fact that they'd been stripped of all their belongings and left to fight for survival. Höss chose to ignore the reality that his entire home was furnished with stolen goods. His wife and children were dressed in stolen garments, or clothing made by desperate inmates.[3]

At times, prisoners took advantage of SS covetousness not only to bribe them for small favours, but also to attempt murder. One early member of the Auschwitz underground bred lice infected with typhus which were handed to the most hated SS in sweaters that had taken their fancy. In another desperate operation, an inmate informer was allegedly murdered with a lice-infected sweater.[4]

When the SS took items from the bulging plunder warehouses it was brazen theft from victims deported to the camp. When prisoners took what they needed to stay alive it was known as 'organising.' Stealing from another prisoner was common, but considered heinous, if they were still alive. Kitty Felix was a German Jewish teenager whose job was shifting corpses from the barrack blocks after the nightly death toll. At just sixteen years old, she learned to steel herself to take clothes from the dead, to keep or to barter for essential food. She was devastated when a sweater she'd organized was stolen by another girl.

'Later I saw her wearing it,' she recalled, 'but never managed to get it back, so had to go on freezing.'[5]

Charlotte Delbo, a French political prisoner deported to Auschwitz in January 1943, was gifted a lovely pink sweater by a friend working in one of the plunder warehouses. Delbo acknowledged that 'the tiniest tatter, or bit of wool, was obtained by infinitely complex manoeuvres.' Esther, the girl who'd gifted her the sweater, disappeared soon afterwards. While the SS might be reprimanded and occasionally imprisoned for theft, prisoners were gassed.

Threat of extreme punishment didn't stop inmates working in the warehouses from smuggling garments out, usually under their own thin dresses. Their desire to trade for bread or give gifts to friends was greater than their fear of death, which they knew was as good as inevitable in Auschwitz anyway.

Charlotte Delbo didn't just appreciate the warmth of her pink sweater. She recognised that it was a reminder of 'a way of life that had been abolished.'[6]

A life before Auschwitz. Normal life. The life they should all have been allowed to live in peace.

Anita had once been dressed in nice clothes bought by her parents or made by her mother. The red sweater that she acquired from Kanada, like Charlotte's pink sweater, belonged to 'before' times.

'It was a nice warm jumper,' Anita said. 'And it cost me a lot of bread.'[7]

Another French political prisoner, Claudette Bloch, worked in an agricultural kommando at the camp. She was no stranger to ingenuity, spending her spare time pulling threads from the edges of garments to sew civilian clothes for an escape attempt that never quite came to pass. Along with other gardeners, she was grateful for the kind gift of sweaters and underwear, 'organized' by male prisoners working nearby. That people with so little could share with others was a great testament to their humanity. Decades after their Auschwitz experiences, Claudette Bloch and Anita Lasker would be linked through clothes. Claudette's camp uniform would one day be on display in a museum case next to Anita's red sweater. Thanks to luck, resilience and friendship networks, they were both survivors.

By seeking out warmer clothes, Anita was, in a way, making her own luck; giving herself a better chance at endurance by the seemingly simple act of swapping bread for a jumper. Not just any jumper. A red one. Red, a vibrant colour. The colour of life and passion. A visible colour, which meant the wearer would never just be drab or anonymous. A protective colour, according to some European traditions. A hopeful talisman, even.

Many decades later, Anita said she couldn't remember why she picked that particular garment out of so many thousands – perhaps it was the bright colour – but she was particularly pleased that it was made from a luxurious yarn that was off limits to prisoners.

It was angora.

Gloriously soft angora wool was such a contrast to other textures in Auschwitz-Birkenau. The splinters, mud, ash and ice. Unknown to Anita when she slipped on her jumper for the first time, Auschwitz and angora actually had a bizarre but significant connection.

Reichsführer Heinrich Himmler, leading Nazi official and dedicated architect of Jewish genocide and exploitation, had a thing for rabbits. Not any old rabbits. Pampered, fluffy angora rabbits.

'We Germans, who are the only people in the world who have a decent attitude towards animals,' he boasted in a 1943 speech. This was the same speech in which he praised the SS elite, declaring, 'Copious breeding should be from this racial super-stratum of the German people.'[8]

Auschwitz was home to three thousand angora rabbits. Three thousand adorable bundles of fur, living their best lives, snug in heated hutches at a sub-camp called Harmęże.[9] They no doubt enjoyed being treated decently, having three hundred female inmates dedicated to feeding, cleaning and combing them.

Himmler saw angora rabbits as the elite of their species, the coney equivalent of the SS, worthy of proliferation. Then there was the not insignificant matter of profit – always part of Himmler's calculations. At a time of extreme thrift and commodity shortages, there was definitely an insatiable market for sweaters, scarves, hats and gloves.

When skinned, angora rabbits provided warm fur to line the coats of German soldiers and airmen. When combed, angora rabbit hair could be spun into a sumptuously soft yarn perfect when combined with wool to create luxury fashion items, or, if excellent quality, for babies' garments. Perhaps Ella Braun even knitted angora yarn for baby Annagret Höss in the commandant's villa.

Angora rabbits were one of Himmler's many agricultural passion projects. He established angora farms in concentration camps and extermination centres across Europe, from Dachau to Treblinka to Auschwitz. He even took his twelve-year-old daughter Gudrun to visit Dachau concentration camp, where she could play with the bunnies. In her diary entry for 22 July 1941, Gudrun wrote about a tour of Dachau, wrapping up with the words, 'It was very nice.'[10]

Himmler's obsession with bloodlines led to rabbits galore . . . and genocide. The three thousand angoras at Auschwitz perversely symbolised the Nazi drive to elevate 'pure' breeds while eliminating those considered unworthy of reproduction. Angoras thrived. So-called 'subhuman' inmates died, or, in the words of one survivor, 'shivered to stay alive.'[11]

A beautifully produced album was testament to his obsession with angora farming, found by a war correspondent at one of

Himmler's properties at the end of the war. The album was even bound in a jacket of woven angora that still sheds hairs when handled.[12] The cover is marked with the SS runes.

In many ways the album isn't so different from the beautiful albums created in Lodz ghetto to showcase the skills of Jewish artisans such as Chana Zumerkorn, stocking maker. Carefully pasted photographs showcase fabulously furry angoras with comical tufted ears. Photos of garments made from angora wool are so enticing you can easily imagine how soft they'd feel to touch. In one picture a woman holds a huge angora rabbit in her arms and carefully brushes its fur.

The camera has also captured black-and-white scenes of heated hutches at Dachau, and rabbits being hand-fed. There is a map marked with angora farm sites, including the one housing three thousand rabbits at Auschwitz. Chillingly, each site on the map is also a notorious Nazi camp.

Himmler's SS 'Angora' album, boasting a total yield of 4730 kilograms of angora wool yarn between 1941 and 1942, which could produce 12,100 sweaters, or 52,500 socks, or 13,100 pairs of thermal leggings.
Wisconsin Historical Society WHI 45431

However, while the Lodz ghetto albums show Jews at work, Himmler's angora album doesn't feature a single camp inmate, despite the fact that it was their job to tend to the rabbits. Just like the musicians of the orchestra, prisoners were considered irrelevant compared to whatever they produced. To Himmler, Jews such as Anita were no more than beasts of burden. Working animals who existed only to live and die in the service of Nazi aims, whether doing hard labour, producing music in an orchestra or grooming rabbits.

Rather like the orchestra, rabbit-tending was a coveted position compared to the crippling, debilitating labour of other work squads. The hutches were built among a pleasant copse of trees. Angora rabbits groomed in Himmler's atrocious empire of suffering had better living conditions than the prisoners who tended them. Workers at Himmler's agricultural sites in the Auschwitz sphere of influence were reduced to killing, skinning and stretching the furs of captured water rats to stitch together for a hint of warmth.[13]

Himmler's angora album has impressive statistics regarding yields. Bags of wool photographed prior to being shipped out of the camp for full production are positively bulging. Given the value and prestige of angora –fashionably, financially and from a fascist breeding perspective – it's not surprising that it was one of the many comforts forbidden to inmates.

No wonder Anita felt an extra frisson of defiance when she took an *angora* sweater to wear under her official camp clothes.

Anita had no qualms about buying her red sweater in return for precious bread. She might have played marching songs for the original owner, at the gates of Birkenau, or beautiful classical music at one of the Sunday camp concerts. Or perhaps the original owner was just ashes in the wind. Only after the war did Anita stop to wonder about the origin of the cello she played in camp. Only when she had the mental space and safety for reflection could she consider that the musical instrument that helped saved her life had almost certainly been brought to the camp by one of the new arrivals too, reduced to carrying only their most precious, most essential items. In this case – a cello.

Some lucky recipients of extra garments acknowledged the sad source of their bounty and grieved for those who had most likely died soon after giving up their clothes. Other inmates couldn't spare the emotion. Survivor Lili Jacobs stated she was 'glad and proud' to wear something brought by another Jewish deportee to Auschwitz, even though this woman's name and fate would never be known. Recovering from her concentration camp ordeal at the end of the war, Lili came across a truly remarkable collection of photographs, eclipsing the photos of Himmler's angora album. These snapshots were taken by a German officer to record the arrival and processing of Hungarian Jews brought to Auschwitz in 1944, during a season of monumental slaughter. The women, men and children follow a horrible sequence of transformation, from their everyday, familiar clothes to dehumanising camp gear, although the camera does not record the fate of the majority, who were stripped and murdered just hours after arriving.[14]

Inmate Kitty Felix, on duty in the Kanada sorting barracks, said they were almost smothered by the sheer volume of plunder at this time. When Anita salvaged her red sweater she was certainly spoiled for choice. There was so much to sort that some clothes were simply dumped on refuse piles outside the camp and left to rot. In just one month 175 sweaters, 2243 socks and 141 mittens were pulled from the rotting mounds, with a view to reusing them somehow.[15] Not for the benefit of prisoners, of course. Kitty herself was reduced to salvaging clothes from the corpses of dead inmates. She knew winter would be fatal without extra hidden layers.

Every day more trucks left the complex 'full of loot for the glory of the German Reich.'[16] The gargantuan bulk of loot gathered from Nazi victims was collected and sorted for welfare organisations who distributed the goods to Germans in need. These included victims of air raids.

Ironically, Regina Feldman, the Polish girl who'd been knitting a red sweater for an SS man at Sobibor extermination camp, and who escaped during the phenomenally daring uprising, found herself on the receiving end of German clothing handouts. A tense series of train journeys using false papers and posing as a Christian brought Regina to Frankfurt-am-Main around the same time as Anita Lasker was being inducted into Auschwitz. It was a long way from her former home in Poland, and not only in terms of miles.

Outwardly, Regina looked like an ordinary young teenager, with her dark hair rolled up and a mismatch of clothes. Inside she felt alone, traumatised, yet resilient. She was hearing German spoken all around her – the language of the murderers in Sobibor. Who could she trust? As it happened, she got lucky. Through a series of mishaps Regina fell into work with a decent German family. She became a nanny, cleaner and cook. Although food was abundant, and her health began to improve, Regina was naturally terrified that the family would discover she was Jewish. As a big industrial city, Frankfurt was a major target for Allied bombing. When the house she worked in was hit by phosphorus bombs intended for the nearby port, the fire that spread destroyed Regina's few possessions.

Reduced to owning nothing more than the clothes she wore – including the coat she'd kept throughout her imprisonment and while in the forest afterwards – Regina was in no position to question the origin of the donations she received as a victim of bombing. Frankly, after what she'd experienced, she deserved whatever help she got. She was allotted shoes, underwear and other clothing. Provenance all unknown.

Anita would eventually get a passing view of the devastation wrought by Allied bombs on her homeland. Like Regina, she was destined to leave Poland for Germany, although not until autumn 1944. She would play her final notes in the camp orchestra and there would be no more music for a while.

For those trapped within the barbed-wire confines of Auschwitz-Birkenau, it was hard to believe the outside world existed; that there had ever been a place or time where music meant pleasure and entertainment, not an incongruous accompaniment to transports, executions and relentless marching.

The scale of the camp was so vast and so monstruous its processes came to seem inevitable, unending. Auschwitz tainted everything, engorged by suffering. People arrived, were murdered and their belongings dispersed. But the system was unravelling even at the height of the killing.

By 1944, rumours around the camp whispered of German defeats and Allied advances. The Birkenau band played on through it all. Anita and the other musicians survived one day at a time, supported by their close friendships and by treats organized from Kanada, such as clandestine towels, bras and bottles of perfume.

The SS grew uneasy, more erratic, even towards the musicians. One day they wanted the distraction that music could offer, the next they were trashing the towels, bras and scent bottles in spiteful block searches. Anita managed to keep hold of her red sweater during these purges, but she and her friends knew how precarious their position was. If the orchestra was disbanded they'd lose all the vital privileges that had kept them alive so far. The gas chambers were only a few steps away.

Sensing the need to find another way to seem indispensable, orchestra director Alma Rosé arranged with inmate Elsa Schmidt, the formidable woman in charge of the Kanada clothing stores, for an abundant supply of knitting wool. Armfuls of yarn in every colour were unloaded onto the table in the music block. Stitches were cast on, and the needles never stopped. Instead of music, the young musicians created scarves and sweaters.

'Now we were a knitting factory,' said musician Fania Fénelon philosophically.[17]

Some worked in a frenzy, as if their lives depended on it. Which, essentially, they did. Some took their time, savouring the familiar rhythms of the domestic task, and smoothing the soft knitted fabric as it grew. How very ordinary it was – like 'before' times – to sit knitting with friends, hearing the time-honoured cries of 'I've dropped a stitch!' The musicians helped each other with snags and patterns, just as they helped each other keep going day to day.

Knitting instead of notes.

It passed the time and helped soothe nerves during upheaval, particularly when the terrible news came that Alma Rosé was gravely ill following a birthday party for Elsa Schmidt. Such was Rosé's status, that SS doctor Josef Mengele was summoned to try to treat her, taking time from his sadistic experiments on camp inmates. Her illness was beyond his medical skills. She died in the company of her friend Manca Svalbova, a young Slovakian Jew known as Dr Manci, although her medical training had been interrupted by deportation. Dr Manci's kindness was legendary in the camp. Her aid linked women in the music block and the hub of resistance in the SS dressmaking salon. One act of generosity was in giving up her own 'organised' sweater for a naked girl who had somehow been reprieved from the gas chamber.[18]

Life for the musicians was increasingly discordant after Alma Rosé's death. Without being defeatist, Anita came to accept that once the Sunday concerts were cancelled and rehearsals dwindled, it was only a matter of time before she too would shed her clothes one final time in the undressing rooms by the gas chamber.

On a fateful day in November 1944 the Birkenau musicians underwent selection. Jews were separated from non-Jews.

'Well, that's it,' they all thought.[19]

It seemed their luck had run out.

In an act of unnecessary cruelty, their precious stock of organised clothes was taken from them and they were issued garments that Anita called 'real monstrosities.' The transition was a shock, and really brought home their loss of status and protection. Somehow, against all odds, Anita held on to her red angora sweater. She'd no idea how much she'd need it over the coming winter.

Her cello was left abandoned in the music block, reduced to a silent piece of wood with strings now there was no one left to play it. Along with her Jewish companions Anita was issued with a blanket and led to a line of freight wagons. At the last moment her sister, Renate, slipped into the huddle of young women, determined not to be separated from Anita whatever came next.

Through her long months in Auschwitz-Birkenau, Anita said they were all 'battling for survival by sheer instinct,' whether that was finding a safer work kommando, nurturing a loyal group of friends or organizing warm clothes.[20] In the final months of war these survival instincts would be needed more than ever.

Under her gruesome new garments and a thin grey blanket Anita still had the protective red talisman of her sweater. Where there was life, there was hope.

We Had Learned to Be Resourceful

I did survive the Holocaust, but only because I refused to die.

— ALICE KERN, BERGEN-BELSEN[1]

When she left Auschwitz, Anita Lasker thought she was escaping the worst possible place on earth. She had to face whatever came next that winter with only the protection of her hidden red sweater and a thin grey blanket.

These blankets, mass-produced in ghetto workshops and industrial factories across Europe, were a defining textile of the war. Not as distinctive as the infamous concentration camp stripes, the blankets were still a constant feature of camp life and death. Piles of loot taken from murdered deportees were bundled in them. Living bodies huddled on them and under them. Blankets shrouded the heads and shoulders of inmates harried along on evacuation marches through bitter weather. They froze in the snow with the corpses of those who perished on the way.

In Auschwitz Anita knew that her skills as a cellist had helped her stand out from the crowd. They made her an individual, not just one of many, like wearing a red jumper in a morass of grey blankets.

Arriving at their next destination it was immediately apparent that everyone would be swamped together in wretchedness.

It was a place in Germany called Bergen-Belsen. Belsen was newly 'upgraded' to the status of concentration camp, where previously it had been a grim holding centre for special categories of 'exchange' Jews who might be of use in Himmler's power plays.

'There was no room for us,' Anita saw at once.[2]

No room, and no amenities. Their blankets were very quickly sodden by catastrophic rainstorms and collapsing shelter. The Nazis were flooding Belsen camp with the human debris of their forced labour and extermination programs. Despite storehouses bulging with clothing supplies, and a nearby bakery capable of producing sixty thousand loaves a day, the multitudes trapped in Belsen had no regular recourse to food or water. Lice, disease and death were the only abundance for inmates. Death thinned the prisoner numbers, but more transports kept arriving. Belsen wasn't, strictly speaking, an extermination centre but 'a camp where people perished.'[3] It was the final destination of Anne Frank, another girl with a red sweater, who was last witnessed clad in nothing but a blanket as she burned with fever, hunger and grief.

Anne Frank died sometime in February or March 1945. At this time Anita was still fighting for life herself. SS staff transferred to Belsen from Auschwitz brought their own brand of terror, whipping and beating starving prisoners who dared to steal so much as a turnip. Anita had to drag herself to stand at roll call no matter how sick or weak she felt.[4] At least the orchestra girls stuck together. They were a family now, pushing each other to endure and survive.

Weeks passed. The new camp commandant, Josef Kramer, wanted to establish an orchestra like the one at Auschwitz, music playing while the prisoners dissolved in malnutrition, dysentery and fever. Anita did not play. Months passed. She existed among mounds of bodies. She was sick. Numb to the horror and decomposition. Slipping away. Tethered by her sister's voice.

Then came the miracle.

The sound of engines outside the camp. Germans dispersing. Voices penetrating the ugly mist of her illness: *Help is here*.

Anita, brought out under open sky by her sister, was one of many thousands of exhausted people still alive at the liberation of the camp.

Men of the British 11th Armoured Division arrived at Belsen on 15 April 1945, with no concept of what they'd find behind the gates, despite the horrible stench contaminating the countryside around the camp. Many later said that what they'd witnessed as they passed into Belsen was worse than any warfare.

It was a hot spring day. There were about sixty thousand living skeletons and thirteen thousand corpses in the camp, often indistinguishable. The faces looking out of barrack windows were like skulls; the people still able to shuffle upright were like ghosts. Yet they had all been individuals before they began drowning in the mire of filth and misery of Belsen. Like Anita, they'd all had lives, hopes and loved ones.

Soldiers recoiled as they looked into Belsen's wooden huts, seeing remnants of human life tangled in dirty grey blankets, or without covering of any kind. A few liberated souls had the energy to reach out to their liberators. Anita was too dazed, too weak, and too full of disbelief.

Renate heard voices through a loud-hailer – *Please keep calm . . . you are liberated*.

Was their ordeal finally over?

There weren't enough blankets for burials. Not enough land for individual graves. Diggers scooped out the earth. Former SS guards were under orders to clear up after their crimes. Without gloves or

A blanket-wrapped survivor in Belsen camp after liberation. Name unknown.
United States Holocaust Memorial Museum, courtesy of Lev Sviridov

masks they pulled at truckloads of naked, stick-thin bodies, swinging them into deep trenches. Former prisoners burned leftover rags and rotten shoes to make fires for their soup.

One man who did get a blanket after death was Adolf Hitler. In the aftermath of his suicide on 30 April 1945 his remains were wrapped and crudely burned in a shell crater in bombed-out Berlin. His ambition, his racial hatreds and his rhetoric had inspired and enabled not a thousand-year Reich but twelve years of persecution and atrocities. He lived a grandiose life gorged on power and sustained by the fanatical obedience of others. After death he was just a corpse wrapped in wool; no state lying-in, no funeral procession, no cenotaph.[5] His reign was over, yet the effects of it were widespread and utterly devastating. The human cost of fascism hits home when each individual life and death is acknowledged. Without Hitler and the cascade of people who followed him, Jock Heidenstein would still be in Berlin with her family, not having a fractured life as a refugee in England. Chana Zumerkorn, stocking knitter in Lodz, would still have her red sweater, and her body would not be mingled with the soil of the Chelmno extermination site. Regina Feldman would still be living in Siedliszcze with her family too, not carrying memories of them stained by her experiences of being a knitter in Sobibor as she negotiated the rubble of existence in Frankfurt-am-Main. Anita Lasker could have been playing her cello at home concerts, wearing clothes her mother had made for her instead of finding comfort from a stranger's red angora sweater and wondering if her fingers would ever have strength again to tear a piece of bread.

Four young lives unravelled, out of many millions.

There would be more human wreckage before rebuilding could begin. In the weeks that followed Belsen's liberation, an estimated fourteen thousand more people died, despite the best efforts of the British Army, and sometimes because of them: stomachs shrunk by starvation simply couldn't cope with the meats or sweets from army ration packs that were pressed upon them by well-meaning soldiers. Mental and physical systems brutalised over many years broke down completely.

Cecilia 'Zippy' Orlin, a volunteer arriving from South Africa to help Belsen survivors, called them 'tortured remnants.' Among Zippy's extensive collection of photographs from liberated Belsen is a snapshot of child survivors bulked out in chubby jumpers and mismatched overalls.[6]

Anita and Renate were two out of nearly twenty-nine thousand 'remnants' moved from the Belsen camp to former military barracks a couple of kilometres away. They passed through what was known as a 'human laundry.' It was a processing that reversed the dreadful dehumanisation of the Nazi system. Instead of undressing for extermination, or stripped and deloused for forced labour, they were disinfected with DDT while naked and given clean hospital blankets for treatment and recovery.

Matron Muriel Doherty travelled all the way from Australia to help survivors. She was overwhelmed with compassion for her fragile new patients, saying, 'I felt nothing we could do for them could ever compensate.'[7]

Through all of this Anita held on to her red angora wool sweater.

What a feeling – to be clean at long last. To be fed regular meals again. True, the diet was limited; too low on proteins, vitamins and fats that would keep starved bodies warm. True, the liberated prisoners were still behind barbed wire. Even so, they were, in Renate Lasker's words, 'slowly changing back into human beings.'[8]

A profoundly important part of the re-humanisation was getting fresh, clean clothes. A United Nations representative touring liberated camps in Germany reported that many Jewish displaced persons – or DPs, as they were known – only had their striped uniforms to wear, or pieces of loathed SS uniforms organised from German stores. Clothing shortages were, at first, so dire that UN leaflets distributed to refugees were being used to pad and patch clothes.

The urge to look civilised and *normal* was incredibly powerful. A big problem was, where to source new garments? Disgusted by German treatment of concentration camp inmates, the British Army were only too happy to force German civilians to make up the shortfall as a kind of collective recompense. Ever-resourceful, Anita's sister, Renate, found herself a job as interpreter for a staff captain driving from one major city to another to collect levies of clothing. A complete outfit was demanded from every German man, woman and child.

One German woman, resentful of the levy, picked out her worst clothing to hand over. She was then surprised to see the quality and quantity of other donations from German civilians. She didn't spare a thought for the victims of Nazism who were to receive the clothes.[9]

A new clothing storeroom at Belsen DP camp was soon filling up with the most bizarre range of garments, including bulbous woolly combinations, antique shifts and worn-through shoes. Rather than piling the donations on tables in a dreary jumble, the used clothes were treated with respect. They were inspected, cleaned, repaired and ironed, then hung on rails just like in a proper shop. The hut was a far cry from the glamour of the KaDeWe department store that Anita had enjoyed browsing during her pre-war sojourn in Berlin. Nevertheless, the enterprise was jokingly named Harrods, after the grand store in London. There was even a wooden signpost directing 'customers' to their transformation.

Han Hogerzeil, one of many heroic aid workers in Belsen, was delighted to report, 'Thousands came, were fitted out and went away utterly transformed persons.'[10]

Discharged patients came to the store wrapped in hospital blankets. They left with a complete new-to-them outfit. In fact, they sometimes left with far more than their official allocation, with a haul of other items hidden in their armpits, under their coats, or simply carried out of the hut with great panache. This was illegal, of course, but Matron Muriel Doherty wouldn't judge.

'One can understand that the people who have struggled for so long for existence still must gather all they can. Wouldn't you?' she later wrote to a friend in Australia.[11]

Nimble-fingered entrepreneurs turned their time and talents to making new clothes as well as acquiring them. Hospital blankets could surreptitiously be cut and stitched into smart suits, with hospital sheets as shirts. Gauze bandages and even unravelled hernia belts were knitted into sweaters using bicycle spokes or wooden sticks as needles, then stitched together with threads drawn from towels and blanket edgings. Enforced idleness was demoralising to people recovering from sickness and starvation; handiwork became a form of therapy. It wasn't long before this energy was harnessed by the Jewish ORT – Organisation for Rehabilitation through Training – supporting the training of new generations of knitters, tailors and dressmakers in ad hoc vocational schools. *Help them to help themselves* was the ORT post-war mission.

Every little fragment was precious in Belsen, as in every camp. Film footage taken just after the liberation show survivors taking care to wash their motley collection of textiles, mushing them in tubs of cold water, then hanging them on fences.[12] These would be clothes which, in their 'before' life, would most likely have been tossed out to the rag man or to second-hand dealers such as Jock Heidenstein's father, Chaim.

Nothing was wasted. One teenager used two wooden sticks to knit up the unravelled wool of German military socks, transforming them into a sweater . . . and a new image for herself.[13] In the surge of post-liberation creativity, oddments of blanket became embroidered gloves and slippers. One girl used scraps of striped uniform material and other rags to fashion sweet little dolls.[14] Another found herself a bag crafted from blanket wool with pretty floral applique, buried in a mound of *Schmatte* – rags and scraps. She said owning a little thing of her own helped her feel human again. More importantly, she could start to gather and keep meagre possessions. It was a small step towards having a normal life after all she'd had to shed along her unwilling journey to Belsen.[15]

In making their own clothes, DP survivors were asserting choice and individuality after years of victimisation.

Survivors also asserted their independence and agency in other ways. Some of the more robust DPs defied their barbed-wire confines to roam the countryside and towns around Belsen, despite British warnings that typhus might still be spread. They broke into German homes, taking whatever they wanted and trashing whatever they didn't. They made their own transformation from being walking *Klamotten* – or rags, as some Germans referred to Belsen survivors – to humans. Angry humans at that.

Anita resisted the urge to steal or take revenge. Her hatred of her persecutors was still strong. Germany should have been her homeland; instead it had caused her family's ruin. Some months after liberation Anita volunteered to be a witness for the prosecution at the nearby trial of war criminals, including men and women who'd been responsible for her own persecution. She identified key perpetrators and was interrogated over her evidence.

Muriel Doherty, so sympathetic to the needs of Belsen survivors, admired Anita at the trial. She remembered that once Anita had finished speaking against the defendants she 'stood for a full three minutes, just looking at them in silence. What a moment of triumph!'[16]

Anita's sense of the trial was somewhat different. A photograph from outside the court building shows her looking very young yet very smart in a shirt and tailored wool jacket. Inside she was riled at her testimony being attacked because she – a prisoner without a watch or calendar or coherent points of reference – could not recall the exact date and time of specific atrocities. She later called the trial 'a total and utter farce,' believing it futile to try to apply traditional justice to events so far beyond normal experience.

During the months following liberation she dressed in her new clothes – including a blouse and navy-blue trousers – and tried to evaluate her own life, and her choices for the future. The European war was over on 8 May 1945, when Germany offered an unconditional surrender, but for Anita, in the strange position of being a German Jew in a hostile homeland, there were still battles to be fought.

On the evening of 8 May 1945, Jock Heidenstein's sister Rita sat down to begin a letter to her parents and brothers – Mania, Chaim,

Anita Lasker and two friends from the Auschwitz women's orchestra
at Bergen-Belsen DP camp after liberation.
Yad Vashem/Holocaust Remembrance Center

David and Michael. It was a letter that would never be sent, since
there was no one left alive to mail it to. She wrote, 'This evening
I heard that this war is over.'[17] Although she couldn't yet compre-
hend the full tragedy of the destruction of Jews in Europe and beyond, she was well aware she was one of the lucky ones. She'd been
saved. She owed her security in part to an inmate of Bergen-Belsen
who continued his dedication to helping others almost as soon as
the camp was liberated. Norbert Wollheim was one of the many
splendid people in Germany who helped organise pre-war Kindertransports that saved Jock, Rita and Stella Heidenstein, even while
he couldn't offer transit to safety for Anita and Renate Lasker and
the tens of thousands of other children at risk. In 1945, after years
of loss and suffering, Wollheim was one of the Belsen survivors
committed to re-clothing other DPs and re-establishing a Jewish
community. Shedding old, grim garments was part of the process
of re-building self-confidence and self-respect. It was hoped that appeals for donations from abroad would make up for the shortfall in

Germany. Soon bundles of goods were loaded on quaysides around the globe, to play their own small but special part in transforming post-war lives.

In Britain work began in earnest to send support for DPs. The public were shocked by graphic radio and cinema reports on conditions at Bergen-Belsen. Despite the fact that everyone had sorrows and struggles of their own, even people who seemed to be getting on with life as normal, it seemed important to spare something for those even less fortunate.

On the surface things were going well for the Heidenstein sisters in England. Rita Heidenstein was happy at the school in Shefford, filling out nicely to be, in her own words, 'a quite nice looking girl,'[18] and still attracting attention from cheeky classmate Henry Mayer. Jock's little sister, Stella, found her own way to cope: ruining her eyesight studying for a school scholarship. Jock herself was pleased to have passed her final school exams and to be based at a hostel in London, thinking of training as a nurse.

'She is always busy,' wrote Jock's sister Rita, to their uncle Oscar in Palestine. 'In many clubs, taking care and being in charge.'[19]

It was a world away from the horrors Anita Lasker had experienced in Belsen, but none of the Heidenstein sisters were unscathed by their refugee life.

On the evening of 8 May 1945, a date celebrated as Victory in Europe Day, Rita sat down to compose a letter in German to the parents she hadn't seen since summer 1939. She hadn't heard from Mania or Chaim since late 1941. She included her little brothers David and Michael in her greeting, asking her parents to tell them 'How I love them and what peaceful happy contented hours would I have had with them, but for my youth being spent in a strange country, torn away from my dearest, missing loved ones.'[20]

There was the faint but tantalising hope that somehow Mania, Chaim, David and Michael could all still be alive, regardless of BBC radio reports about places such as Belsen and Auschwitz. Anita Lasker, having lived through the horrors of both camps, wasn't optimistic about being united with her parents again.

Whatever anxieties Jock had about her missing family she kept private, as was her nature. She and her sisters also carried the grief of losing relatives closer to home. In May 1940, her grandparents Sara and Josef had miraculously managed to escape the German occupation of Belgium to find refuge in England. Sadly, in December 1940 seventy-year-old Sara died of pneumonia.[21] Her husband, Josef, once a thriving rag merchant in Berlin, was cared for by Jock's aunt Lottie, who also had charge of her two children. All were reliant on handouts from Polish and Jewish charities. Their poverty is clear from poignant details from their case files, which reveal a meagre but appreciated dole of one pair of socks, one shirt, one pullover and one blanket.[22]

When people have next to nothing, anything extra is precious.

By 1944 Josef was entirely dependent on his daughter Lottie's care. She moved with him and her children to a basement flat in London, which she kept spotless despite a painful lack of resources. She was desperate to find him a place in a care home or hospital, with no luck.[23] It speaks volumes that beyond the Nazi sphere of influence, old and sick Jewish people were seen as vulnerable adults deserving of care, rather than prime targets for extermination. As it happened, Josef Heidenstein did not escape Germany's reach. On 2 July 1944, he was injured during one of the deadly V1 rocket attacks on London.

'Ghastly sights everywhere,' wrote Stella Heidenstein's foster sister Betty.[24]

However, in contrast to the bodies swung and tumbled into mass graves, or incinerated in the infamous camp crematoria, Josef Heidenstein's body was treated with respect. He died in the company of loved ones, in bed, under a hospital blanket; not left naked, or just wrapped in a concentration camp blanket, denied any kind of help. He was buried in an individual grave with proper religious attention.[25]

When the rockets stopped falling and the war ended, the youngest Heidenstein sister, Stella, was still living with the Adler family in Hackney. Losing her grandfather was one more thread broken that attached her to her former life in Berlin. As she walked to school, on errands or out to play, Stella might have spotted posters put up around London showing a stylised gaunt figure with the plea *Give Clothing for Liberated Jewry*.[26] At age thirteen she was old enough to appreciate how lucky she was to have been spirited out of Europe in 1939. She'd been away from her parents for nearly six years. Her memories of them would be wisps and yearnings only.

After six years of war, most people had very little surplus, but they gave what they could. Those, like Jock, who'd escaped the worst of Nazi persecution, or who'd never directly suffered from it, found that they could feel slightly less helpless if they could donate something – a few coins, or a few bits of clothes. Despite wool being in short supply, eager knitters gifted patchwork cot covers for the children's ward in Belsen. Others followed printed patterns to make children's garments, advertised as 'Clothing for Liberated Europe.'[27] Did Jock knit anything to send? She never said. Often these kind deeds were done in silence.

Dr Solomon Schonfeld, the unstoppable Orthodox rabbi who'd championed the Heidenstein sisters in England, also dedicated his formidable energies to providing kosher food and much-needed clothing to the Jewish remnants of Europe. Even before Hitler's death and the official end of the war, the clothing committee Schonfeld established had collected an extraordinary number of garments for DPs, including 300 woolly pullovers and 100 army blankets. Over the following months the tally increased to a total of 130,000 garments sorted, fumigated, repaired, packed and dispatched by a full-time team of trained staff. Off they went to re-clothe Jewish Germany, Poland, France, Holland, Italy, Greece and Czechoslovakia.[28]

In all likelihood, Stella Heidenstein's little red sweater – identical to those worn by Jock and Rita – would long since have been unravelled and repurposed when outgrown, or passed on to a needy neighbour. How poignant to imagine that Stella might possibly have tucked it into one of Schonfeld's parcels bound for DP camps and orphanages, perhaps even to Belsen, for one of the innumerable children who weren't lucky enough to gain precious refugee status.

Among surviving film footage of rehabilitation efforts in Belsen is a clip of a young boy being eased into a new, clean jumper. It is a moment of absolute tenderness in contrast with all that the child had endured. Soft yarn, from donor to recipient, connected very different experiences of war.

While Renate was rumbling around the shattered country in an army lorry, collecting clothing for DP survivors in Belsen, Anita had a mission of her own. Clean, fed, dressed and housed, she immediately turned her attention to making connections. Specifically, communicating with England.

Fania Fénelon, one of Anita's companions in the Auschwitz orchestra, had already sent her voice out over the airwaves. She sang the British national anthem and the French *Marseillaise* for BBC radio at the liberation of Belsen, receiving an old lipstick for her effort. 'I couldn't imagine anything lovelier,' Fania remembered, 'three quarters used as it was and despite its uncertain pedigree.'[29]

Anita recorded a message in German to be transmitted on air to her older sister. Like the Heidenstein sisters, Marianne had escaped to England before the war. Since then there had been no news.

What joy, what *incredulity* Marianne must have felt to hear Anita after so long. To know both sisters were alive. To have hope fulfilled. Happiness was possible. Pages of emotion-filled letters followed.

Anita was ecstatic to report, 'I have a cello!'[30]

She'd already had the pleasure of hearing Yehudi Menuhin and Benjamin Britten performing a concert in the former Officer's Ballroom at Belsen, where the beds and blankets of a makeshift hospital had been cleared away. On 4 July – appropriately Independence Day in the US – Anita played in front of the public as a free person, not a Nazi prisoner.

Renate was happy to review Anita's performance, telling Marianne, 'She plays as beautifully as ever.'[31]

The notes of a Bach sonata were coaxed from fresh cello strings supplied by Marianne in England.

'Please don't send us any clothes,' Anita wrote. 'We get everything we need.'[32]

In that sense, Anita and Renate were relatively spoiled. On Anita's twentieth birthday on 17 July, her gifts included blouses, underwear, slippers and two dresses. However, she did still ask Marianne to source some swimming costumes. Such an uplifting symbol of life returning! Despite her sartorial 'riches,' and despite her claim that 'the less one possesses the happier one feels,'[33] there was one garment Anita kept hold of.

Her red angora sweater.

Not only did she keep it, she mended it. The darns on the sweater sleeves are stitched in a yellowy lattice that stands out against the bright red. There are still significant holes, both where the wool has been worn through, and where stitches have snagged.

Anita wore the red sweater incessantly until liberation, out of sight so it wouldn't be confiscated. When it was no longer needed on a practical level, since Renate was on the case sourcing sweaters and winter coats for when the weather turned cold, she saved it anyway. It was a reminder of past experiences, even as the future unfolded.

Like the sweater, Anita's life had been unravelled, but not beyond repair. The question was, how could she assemble all fragments to go forward?

Gena Turgel, another young Belsen DP, reflected on survival and resilience, saying, 'We had learned to be resourceful.'[34] This resourcefulness would be needed in the post-war years as she, and the many thousands of others like her, including Anita Lasker, Jock Heidenstein and Sobibor survivor Regina Feldman, looked to find their path and their place in the years ahead.

Memories Become Your Possessions

My greatest joy has been the photographs.
– ANITA LASKER[1]

Of all the things the Nazis and their collaborators stole from their victims, personal photographs were among the debris they valued least. Of all the things survivors craved as they rebuilt their post-war lives, photographs were among the most precious.

What did murderers and robbers care about faces and places in pictures, gathered in mounds on the ground like autumn leaves ready for a bonfire? Let the paper blister and curl in fire. It was nothing to them that black-and-white tones captured memories, that they could prove there had once been homes, holidays, holy days and loved ones.

As strong as her need for food, clothes and music, in Belsen DP camp Anita Lasker was desperate for photos. Her sister Marianne in England couldn't send too many, or quickly enough. She saw again her home on Kaiser Wilhelmstrasse in Breslau. The Lasker family gathered for cake, coffee and laughter. Herself as a girl with a cello wearing the dress her mother had made. All things that existed a little longer because they were caught on camera and held in the memory. Just brushing fingertips over them helped create a sense of connection.

In England, the Heidenstein refugee sisters had few photographs to cherish. Each one was infinitely precious. They had no pictures of themselves as a family together in Berlin. No portraits of their parents even. No wedding photos showing extended family. Just the studio shots of their little brothers David and Michael, taken in the summer of 1939, when Auschwitz was just a town in Poland, and cattle travelled in freight wagons, not people.

With their grandparents dead, the Heidenstein girls were a generation without elders. They had to make new memories. They featured in photographs their parents would never see. Jock, at the Jewish Secondary School with her classmates, growing taller and wiser every year, then leading study circles and youth groups for a London synagogue.[2] Rita, leaving school to work as 'house mother' at a hostel for young Holocaust survivors, in a smart wool skirt and dark jumper, surrounded by emotionally dishevelled teenagers who'd endured what she had so narrowly escaped. Stella, the girl with a loving foster family, looking out on the world with new prescription glasses and a fresh sense of style.

Jock still had her dainty album of passport-sized photos showing her friends from Berlin school days. The faces of her friends never aged. Helene Kiwowicz, Helen Sternlicht, Martl, who wrote *forget-me-not* on her photograph, and little Mimi Sternlicht, who had been so desperate to get to England herself, back in the summer of 1939 when such escapes were still possible. Only after the war did Jock understand what had happened to all the faces in the photos. Their fate could have been hers.

Rita Heidenstein wrote to the Jewish Refugees Committee at Bloomsbury House in London to beg them for any photographs of her parents which may have been included with the paperwork submitted back in Berlin, when the girls first applied for places on the

Kindertransport. She received a reply in October 1945, regretting that only one photo of her father had been found . . . which was subsequently lost.

'We do hope that you may soon have direct news from your parents,' added the committee secretary.[3]

For Regina Feldman, whatever photographs the family might once have possessed, whether displayed in frames on a sideboard, or layered in a keepsake box, these were all long gone. Leaves blown away in a storm. From her time in the sorting sheds at Sobibor extermination centre, Regina knew that even the most cherished mementos would be dispersed or destroyed by the SS. At Sobibor she'd been offered the shoes of her murdered sister to wear. She'd been forced to let fall her mother's wedding ring. Even the red sweater she'd knitted had to be given up to an SS man to wear.

What Regina did still have, and what she could still wear as she emerged into the post-war world, was the same tweed coat she'd worn since leaving her home. The woven threads had to be brushed to sweep away rubble dust and the smoke of many fires. By day the US Air Force had bombed the city of Frankfurt-am-Main, where Regina worked in the guise of a Polish Christian. By night the British bombers came. In April 1945, when Anita emerged from the stinking barracks of Belsen to see what freedom looked like, Regina was picking her way through the ruins of a liberated Frankfurt.

'The plight of the Germans helped me to get over whatever I lived through before,' she said, with remarkable compassion.[4]

During the war she'd been so busy helping the German family who'd taken her on – the Hildmans – it didn't leave room for post-war plans. Once Americans came riding on their jeeps through the rubble, Regina knew it was time to move on. On hearing her story, and learning her true identity, Mr Hildman helped her pack a few essentials to leave. In June 1945 she was registered at Wetzlar DP camp, still under her assumed name of Regina Wojcisyzn, not her birth name Riva Feldman, but at least she could live openly as a Jew, among about four thousand others who understood something of the trauma she'd survived.

Regina played her own part in re-clothing and re-humanising survivors. As shiploads of donated clothing arrived from the US, she helped sort and dole out garments to DPs in need, under the aegis of UNRAA, the United Nations Relief and Rehabilitation Administration. She worked with friends and found a sense of purpose. She also gained an admirer: a young Polish soldier called Kazimierz Cybula-Zielinski came to the UNRRA warehouse looking for sports kit – a vivid example of how much DPs were ready to embrace life and culture after liberation. Regina caught his eye. One meeting led to many, all scented with the tang of Regina's nervous chain-smoking. Many meetings led to a marriage proposal from Kazimierz. Regina accepted.

It was in Wetzlar DP camp that Regina made a surprising discovery in her own wardrobe, all because her beloved tweed coat was in need of renovation. The tried-and-tested remedy for worn coats

Regina Feldman in the UNRRA clothing store of Wetzlar DP camp.
Sydney Jewish Museum Collection, donated by Ms Regina Zielinski
(M2010/063:001)

was to unpick them and 'turn' the pieces, reversing the fabric so that the shabby outside became the inside. As she stitched the sections back into place she found an earring hooked into a pocket lining – a tiny diamond that had escaped robbery on the cart trip to Sobibor. It had originally belonged to her great-grandmother. Now the one earring and her revamped coat were all the tangibles left of her Polish childhood.

The sight of civilians – especially women – picking over rubble to salvage scraps was all too common during the war years and the re-construction that followed. They were attempting to re-assemble lives blown up by bombs and perforated by gunfire. One writer in London observed the care required to glean 'broken orna-ments, odd shoes, torn scraps of the curtains that had hung in a room.'[5] It was no different in Germany. Women searched for loot in the rubble, using prams, barrows and folded aprons to carry their shabby hauls. The term for rubble-woman thrift, where dish-cloths and military blankets were transformed into wearables, was *Lumpenkleider* – rag clothes. Once only fit for rag traders like Jock's father, Chaim, shabby used clothing was the new street fashion, even when streets were in ruins.

'We only wear our oldest clothes all day long, coats on top, and nobody cares what one looks like,' said one German housewife, re-building a home out of charred materials.[6]

Rebuilding a home was all very well for those still living in the footprint of their old dwelling. What about Jewish survivors who had no home to go back to? The building might still be standing, the curtains might still be hung at each window, and ornaments still on display, but other people would be living in the rooms, draw-ing the curtains and dusting the ornaments.

The apartment in Breslau where Anita Lasker had grown up, on Kaiser Wilhelmstrasse, was unscathed by conflict, but the Lasker family had long since moved out and been dispersed. She didn't have the means or the inclination to move back in. Anita watched army trucks and lorries decorated with garlands and flags depart Belsen DP camp carrying repatriated survivors. Jock watched the post, hoping for a letter, a postcard, a telegram from her parents – any sign that they were among the human flotsam of the war in Europe.

The building in Berlin where Jock Heidenstein had grown up, on Linienstrasse, had become headquarters for Soviet police administration of the city's Mitte district. Hardly a place to live, even if she thought of taking up life in Germany once more.

Regina Feldman often thought of her family home in Siedliszcze. To help with her homesickness, a kind friend sent her foliage from the acacia trees that grew outside the house she'd once lived in. She was due to return to Poland from Wetzlar DP camp and was just waiting for a date and transportation. A reunion with her cousin Zelda Metz, another Sobibor survivor, dispelled that dream. Zelda told her to forget the whole idea. There was nothing for her in Poland except haunted views and the danger of continuing antisemitic violence.

Decades later Regina was still trying to come to terms with the fact that all her family perished in the Holocaust. In her words, 'I have not found anybody so I'm the only person.'[7]

Uprooted survivors searched for fragments of their families.

Where were they?

What had happened to them?

From her time in Sobibor, knitting for the SS, Regina knew the terrible truth of her family's last moments. Anita had lived in sight of the lines for Auschwitz gas chambers. Auschwitz hadn't been the final destination for her parents and other relatives, but she learned enough to piece together the probability of their fate: undressing after digging their own graves.

For the Heidenstein sisters, only learning about extermination centres from news reports and the expanding ripples of survivor accounts, there was still a spark of hope. Of their extended family, spread across Germany, Belgium, Poland and Russia, surely some of them lived? Of the millions missing, surely there would be traces of Mania, Chaim, David, Michael . . . aunts, uncles, cousins and school friends?

Fragments of Heidenstein family correspondence testify to the efforts made to piece together stories of those no longer able to tell their tale. Some are official printed forms. Personal details look all the more poignant for being filled in by hand on these documents – names, birthdays and last known locations. The Red Cross and Centra Tracing Bureau, known as the International Tracing Service after 1948, had a deluge of enquiries to sort through, each charting individual tragedy.

The Heidenstein names were fed into a system, to wait for a response. 'It was difficult to relate the humdrum routine of the filing clerk to the horror stories coming out of Germany,' said one organiser.[8]

The results were inevitably negative. After eighty years the evidence speaks of absence. The branches of Jock Heidenstein's family tree, extending across the Fink, Schwartz and Kapelner families, were cut off in Auschwitz and Treblinka, and at other sites of pogroms and mass executions.

Then there are the typewritten letters, so very formal in style yet so very emotional in their implications, sent by Jock, Rita and Stella over several decades.

'I confirm that I last saw my brothers, Michael and David, when I left my home in Berlin for England, in January 1939,' writes Jock in 1967, in correspondence dealing with Statutory Declarations of death.[9] In the same year, Jock wrote to her aunt Rosa, who'd miraculously escaped from Berlin to the US in 1941. A postscript after a polite letter reveals something of Jock's emotions.

'PS. I am wondering whether you ever heard anything more about my Mother, after you left???'[10]

What a world of loss in these simple sentences. It was a loss that the ones who lived had to hide from public view, without psychological or therapeutic support. It would be decades before there was even a widely recognised collective name for the system and experience of atrocities – the Holocaust – let alone a consistent recognition of the ways in which emotional trauma tore at the soul.

These wounds couldn't heal, but life went on, and it deserved to be lived to the full. Each of the girls who'd made or worn the iconic red sweaters would find her own path to fulfilment.

Among the pleas for information and clarification are letters about possible restitution, including for the Nazi appropriation of the Heidenstein clothing warehouse near the river in Berlin. In losing their parents, the Heidensteins also lost whatever generational support they might have received to set them on their adult paths. Refugees and survivors were often bewildered by the scarcity of compassion and nurture on offer as they tried to make their way in the world once again.

One girl coming from Auschwitz to England was desperate for an education, having missed six years of school. She was met with indifference. 'There was nothing doing. Cast-off garments from the past, yes. Help for the future, no.'[11]

Anita Lasker found the bureaucracy of being a refugee irritating in the extreme. She was eager to leave Germany to join her sister Marianne in England but felt thwarted by all the restrictions. Nobody official seemed to understand what it meant to have been stripped of citizenship by one's own country, or to be tormented almost to the point of death in her own homeland.

It was glorious for her finally to make it across the Channel to Britain, even if it meant wrestling with more rules in order to do what she truly loved most – play the cello. In this she succeeded, her ambition matched by her talent. A demanding concert schedule took her to many different countries except, at first, Germany, because there, as she put it, 'It would be possible to meet the person who had murdered my parents.' One day in Paris she reconnected with a former pupil from her old school in Breslau, humorously remembered as 'the fat boy who played the piano.'[12] From this inauspicious background, Anita and Peter Wallfisch were eventually married, and life became even more full, with children as well as music.

And still she kept her worn red sweater.

The Heidensteins were tremendously lucky to have threefold support. Jock and Rita were buoyed by friendships formed at the Jewish Secondary School in Shefford, their rural haven of faith, study and fun. Stella was warmly, fully embraced by the Adler family, who had fostered her since summer 1939. This embrace was wide enough to include her two big sisters, who featured in photograph albums of the Adlers and their friends. Then there was the incomparable influence of Rabbi Dr Schonfeld. He'd been fighting on behalf of the Heidensteins since the frantic days of the Kindertransports, through the hardships of war and then in the post-war revival. In later years he never felt he'd done enough. Who could, in the face of so much need? Schonfeld saved and secured many, many lives before, during and after the war. He also officiated at Rita's wedding in September 1951 – a celebration of love and new beginnings. Stella and Jock were present, of course. Stella in a sensational striped skirt with stiff petticoats, and Jock looking smart in a dark suit and wedding nosegay.

Rita Heidenstein never struggled to attract admirers. She balanced her job in a Jewish care home with a craving for fashion and fun. At one point, like many young women, she took to wearing all black. Jock, nicknamed 'the great big boss,' told Rita she looked 'just like a maid on her day off!'[13]

Irrepressible, Rita dated as she pleased, receiving ten proposals of marriage until finally rewarding the persistence of Henry Mayer, the same boy from Shefford school who'd once announced 'I'm going to marry you one day!' She made a beautiful bride, with her dark hair set off by a bridal headdress and veil. She didn't have a penny to her name – and if she had she might well have spent it on hats and gloves instead – so the wedding dress was borrowed. She carried a large bouquet of roses and foliage. She carried memories of her parents' love.

While Rita chose marriage to give her a sense of stability and safety, Jock's youngest sister, Stella, chose travel and adventure. Work was the centre; people were part of the whirlwind. With her energy and intelligence Stella was a prize for everyone who employed her, from renowned publisher Andre Deutsch – the watchword for any query at the fledgling company was 'ask Stella' – to world-famous violinist Isaac Stern, who actually headhunted Stella as his personal assistant.[14] Stella eventually found her professional home back in the world of publishing. She helped establish Universe Books, with a brilliant range of colleagues and a shoestring budget.

Fragments of Stella's post-war life include polaroid pictures of touring Washington, D.C., picnics in Israel and beaming on skis on a snowy mountain slope; postcards from Hawai'i and high-rise hotels of the Californian coast; business letters crackling with competence. Work was so all-consuming a colleague had to send her a mantra while she took a few days holiday – 'I am here to enjoy myself.'[15] For her, work was described as a blitz and a battlefield.[16] It's encouraging to know that Stella occasionally took time to indulge herself. On one intense work trip she mitigated a frustrating day by buying a golden Christian Dior chain belt, 'just to get away from the damn phone.'[17] She also loved to escape into the world of books, with Jane Austen as a firm favourite.

When in London, Stella joined Jock and the Adler girls for

jaunts around the capital. Everything was interesting to her, whether Japanese art or Egyptian archaeology. However, one place Stella did not like to visit was Germany, her country of birth. Attending the Frankfurt Book Fair was a duty, not a pleasure. Although usually seen as quite a gentle person, there was a fierceness to her, and a legacy of pain. If the subject of the Holocaust ever arose in a conversation she straight-up stated, 'My family was murdered by the Nazis.' She lived her history every day. It was always with her, for all she moved in a new world of computers, tape cassettes and miniskirts.[18]

As for Jock, who learned to be sensible and responsible far too early, she kept busy, morning to night; always full of energy, always doing. Formidable in her own way, those who knew her said she would march into a room, with purpose. She was also good-hearted and completely trustworthy. She eventually began work as PA for Ralph Kohn in London. As a boy, Ralph had, like Jock, escaped Nazi persecution in the nick of time. He was on the very last boat out of Holland, the SS *Bodegraven*, which brought him to England as a refugee. His wife, Zahava, had, like Anita Lasker, survived Bergen-Belsen camp. As a girl Zahava and her family had been incarcerated in Belsen's 'star' camp – a holding pen for mainly Dutch Jews who might be used for exchange. There was so much the three of them might have talked about, but Jock did not share many details of her past life with Ralph or Zahava. Their daughter called Jock 'a very, very private person.'[19]

Jock chose not to marry. Was she lonely, or simply self-reliant? Faith was at the centre of everything. She nurtured a wonderful community in the Stoke Newington area of London, her life interwoven with friends and fellow worshippers in her local congregation. Dressed conservatively – long-sleeved tops and skirts, never trousers – she took the tube into work, or to enjoy the city's theatres, concert halls and galleries. She cooked, baked and nurtured her garden. She knitted.

And still she kept her little red sweater.

Regina Feldman, married as Regina Zielinski, had no red sweater to keep from her time in Sobibor. The striped jumper she'd knitted while bearing witness to the tragedy of extermination there only held value in that being required to knit it kept her from joining lines of denuded people being marshalled into Sobibor's gas chambers. What she did have post-war was a new husband, and fingers busy knitting clothes for her little son, Andrew, first of a new generation. A boy without grandparents, uncles or aunts on his mother's side. In 1949 Regina and her compact family joined hundreds of other refugees on a ship to Australia.[20] She wanted to be as far away from Germany as possible. She actually knelt and kissed the ground on arrival, it was such a tremendous relief to reach the sanctuary of Australia, even if the little family had to live in a migrant camp for a while, bundled in sleeping bags. Her cousin Zelda, another Sobibor survivor saved through knitting, eventually made her home in Australia too. New beginnings on a new continent.

If only mental and physical trauma could have been left behind in Europe too. Regina's experiences could not so easily be sloughed off. Through pregnancy, labour pains and childcare, through illness, financial hardship and lonely times, she knitted. As she knitted there were also joys and triumphs. She'd found her place, and she was grateful to be starting life again in a free country.

For many survivors, the newly established state of Israel was seen as the ultimate haven. A place where all Jews were welcome, even if life there would mean hard graft and austerity at first. As Jock Heidenstein established her life in London and Stella found a tiny apartment amidst the dazzle of Manhattan, Rita and her new husband founded their new home in Israel. When the babies came – Mira, Adina and Tamar – Rita learned to be a mother without a mother to help her. She'd lost one layer of family. Her goal was to nurture a new generation.

Despite a tight income, Rita accumulated possessions, including an impressive tally of eighteen hats shipped over to Israel when she moved. What she shed was any sense of being German. As a little girl, fresh off the Kindertransport train, she'd struggled to learn English. At home in Israel she clung to English manners and an English way of dressing. From labouring over pencilled notes to her sisters during the war, she graduated to lively scrawls of biro writing on aerogrammes. She saved up for new furniture and tied bows in her daughters' hair. She kept the box of her mother's last letters from Berlin next to her bed.

Among the precious possessions survivors carried across railways and sea waves to Israel was Chana Zumerkorn's red sweater.

Josef Zumerkorn, one-time resident of Lodz in Poland, son of Dvora-Gitla and David, brother to Chana and Nechama, had already covered countless miles in his six years of war. Escaping antisemitic violence in his hometown, he suffered more brutality when he headed east into Russia. He also experienced great hospitality, finding loyal friends on his journey, and ultimately a new partner in life when he married Nechama Paskovitz in 1942. She'd been with him through every kind of bitter experience, including harsh Russian winters. In this cold exile she gave birth to their first child. Daughter Miri was welcomed to the world in January 1944 and no doubt swaddled in whatever woollens were at hand.

As the German army were forced to retreat from Russia following a series of disastrous losses, Josef's thoughts turned to his homeland, and to all that he'd been forced to leave behind. In his words, 'Not only me, all the people who were in Russia, we wanted to return to Poland.'[21]

Somehow evading the checks on Russian trains, during which Jews were removed from carriages and killed in random pogroms, Josef, Nechama and Miri reached liberated Poland. It was not a rosy homecoming. The tiny apartment he'd shared with his family in Lodz had long since been home to new people. The only familiar faces in the old marketplace outside would be conjured up from his memories. The 1943 Baedecker's tourist guide that had laid out a Germanised view of the occupied town was maybe obsolete, but when the Nazis withdrew from Polish territories anti-Jewish virulence did not leave with them. Josef faced murderous threats from Poles who had been more than happy for Jews to be taken away to extermination centres such as Chelmno, where Josef's sister, Chana, was killed.

Leaving for a new start wasn't done on a whim. It was a survival strategy.

In 1949 Josef added more miles to his life journey, reaching Marseille in France to take the *Negba* to Israel. By this date he had celebrated the birth of a second daughter, Gitl, named for her grandmother. Gitl was not quite a year old when the *Negba* docked in the port of Haifa. She had no idea that as the Zumerkorn family descended the gangplank into a new country and their new life, her father, Josef, had something very special and very secret packed in his luggage: the red sweater Chana had pressed upon him in their final fraught moments together. It was frayed but still vibrantly colourful.

'I'm sure you will need this,' Chana had told him when they parted, back in November 1939.

'The wanderings of the sweater were my wanderings,' Josef wrote, years later.[22]

In his post-war life, Josef put Chana's red sweater away. He did not speak of it and did not show anyone, not even his wife. It was precious yet painful.

With only a suitcase or a trunk or a backpack to pass through customs it might seem that refugees travel light – Rita Heidenstein's hats notwithstanding. What they hold in their hands is nothing compared to what is carried in the heart.

'Memories become your possessions,' said Estelle Glaser Laughlin, another young Jewish survivor from Poland.[23] She knew what it was like to be 'sorted like rubbish' by the Germans, then loaded into a freight train like 'bundles of waste.' She learned the hard way that even when treated as walking rags, owning nothing and having power over nothing, there was still something that could be salvaged – the memories. But memories are fickle. They can fade over time, particularly without something to tether them. Or they can be buried under mountains of other experiences if grief and mourning were too painful to face.

Chana's red sweater, Anita's red sweater, Jock's red sweater – all three represented a link to the past, both sad and life-affirming.

Years passed. Decades passed. The red sweaters were stored out of sight, not out of mind. Anita, Jock and Regina's lives were filled with many new possessions – little things that had meaning or were useful, or were simply the comforting clutter of everyday life. Babies grew, toddled, then strode out into jobs and partnerships of their own. Knitting fingers maybe slowed and stiffened a little. The question became, how could memories be passed on to the next generations?

It was time for the red sweaters to take on a new role; to share their stories around the world.

So Many Missing Things

Jewels of beauty ... treasures of colour ... revelations of texture.

– 1950S ADVERT FOR BERNHARD ALTMANN CASHMERE SWEATERS

1950s Bernhard Altmann magazine advert featuring a bright-red cashmere sweater.
Lucy Adlington personal archive

What a riot of knitting there was after the war! Once shop shelves were re-stocked and yarn was off the ration it was so exciting to see new colours on display and new patterns to knit up.

Those with money – or who were particularly nifty with home embellishments – could indulge in dynamic new knitwear styles. The 1950s boasted batwing sleeves, long-line sweaters and double-the-wool twin sets. For extra luxury, additions of mink collars and diamante clasps, or crusts of brilliant embroidered beads. By the 1960s, youthful vitality was all the buzz in knitted goods: bold, bright and fun.

Exciting new blends of cashmere, mohair, Lurex and acrylic out-dazzled older fashions. Who wanted to look back when the future could be brighter and better? In the immediate post-war decades it seemed the world wasn't interested in Jock Heidenstein's stretched sweater, Anita Lasker's darned sweater, Chana Zumerkorn's frayed sweater, or the implications of socks and sweaters knitted by Regina Feldman in Sobibor. People were still healing from the past. Or hiding from it.

Poor Chana was forever trapped in the past, her future stolen in the wooded grounds of Chelmno. Survivors such as Jock, Anita and Regina had to carry the past like a weighted backpack that was always there, even if it wasn't always seen.

However bright the colours and inventions of the post-war age, the past was ever-present. Behind some of the most iconic knitwear names, there were stories of refugees – Jewish artisans and entrepreneurs forced to flee persecution before the war, who turned their talents to textiles in their new homes.

Maria Altmann, niece of Adele Bloch-Bauer, who posed for Gustav Klimt's iconic *Woman in Gold* portrait, helped pioneer the surge in popularity of cashmere knitwear in North America post-war. This was via her brother-in-law Bernhard Altmann's company, originally based in Vienna but forced, through antisemitism, to relocate abroad. *The world offers none finer*, boasted Altmann adverts in major US magazines.

A Jewish refugee was behind the original knitted Kangol angora berets, worn by the fabulous Elsa Schiaparelli, Greta Garbo and Marlene Dietrich, then taken up by 'youthquake' designer Mary Quant in the 1960s. This angora was a world away from the red angora that kept Anita Lasker warm in Auschwitz.

The legendary Pringles cardigans and sweaters could also be credited to a Jewish refugee. Pringles knitwear went on sale in post-war Paris at outrageously high prices.[1] Grace Kelly and Audrey Hepburn loved their twinsets in the 1950s. To the great joy of ordinary British shoppers – thanks to Jewish talents behind the scenes – affordable and washable lambswool sweater sets graced the rails of Marks and Spencer stores.

It took time for new generations, enjoying new fashions, caught up in their own dreams and dramas, to give the past prominence and to form questions about the actions and experiences of their parents or grandparents during the war years. By the 1970s and 1980s – eras of big knits and exuberant jumper drama – there were listeners for those ready to talk.

It often began among family. Children overheard adults talking and picked up disturbing concepts such as *deportation, concentration camp, selection*. Questions were sometimes answered; sometimes shrugged off with a resolute *We don't talk about it*. There could be painful, cloying silence. Or the talking might be compulsive. A need to find words for experiences that were almost unimaginable to anyone who hadn't lived through them.

Filmmakers and publishers played their part in sharing the memories of those who'd survived more widely. At a distance of three or four decades, it was perhaps easier for readers and viewers to face the reality of what had become termed the Holocaust through books, movies and documentaries. Late in the twentieth century, meaningful efforts began to record and archive survivor testimonies, a process that continues today. Words, images, documents, objects – by the twenty-first century the gathering of fragments became even more imperative as the numbers of survivors dwindled.

In the post-war years, Jock, Anita and Regina all laboured to craft meaningful lives. Each found a way to hold on to the past while forming a future. Each in her own way contributed to memorialisation and to vital Holocaust education. 'The millions who were murdered rely on those survivors to bear witness to their existence,' Anita wrote in her memoir.[2]

Inevitably all new fashion trends depended on the labour of a multitude of makers, whether weaving, stitching or knitting. Starting her new life in Australia as Mrs Zielinski, Regina's deft fingers knitted at home for her growing family, while working at a machine to bring in an income. She was naturalised in 1957, the same year that the Zielinskis moved into a self-built house. The same hands that had made socks and sweaters in Sobibor, and sorted through the clothes of murdered deportees, and pounded the laundry of SS murderers, came to make beautiful wedding dresses, dainty children's clothes for the Gay-Worth company and eventually nightwear and lingerie for the Ralstan brand.

Regina's work brought her a very subtle kind of memorialisation. She had to add her initials to the labels of Ralstan garments she completed, for accountability. After her retirement in the late 1980s Regina was chatting with a friend who praised the quality and longevity of a Ralstan dressing gown. Looking inside the garment, both women were delighted to find that the label was marked 'RZ' for Regina Zielinski. Regina's handiwork had been credited, a rare occurrence in the garment trade.

Being called to testify at post-war war crimes trials was a different kind of memorialisation. While it put Regina in the spotlight and helped in attempts to bring perpetrators to justice, it also set on record what Regina had endured, and what she had witnessed. It ensured that victims at Sobibor – her own family included – would be remembered. She may initially have been reluctant to testify, but it was worth the trauma of coming face-to-face with the men who'd once set her to knitting while they facilitated mass murder. Of course most perpetrators of the Holocaust were hugely reluctant to speak in public about their actions until forced to do so under oath in court. Whichever SS man made Regina knit him a striped red sweater in Sobibor, he certainly wasn't like to conserve it as a memorialisation of his crimes. In the unlikely event that this jumper survived – perhaps worn by Karl Frenzel as he tried to dodge accountability after Germany's defeat, or Gustav Wagner, spotted lurking in Uruguay post-war, 'looking like a beggar, with torn clothes and shoes'[3] – it would not be accessioned into a museum collection and curated in honour of the wearer. Regina, the knitter, had words, not wool, to represent her experiences.

Hella Weiss, Regina's friend from Sobibor who became a decorated war hero after their escape, also testified in court. Hella was one of those who needed to talk about her past, even as she lived in the present moment as a mother, homemaker and café owner. Like Regina, Hella also continued to use crafting skills in her post-war life, teaching her young girls how to knit and making memorable fancy dress costumes for them during Purim festival celebrations. Stitches were mixed with stories. While Regina acclimatised to Australia, Hella had made her home in Israel, married to another army veteran who'd fought the Nazis. None of the knitwear from these early years of Hella's married life survive. When her daughters grew out of things, they were passed on to others in need.

Hella was used to letting go of possessions. The only mementos she salvaged from Poland when she left were photos of her in a Red

Army uniform, and her medals. In Israel she moved so many times it was hard to hold on to things. For Hella, talking with other Sobibor survivors was one way of keeping connected to the past, when there were no relatives left alive.

Her daughter Miriam said, 'They were family. They had no other family.'

After the war crimes trials Hella was approached to share her story with the wider world in a different way – for a 1987 film portraying the Sobibor uprising. She sat to watch the finished result with her daughters. It was an eerie and emotional experience. Even Miriam, already familiar with her mother's story, reacted with disbelief at the events portrayed: 'You see the men, and you can't believe these men do so many evil things.'[4]

One way to combat the disbelief of strangers was through education. Both Regina and Hella gave recorded interviews about their experiences. When the Sydney Jewish Museum opened in 1992 Regina volunteered as a guide. It was incredibly moving for museum visitors to hear Regina's extraordinary story in person. From 1995, after a move to Adelaide, Regina spoke to countless school classes, youth groups and at adult events. Out of the desolation of her Sobibor experiences, she found purpose and very receptive audiences.

And she kept on knitting.

Regina's legacy went beyond words. In 2013 a crafter named Heatherly Walker was so moved by the stories of the Sobibor knitters she created a special pattern for Remembrance socks as tribute to Regina. Hidden within the pattern are Jewish stars.[5]

Regina died in 2014, not long after being awarded the Knight's Cross of the Order of Merit of the Republic of Poland in recognition of her courage during the legendary Sobibor uprising and for her remembrance work. Over seventy years before, Regina heard Sasha Pechersky, one of the instigators of the rebellion, standing amid the turmoil in the camp shouting, 'If only one of you survives, then you will be able to tell the story of what was happening here.'[6]

It falls on those who remain to keep sharing the histories of the ones who cannot.

Regina wasn't the only one telling her story. In addition to her talents as a touring musician and founding the English Chamber Orchestra, cellist Anita Lasker, married as Mrs Lasker-Wallfisch, became an influential speaker on the subject of Holocaust remembrance and education.

Following a surge of interest in the Auschwitz musicians, Anita gathered up her memories and laid them out in an autobiography. Her writing snaps with dry humour and controlled anger. It honours her belief that Holocaust history must be personalised, so that victims are acknowledged as human, not just a tiny digit in an overwhelming mass of statistics. During an interview recorded for the Shoah Foundation, she emphasised, 'We were actually people and totally normal people, nothing wrong with us, coming from totally normal families.'[7]

When Anita was awarded the Officer's Cross of the Order of Merit of the Federal Republic of Germany it was in recognition of keeping the memory of the Holocaust alive for future generations. Some come to Anita's story not through her words or music, but through seeing the red angora sweater she'd salvaged in Auschwitz, on display at the Imperial War Museum in London. When asked about her decision to donate the sweater Anita's answer was characteristically practical: 'What else would I do with it?'[8]

Despite . . . no, *because* of its darns and dilapidation, it is a powerful artefact in the shadows and stories of the museum's Holocaust galleries.

Of all physical memorials, it is often the smallest, ordinary, personal things that make the most powerful connections. When Anita left Auschwitz with her precious sweater in 1944 the camp still held so many objects that had outlived their owners. On liberating Auschwitz in January 1945, the Russian army found 1.7 million items of clothing on-site. Belongings found spilling out of bulging plunder warehouses in concentration camps needed no words to communicate the sorrow of loss and the evil of mass murder. Socks without warm feet. Jumpers without warm bodies. Mittens without busy fingers. Buttons, thimbles and darning mushrooms whose original owners were beyond making or mending.

Anita's sweater now plays its part in humanising statistics; in highlighting the individual among the millions. It represents her and the nameless person who'd originally been stripped of it, and all the girls or women persecuted by the Third Reich who might have made or worn it.

It hadn't been easy for Anita to return to her homeland, where there were so many personal reminders of what she'd lost and what she'd suffered. What changed over time wasn't only Anita's appreciation that Germans born after the war were not guilty of wartime crimes, but also that these new generations were willing to engage honestly with their country's past. This wasn't only via war crime trials, restitution and reparation initiatives, or extensive education programs. Gradually Germany, and countries once occupied by the Nazis, began taking steps to ensure there were solid, public reminders of the people who lived, resisted, suffered and died in the Holocaust.

Jock Heidenstein's red sweater found a home for a while in a large, glass suitcase.

It was the artistic creation of sculptor Flor Kent. Kent collected a range of artefacts from those who'd been saved on the Kindertransport to London. These were set on display in a suitcase-shaped case just outside Liverpool Street Station in London – the dispersal point for many Kindertransport refugees, including Jock's sister Stella. Kent also gathered fragments of the histories behind each artefact. When donating her mementos from a childhood in Berlin, Jock shared a few scraps of her own story, about the three Heidenstein girls being dressed in identical red sweaters before they left Berlin, and about her own little suitcase, with its meagre contents.[9]

Travellers streaming in and out of the station could stop to look through the glass, and think of refugees paused in their own fraught journeys. Their gaze might be caught by the bright red of Jock's jumper, then held by the poignant implications of such a small, fragile garment.

Jock chose not to discuss her history in public. She let her little red sweater do the talking.

Ten thousand miles from London, in Australia, Regina's son, Andrew, reflected on his mother's life, writing that there were 'so many missing things,' thinking of a home without heirlooms or photographs from past generations.[10] Of all the missing things in the lives of Regina, Jock, Chana and Anita, it is sad and beautiful that something as humble as a woolly jumper did survive to help tell their stories.

Postscript

What's left of us when we're gone?

Most obviously, our possessions. The debris of our years interacting with objects.

This could be anything – furniture, books, baby teeth, bedding, boots, jeans or jam jars; papers, plants, pants or pets. Things we have touched. Things we have hoarded. Things we forgot we even owned.

Those who outlive us face the task of sorting through both treasures and tat – sometimes one and the same, depending on the value we give inanimate things. There will be heirlooms with financial worth, and other items which are priceless because of sentiment. There'll be everyday objects dispersed around family and friends, or passed on to a charity shop where strangers will pick things up or pass them over. Or junked items, thrown out as rags and trash.

Clothes are an interesting aspect of the sorting. They are at once disposable and meaningful. Intimate personal things that may still hold the shape and scent of our bodies, yet simultaneously just fabrics, stitches and embellishments. Clothes can be fragile, prey to nibbling larvae, strong light, damp and decay. They can also be remarkably tenacious textile evidence of all our activities, from work, play, travel and weddings, to sickness, sleep and funerals.

Then there is legacy. An interesting concept. Does it mean a name? Fame? Achievements? Endowments? Or can it be quieter and wider than that? A connective effect of our lives on those around us, or even on those who've never met us? The loop and tension of one stitch might seem very little on its own, but that yarn links hundreds of other stitches until fabric is formed. For humans, that fabric is community.

Reflecting on moral life in the concentration camps, philosopher Tzvetan Todorov wrote, 'History may remember the names of poets and scholars and not those of the people who brought them tea in their bedrooms or sewed on their buttons.'[1] Literally and symbolically we need tea and buttons as much as poems and studies. Like the soft, subtle power of a woolly sweater which can hold warmth, memories and meaning, our lives have impact in unmeasurable ways.

This book began because I was curious to discover the history behind a name and a garment: Jochewet Heidenstein's red sweater. An object left of someone's life, belonging to a girl I never met, and who I came to know only through the fragments of her life that remain now she's gone.

Jock's jumper now features in a museum collection because of a significant historical event – she was lucky enough to escape Nazi Germany on one of the Kindertransports – and because towards the end of her life she had the opportunity to donate it to a Kindertransport memorial. If it weren't for this historical context, and the existence of an object to tether the history, Jock would only be known to her family, friends, colleagues and fellow congregants. This doesn't mean her life is less worthy of remembrance.

Jock was a girl who inspired loyal friendships. A classmate from the Jewish Secondary School remembered the 'genuine delight' that Jock kept in touch when they were out in the world.[2] Jock became a woman who earned love from her young relatives, taking them on mini adventures, always remembering their birthdays.

'She was such a strong personality,' said her niece Tamar. 'Full of life. Full of energy.'[3]

Isn't this worthy of being called legacy too?

When Jock was assailed by cancer at the end of her life, it was hard for relatives to believe that such a robust, energetic woman could be slowed down. That she would, inevitably, have to let go of life. She was surrounded with loving care to the very last moment, on a warm but mizzling day in October 2004.

One of Jock's fragments – her red sweater – would end up safely nestled in tissue paper in the collections store of the Imperial War Museum, not so far from the display showcasing Anita Lasker's.[4] It might so easily have been her companion on a deportation train to Auschwitz back in 1942, rather than an escape train to England in 1939. It could have been removed in a gas chamber undressing room, piled high with other woollens, unravelled, lost, left to moulder. It could have been one of the garments conserved post-war in specialist laboratories of the Auschwitz-Birkenau State Museum, becoming an artefact without a name, viewed through glass on-site at the camp. Jock's fate could have been so very different.

But Jock lived, thanks to the selflessness of her parents in letting her go while there was still a chance to leave Germany, and thanks to the courage of countless people who laboured against the odds to give refugees a chance of life in a new country.

Her mother's belongings were all stolen by the Gestapo. Jock was able to will her possessions to family and friends. After her death they were gifted traces of her life – clothes, linens, a special clock, bits of jewellery, a new Siddur. She left bequests to the precious relatives who had survived the Holocaust, stating, 'They well know that they are all very much in my heart and mind.'[5]

Each of the Heidenstein girls was able to accumulate experiences and possessions. For Rita, the middle sister, her most precious belongings were letters from her mother, Mania, and a delicate little comb set she brought in her luggage on the Kindertransport. Although her memories began to unravel towards the end of life, these special objects remained until and beyond her death in 2015.

In uncovering Jock's story, there are many other encounters

that can be considered legacy, such as the powerful generosity of Debbie Adler, the woman who took in the youngest Heidenstein sister. Herself a refugee, Debbie Adler opened home and heart to the little German girl. In a eulogy read at Stella's funeral many years later, it was revealed that Debbie saved every penny she'd ever been given to pay for Stella's keep, and passed it on to Stella when she needed money to visit her sister Rita in Israel. A gesture too small for a commemorative plaque on her house, yet so big in emotional terms. Debbie's kindness was repaid whenever Stella returned to London: she was taken out for fancy afternoon tea at the Dorchester hotel.

Tragically, Stella's life ended the moment she stepped off the balcony of her riverview apartment in Manhattan, on 15 October 1993. She'd long been tormented by health issues, including the unbearable pain of an inoperable tumour. Tributes at her memorial service – punctuated by sounds of New York traffic outside – spoke of her courage and her curiosity. Of the sunshine of her character . . . and the bitterness she also had to carry in her life.

'We are all unique to those who love us,' commented one of Stella's mourners.[6]

The task of those who live on beyond those who survived the Holocaust is to ensure that this uniqueness isn't lost; that history is humanised. That we all feel the sense of connection rather than 'othering' victims.

After death, Jock's legacy was quiet but enduring. She directed that the inscription on her grave marker would be a *never forget* for those who couldn't tell their own stories. The headstone stands amid a crowd of grey memorials in a Jerusalem cemetery. It reads:

In memory of the martyrs who perished in the Holocaust
Parents Chaim and Mania
Brothers Michael and David

and family members
Heidenstein Fink and Schwartz[7]

The story of the Heidenstein sisters touches on a myriad other existences. The stitches in Jock's life fabric loop in with Dr Solomon Schonfeld, the rabbi who worked to save and support as many Jewish lives as possible. With Norbert Wollheim and his team, who laboured to route escape trains for at-risk children in Germany. With Dr Erna Davidsohn, who escorted Jock on one of these Kindertransports, only to die herself in Auschwitz.

It is the same for Anita Lasker, Chana Zumerkorn and Regina Feldman.

There are so many ways in which individual stories are valuable. Fragments contribute to a whole, in this case, to an appreciation of the scale and impact of the Holocaust. The entirety of experiences can never be known, not when so many lives were impacted and when in so many cases there are no fragments left at all – a void. Holocaust scholar Dr Lore Shelley dedicated her post-Auschwitz life to collecting stories from other survivors. She believed in 'the right of the individual not to be overlooked.'[8] Testimonies, memoirs and histories exist in defiance of Nazi aims to lump victims into one featureless mass then erase them.

Jock, Anita, Chana and Regina were four girls out of millions whose stories could be written. Four girls whose lives have been traced in these pages because of the simple connection of a red sweater. Because of a humble, seemingly insignificant garment that would not ordinarily feature as an heirloom or a museum exhibit.

For any human being it shouldn't matter who they are, what they do, have done or might one day achieve. Nor should the value of their lives be judged through the stained filter of bigotry. The Nazis persecuted Jock, Anita, Chana and Regina through manufactured fear, stoked-up hatreds and inflamed greed. Not because of who they actually were; not because of accolades they'd received or crimes they'd committed. Simply for being born Jewish. For existing.

The legacy of this persecution is, at one level, trauma and loss. Trauma was physical and emotional. Wrecked health. Nightmares after suffering. Pain after bereavement.

What the stories of the red sweaters reveal is that underlying the persecution is something more enduring and more powerful.

Many kinds of love.

Love that welcomed refugee children into a home. Love that fought to protect children still at risk. Love for home pleasures and the little rituals of family living. Love of friends, through thick and thin, when bombs fall and to the last piece of bread. Love of siblings, at reunions or at final partings. Love of God, of learning, of music, of knitting . . . Endless examples of love that could never be entirely unravelled.

If you ever get the chance to see one of the red sweaters on display in an exhibition, think of that love.

Next time you pull on woollens of your own, remember Anita Lasker easing her angora sweater out from the piles of plunder in Auschwitz and wearing it hidden from sight.

Remember Regina Feldman aching with love for her murdered family as she sat in the horror of Sobibor knitting a striped pullover for the SS.

Remember Chana Zumerkorn passing her lovely warm jumper to her brother, Josef, as he set out on a chilling journey into the unknown.

Think of Mania Heidenstein, dressing her three girls in identical red sweaters before waving goodbye at a Berlin station, then writing to say, 'You are very loved, my child.'[9]

Hate, hard as bullet-pitted concrete or spikes of barbed wire, is endlessly renewable. I'd like to think that love, soft and fragile like woollen yarn, lasts longer.

Acknowledgments

I owe a big thank you to the many people who've helped bring this book to readers.

To my stalwart companions on research expeditions – Elsie Walton, Lucy Ridley and Derek Muir.

To those who generously agreed to be interviewed and/or to share their memories – Anita Lasker-Wallfisch, Eran Kahanov, Miriam Kahanov, Yaffa Miller, Diana Young, Elaine Butchins, Myriam Lucas, Nicole Klynman, Bernard Diamond, Drora Goshen, Tamar Abrams, Mira Epstein, Sidney Cohen, Gil Park, Adele Ursone, Dorothy Caesar, Cynthia Cook, Hannah and Johnny Chody, Hephzibah Rudofsky and Jeremy Schonfeld.

To those who gave valuable assistance relating to research, connections, archives and collections – Professor Konrad Kwiet at Sydney Jewish Museum, Sarah Maspero at Hartley Library Archives & Special Collections, Dr Maria Castrillo and James Bulgin at the Imperial War Museum, Carol Sklinar, Maxine Willett, Franz-Josef Wittstamm, Lesley Urbach, Sigal Rosh and Nogaz Eliash. Also the numerous staff labouring to create and maintain digital archives at the Wiener Holocaust library, the Arolsen archives, the Association of Jewish Refugees, Yad Vashem, the United States Holocaust Memorial Museum, the Ghetto Fighters' House Museum, and Lodz State Archives.

To those who helped with document deciphering and translation – Katherine Schober of Germanology Unlocked,

Tammy King, Helen and John Westmancoat, Magdalene Zentek and Hannelore Sowodniok

To those who generously shared their impressive knitting knowledge – Helen Betts, Sarah Beedle, Kirsty Shipton, Anne Drew of Cymbal Knits, Tanya Singer of Knitting Hope and Faye Levinson.

To those working tirelessly in the world of publishing – Kate Shaw of the Shaw Agency, Sara Nelson and colleagues at Harper-Collins, all at Ultimo Press, Allison Hellegers of the Stimola Literary Studio, the dynamic team at ILA agency and diligent picture researcher Jane Smith.

To those at home who offered patience, love and cups of tea – Richard, Jay, Jasper, Esmé and Simon.

To all of you – my gratitude and appreciation. I could not have written this book without you.

Notes on Sources

INTRODUCING FOUR GIRLS

1. Anita Lasker-Wallfisch, *Inherit the Truth 1939–1945*.
2. Jochewet 'Eva' Heidenstein was known as Joch and Jock after her arrival in England. For consistency I've chosen the spelling Jock. Although she later shortened her name to Heiden, I've retained Heidenstein for consistency.
3. Jochewet Heiden, red sweater, Imperial War Museum collection EPH 3909. Information supplied by Flor Kent.
4. Josef Zumerkorn written testimony, Yad Vashem, submitted 12 June 2011, Item ID 9698712.
5. Josef Zumerkorn written testimony, Yad Vashem.
6. From a speech given by Chaim Mordechai Rumkowski in the Lodz ghetto, 17 January 1942.
7. Regina's birth name was Riva 'Rivka' Feldman, also spelled Riwka. In 1943 she was compelled to use the name of a Christian friend, Regina Wojciszyn. I've used Regina throughout this book for consistency.
8. Regina Zielinski née Rivka Feldman, 1983 interview with Julius Schelvis, www.sobiborinterviews.nl. As noted above, although Regina was born Riva, affectionately known as Rivka, her later adopted name of Regina has been used for consistency.
9. Regina Zielinski, 'Holocaust survivor Regina Zielinski receives a medal for bravery and heroism.' *Daily Telegraph*. Australia, 26 August 2014.

CHAPTER 1: END OF THE OLD, BEGINNING OF THE NEW

1. Paul Tabor, *The Nazi Myth*.
2. Jochewet Heiden acquisition note, Imperial War Museum Legacy ID 1464, Item #EPH 3909 (2003).
3. 'Hope for thousands – a Tour of the Jewish Winter Aid,' *CV Zeitung* 28 January 1937. *Central-Verein-Zeitung* was a newspaper of the Central Association of German Citizens of Jewish Faith. It is available digitally via the Jewish Virtual Library, jewishvirtuallibrary.org, a project of AICE.
4. As early as 1933 the Nazi Party – NSDAP – declared 'No Jew can be a German National,' quoted in *Documents on the Holocaust*.
5. Paul Tabor, *The Nazi Myth*.
6. 'Rag' didn't just refer to torn oddments of fabric. It was a term for the clothing trade in general, and for used clothing in particular.

7. Described in the 1916 Berlin & district directory as *Lumpenhandlung en gros*.

8. Josef Heidenstein was born in 1866. He was married to Sara Schwartz, born 1870. Their sons were: Leo (dates unknown), Wolf (born 15 December 1890), Oscar (dates unknown), Chaim Jakob (born 9 December 1897) and Juda (born 22 December 1900). Josef and Sara had at least one daughter – Lieba, born 19 September 1899. Leo Heidenstein lived north of Berlin in Schwerin. He dealt in ready-to-wear clothing and shoes, but fell afoul of the Nazis as early as March 1933, when he was accused of hiding Communists in his house. His fate in ensuing years is unknown. His son, Hermann, was born in July 1933. Hermann survived the war as a forced labourer and died in France in 1999.

9. *Deutsche Hauswirtschaft*, January 1937, *Einiges über das Sammeln von Altmaterial und Rüchenabfällen*, January 1937.

10. Heike Weber, 'Nazi German Waste Recovery and the Vision of a Circular Economy: The Case of Waste Paper And Rags.'

11. Martha Brixius, quoted in Alison Owings, *Frauen: German Women Recall the Third Reich*.

12. Versandhaus Quelle Wolle-Müstenbuch #24.

13. Gross-Versandhaus Quelle #61. Quelle advertised sundry craft products, including spiral wool holders and wooden wool winders. They also ran ads for Dukaten wools. Dukaten still trades today. Gustav Schickedanz gave evidence at post-war trials and confessed more than 85 percent of his business expansion after 1933 was from Jewish confiscations. Through all its commercial manifestations Quelle has generated vast fortunes for the associated Schickedanz family. Information courtesy of Uwe Westphal, journalist.

14. Juda Heidenstein, born 14 March 1917 in Prezmysl, Poland. His parentage cannot be confirmed. He is listed as living with Wolf and Tauba during the May 1939 German Minority census.

15. *Deutsche Hauswirtschaft*, 'Our Sewing Corner,' September 1941.

CHAPTER 2: WINTER CAN GET GRIM

1. Anita Lasker-Wallfisch, *Inherit the Truth 1939–1945*.

2. The photograph was taken sometime in 1939, in the Lasker apartment on Kaiser Wilhelm Strasse, Breslau. From the IWM 92/31/1 file 1925-1945.

3. Letter from Edith Lasker to Marianne Lasker, 15 January 1941. Quoted in *Inherit the Truth 1939–1945*.

4. Simone Ladwig-Winters, 'The Attack on Berlin Department Stores (Warenhäuser) after 1933.'

5. Helene 'Hella' Sternlicht was born 29 June 1925 in Berlin. She lived with her sister, Mimi, brother, Leo, and parents in the same building as the Heidenstein family. Helene Spitz Kiwowicz lived on Dragonerstrasse 44. Her father was a ritual slaughterer by profession.

6. Stephan Landwehr, interviewed by Renuka Rayasam, *Der Spiegel*, 'Old Jewish Girls' School Reborn as Berlin Hotspot,' 20 April 12, accessed 2.3.23.

7. Meta Wollny, born 8 April 22, Mädchenvolksschule der jüdischen Gemeinde Zeugniss, Sommer 1936. Metta's father was a tailor from Breslau. Meta survived the war and died in 2000.

8. *Inherit the Truth 1939–1945.*

9. Günter Morsch and Astrid Ley, ed., *Sachsenhausen 1936–1945. Events and Developments.* This was on the night of 18 January 1940. The mortality rate that January was seven hundred people – the highest total yet. Chaim was still alive at this time.

10. Rudolf Höss memoirs, *Death Dealer.*

11. Ursula Mahlendorf, *The Shame of Survival: Working Through a Nazi Childhood.*

12. Marta Jacobowitz, born 5 April 1883, in Pudewitz. Deported to Lodz 1 November 1941. Murdered in Chelmno, 9 May 1942. Her husband, Isidor, shared the same fate. Le Mémorial aux juifs assassinés dEurope (Berlin), Wikimedia Commons.

13. IWM EPH 3908.

14. Gertrud Sholtz-Klink, 'Tradition heißt nicht Stillstand sondern Verpflichtung. Frauenkundgebung Reichsparteitag Großdeutschland 1938.'

15. Adolf Hitler speech at the 1934 Nuremberg Rally, quoted in Wendy Lower, *Hitler's Furies.*

16. These efforts and more detailed in Christoph Kreutmüller, *Final Sale in Berlin: The Destruction of Jewish Commercial Activity 1930–1945.*

17. *Het Rejk der Vrouw* – Woman's Realm - 30 October 1943.

CHAPTER 3: WHEN YOU HEAR YOUR NAME, PLEASE COME FORWARD

1. *Jewish Chronicle* 18 November 1938.

2. *Jüdisches Gemeindeblatte für die synagogen gemeinde Breslau,* October 1938.

3. Eleanor F. Rathbone, *Rescue the Perishing: A Summary of the Position Regarding the Nazi Massacres of Jewish and Other Victims and of Proposals for Their Rescue,* June 1943.

4. In Germany, notable aid workers included Käthe Rosenheim, Herta Souhami, Norbert Wollheim, Cora Berliner and Hannah Karminski. In England a few standout staff are Dorothy Hardisty, Lola Hahn-Warburg and Elaine Laski.

5. Conversation with Jeremy Schonfeld, August 2022.

6. Conversation with Jeremy Schonfeld, August 2022

7. Conversation with Jeremy Schonfeld, August 2022. The house in question was on Lordship Park in North London. It's likely Jock had a spell here before being allocated a foster home.

8. Rabbi Dr Solomon Schonfeld, *Message to Jewry.*

9. Elaine Blond, *Marks of Distinction: The Memoirs of Elaine Blond.* Blond

volunteered for the Central British Fund. She described scenes of 'human jetsom' at the Fund's offices as 'heartbreaking.'

10. *Zum Andenken von Deiner Freundin, Helene-Kiwowicz. Berlin N. 54 Dragonerstr 44. Berlin, den 15.1.1939.* IWM EPH4194, donated by Jock Heiden, 2003.

11. *Zur Erinnerung am Hella Sternlicht.* IWM EPH4194.

12. *1939 Das Datum, ach ich Weiß es nicht, ich glaub es heiß Vergißmeinicht – Deine Martl.* EPH4194.

13. Bertha Leverton and Shmuel Lowensohn, eds., *I Came Alone.*

14. For example, joining Jock on her transport was fourteen-year-old Ruth Heymann from Breslau, noted in the Breslau community bulletin for being a good tennis player.

15. Jochewet Heiden acquisition note. IWM.

16. Anne Fox, *My Heart in a Suitcase.*

17. Jochewet Heiden, Imperial War Museum collection, EPH 3910.

18. Mark Jonathan Harris and Deborah Oppenheimer, *Into the Arms of Strangers: Stories of the Kindertransport.* Norbert Wollheim gave up his chance to escape to England on the final transport in late August 1939. He didn't want to be separated from his wife and child. They were all deported to Auschwitz in March 1943. Only Norbert survived.

19. Veronica Gillespie, 'Working with the Kindertransports,' *This Working-Day World, Women's Lives and Culture(s) in Britain 1914–1945.*

20. Elaine Blond, *Marks of Distinction: The Memoirs of Elaine Blond.*

21. Ruth Neumeyer, from Munich. IWM. Of the ninety-three children on Jock's transport, the majority – 73 percent – were from Berlin. The remainder joined from Breslau, Hamburg, Hannover, Stettin, Nuremburg and Rostock.

22. *Läkartidningen* 43 2006 volym 103, accessed 20.7.22.

23. Erna Davidsohn was born in 1897 in Berlin. A Stolperstein in the city commemorates her existence and her deportation to Auschwitz, where she worked alongside Dr Lucie Adelsburg (whose memoirs describe the lamentable state of so-called health care in Auschwitz) before her death from typhus. Fridolin Friedmann, born in 1897, was able to stay in England in 1939. When the war ended he took charge of reception centres for child Holocaust survivors. Dora Segall survived the war and did post-war work with the Leo Baeck Institute. Irma Zancker was born in 1901. She was deported to Theresienstadt camp in June 1943, then on to Auschwitz and death in October 1944. A Stoleperstein is installed outside her former home in Hamburg. Her son, Claus, was saved by the Kindertransport in 1939. The fate of Dorothea Magnus, born in Hamburg in 1876, is unverified, but likely to be grim.

24. The *Manhattan* worked the New York-to-Hamburg route, with a stop at Southampton. It had the honour of carrying the US Olympic team to Ger-

many for the 1936 Olympics. After the outbreak of war it took passengers fleeing Europe to the US, until it was assigned to the US Navy in 1941. One child on the 16 January Kindertransport voyage remembers the ship as the SS *Normandie*, a similarly modern luxury liner.

25. Hamburg details from the memoirs of Irene Katzenstein, *Voices of the Kinder* (Kindertransport Association), accessed 20.7.22. Irene notes her journey date as 19 January, but she is officially listed as joining Jock Heidenstein on 16 January. Transport of 93 German Jewish Children with 6 Adults from Germany to England – 16th January 1939 USHMM ID 40222.

26. Wolfang Dieneman was born in 1929 in a town northeast of Dresden. His sister, Ursula, was five years older. Their father was arrested during Kristall-nacht roundups and sent to Sachsenhausen, being released after six weeks. Under no illusions about Nazi treatment of Jews, their father had sent a postcard from the concentration camp with the terse instruction, 'Get the children out as quickly as possible.' He was eventually able to join Wolf-gang and Ursula in England, along with his wife. Interview conducted by Andrea Hammel with William Dieneman, Aberystwyth University, 14 June 2011, accessed 20 July 22. Wolfgang's account of seasickness on the Channel crossing is corroborated by Irene Jacoby, born 1926 in Berlin. Her father avoided the 1938 roundups, but still took her to Hamburg to join the Kindertransport there. She said it was a 'terrible voyage.' 'We were all sick and they had made a special party for us. Whoever had organised the transport wanted kids to be happy and most of the kids never made it to the party.' USHMM interview with Irene Buchner née Jacoby, accession 30 July 1987, Number 1993.A.0088.110, accessed 20 July 2022.

27. Elaine Blond, *Marks of Distinction*.

28. Jock's ID card reads, 'This document of identity is issued with the approval of His Majesty's Government in the United Kingdom to young persons to be admitted to the United Kingdom for educational purposes under the care of the Inter-Aid Committee for children. This document requires no Visa. Jochebeth Heidenstein 29.7.27 Foreign Office Passport Control Dept (stamp) Stamped with 2241.'

29. Gideon Gehrendt, *I Came Alone*.

30. Letter from Edith Lasker to Marianne Lasker, 19 June 1939, quoted in Anita Lasker-Wallfisch, *Inherit the Truth 1939–1945*.

CHAPTER 4: WE DO NOT KNOW WHERE IT WILL END

1. Anonymous, in *We Came as Children: A Collective Autobiography*, ed. Karen Gershon.

2. In conversation with Anita Lasker-Wallfisch, 13 March 2023.

3. Letter from Jock to Mrs Adler, 26 January 1940; letter from Rita to Stella, 4 November 41. Private collection.

4. Jock was given a home by Mrs R Cohn of 81 Reighton Road. As guarantor,

Mrs Cohn was required to provide fifty pounds to cover Jock's expenses. When Mrs Cohn failed in this financial promise, Rabbi Schonfeld had to find alternative funding for Jock's basic needs.

5. The Dimant hometown was Jēkabpils on the Daugava, although there were also family connections to the great port of Riga.

6. Video interview with Betty Young née Adler, undated. Private collection.

7. Video interview with Betty Young.

8. Letters between Rita, Jock and Stella Heidenstein 1939–42. Private collection.

9. Letter from Stella to Rita, undated. Private collection.

10. Letter from Stella to 'parents and relatives,' undated. Private collection.

11. Letter from Mania Heidenstein to Rita Heidenstein, dated 27 August 39. Private collection.

12. Wyberlye House was on Leylands Road, Burgess Hill, Sussex. The matron was Miss Hilda Josephs. The enterprise was supported by the Movement for the Care of Refugee Children from Germany and B'nai B'rith.

13. Testimony of Ester Friedmann, Interview 18331, Visual History Archive, USC Shoah Foundation, quoted by Lesley Urbach in 'Wyberlye Ladies Convalescent Home, Burgess Hill,' *Jewish Historical Studies* 51, UCL Press (2020).

14. Ester Friedman née Müller, Interview 18331, *Visual History Archive*, USC Shoah Foundation, quoted by Lesley Urbach, 'Wyberlye Ladies Convalescent Home, Burgess Hill.'

15. Lesley Urbach, 'Wyberlye Ladies Convalescent Home, Burgess Hill.'

16. Betty Young, in conversation with Elaine Butchins, Diana Young and Myriam Lucas, recounted to the author 13 June 2022.

17. Details shared by Bernard Diamond, in conversation with the author 1 June 2022, and in Betty Young's memoirs.

18. Letter from Stella to Rita, undated. Private collection. By 1945 Stella was actually re-learning German in school. Her school report notes her level as 'good' only, not excellent, and certainly not fluent.

19. Letter from Jock to Stella, 26 January 1940. Undated letter from Rita to Stella. Private collection.

20. Letter from Jock to Stella, 17 February 43. Private collection.

21. Letter from Mania Heidenstein to Rita, 27 August 1939. Private collection.

22. Letter dated 19 June 1939. Private papers of Mrs A. Lasker-Wallfisch, Documents.2074 IWM, 1988.

23. Letter from Dr Alfons Lasker, Breslau, 12 August 1939, to Reverend and Mrs Fisher, quoted in *Inherit the Truth 1939–1945*.

CHAPTER 5: WEATHER THE STORM

1. Rabbi Chiel Teichteil of 42 Stepney Green. Jock's host family invited her to the wedding of their daughter, once she'd recovered from her illness. Jock's

sisters were very surprised to learn that Jock wore a dress with a train at the wedding – it seemed out of character for her.

2. Leo Heidenstein, in the 1930 Berlin business directory, listed as a rag dealer on Gipsstrasse 14 N. 54; *Lumpen- (Hadern) – Grosshandlungen und Sortieranst.* 1933 Mechlenburg-Schwerin business directory, *Konfektions-und Schuwarenhaus.* Leo's son, Hermann, was born 3 August 1930 in Schwerin. When he arrived in Krakow, Leo gave his address as Kupa 16, site of the beautiful sixteenth-century Izaak Synagogue, next to the fish market in the Jewish district of the city.

3. Mania Heidenstein letter to Rita Heidenstein, 27 August 1939. Private collection.

4. Mania Heidenstein letter to Rita Heidenstein, 2 July 1939. Private collection.

5. Mania Heidenstein letter to Rita Heidenstein, 8 April 1940. Private collection.

6. Lotte and Jacob had two grandchildren, David, born 1922, and Celia, or Cilly, born 1927 – Jock's cousins.

7. Letter from Lotte (Libe) Kapelner née Heidenstein, 24 October 1939, to Rita Heidenstein at Wyberlye House. Private collection.

8. Undated letter from Stella to Oma and Opa. Private collection.

9. Undated letter from Mania Heidenstein to Stella Heidenstein, from Berlin. Private collection.

10. Mania Heidenstein letter to Jock, 2 July 1939; Mania letter to Rita, 1939. Private collection.

11. Melanie Lowy, *A Childhood Memoir: A Double Childhood.*

12. Dr Judith Grunfeld, *Shefford: A Story of a Jewish School Community in Evacuation 1939–1954.*

13. Rabbi Dr Solomon Schonfeld, *Message to Jewry.*

14. Dr Judith Grunfeld, *Shefford. A Story of a Jewish School Community in Evacuation 1939–1945.*

15. Frieda Korobkin, *Throw Your Feet Over Your Shoulders. Beyond the Kindertransport.*

16. Jock Heidenstein to Debbie Adler, 11 June 1941, from 41 Henlow Road, Clifton. Private collection.

17. Jock to Mrs Debbie Adler, 26 January 40. Private collection.

18. The paper is an incomplete copy of a Hebrew newspaper from 31 January 1940, in which the office of the World Jewish Congress reports that 'as a result of its efforts it is possible to save a number of Jews imprisoned in Nazi Germany in Sachsenhausen camp' and appeals 'to the relatives of the victims to immediately come up with the money needed to leave: 200 dollars for every man.'

19. Mania Heidenstein to Rita Heidenstein, 8 April 1940. Private collection.

20. Poem penned by Hermina Wolf, 19 January 1951, on the occasion of Rita Heidenstein's wedding.

21. Melanie Lowy, *A Childhood Memoir: A Double Childhood*.
22. Melanie Lowy, *A Childhood Memoir: A Double Childhood*.
23. Letter from Rita Heidenstein to Jock, 24 January 1942. Rita was billeted with Mrs Simmons and her husband (in the Royal Sussex Regiment) of 2 Westwood Cot, Rotherfield in Sussex.
24. Tamar Abrams, daughter of Henry Mayer and Rita Mayer née Heidenstein, in conversation with the author 9 February 23. Henry teased Rita at school and called her 'Fat Legs.' His courtship technique took a bit of working on, but he got it right by 1951 and his marriage to Rita.
25. Letter from Mania Heidenstein to Rita, 8 April 1940. Private collection. The Nazis deliberately kept relatives in the dark about the state, place and fate of the loved ones in the concentration camp system.
26. Letter from Mania Heidenstein to Rita, 3 June 1940. Private collection. Jock's uncle Wolf, rearrested with Chaim, was transferred from Sachsenhausen to Dachau, arriving 3 September 1940, prisoner number 17293. He died in Dachau 15 May 1941. Juda Heidenstein, born 1917, presumed to be the son of Wolf and Tauba Heidenstein, died in Gross-Rosen camp on 17 December 1941. Chaim's brother Juda was lost in Russia along with his wife, Esther.
27. Rabbi Dr Solomon Schonfeld, *Message to Jewry*.

CHAPTER 6: WHAT IS GOING TO HAPPEN TO US NEXT?
1. Anne Frank, *The Diary of a Young Girl*, ed., Otto H. Frank and Mirjam Pressler.
2. Sue Milkes in conversation with the author, 25 February 2022, remembering Phyllis Goldhammer: 'She made the most beautiful blankets for her great-grandchildren.'
3. Anne Frank, *The Diary of a Young Girl*, 21 September, 1942. 'I've come to the shocking conclusion that I have only one long-sleeved dress and three cardigans to wear in the winter. Father's given me permission to knit a white jumper; the wool isn't very pretty, but it'll be warm, and that's what counts.'
4. Anne Frank, *The Diary of a Young Girl*, diary entry for 11 April 1944 regarding clothes worn during a night-time burglary attempt in the Annexe building.
5. Anne Frank, *The Diary of a Young Girl*.
6. Letter from Jock Heidenstein to the Adler family, 26 April 1942. Private collection.
7. *Knitting for All Illustrated*, Margaret Murray and Jane Koster.
8. Stella Heidenstein undated letter to her sister Rita; Mania Heidenstein to her daughter Rita, winter 1939. Private collection.
9. Anna Freud and Dorothy T. Burlingham, *War and Children*.
10. Sidney Cohen, conversation with the author, 29 May 2022.
11. Debbie Adler, conversation with the author, 1 June 2022.

12. Anna Freud and Dorothy T. Burlingham, *War and Children*.

13. Jocheved Eva Fink was extraordinarily resilient. She had to be. She endured years of wandering before finally escaping Europe for a new life in Israel. The information about the Ukrainian pogrom of Eva's family was shared by one of her classmates after the war, and passed to Eva's daughter Drora Goshen. Drora said her parents, both Holocaust survivors, 'did not talk about the past. Only about the future' – interview for moment.mag.com, 13 September 2023, 'Crossing the Krimml Pass.'

14. 'Our Sewing Corner,' *Deutsches Hauswirtschaft*, September 1941.

15. Sometimes just one person could make a significant difference to the general treatment of Jews in an area. A German officer named Albert Battel managed to block the SS liquidation of Jews in Przemysl, hometown of Jock Heidenstein's father, uncles and aunts. He commanded a detachment that used army trucks to rescue one hundred families destined for Belzec extermination camp. He couldn't save all the Przemysl Jews, but he did what he could. He was posthumously recognized as Righteous Among the Nations by Yad Vashem in 1981. This information from Israeli researcher Dr Zeev Goshen.

16. *Deutsches Hauswirtschaft*, 'Vorweihnachten im kriegswinterhilfswerk,' December 1939. The same magazine contains an articles on how to turn a man's raincoat into a pinafore and a grocery bag, and how to craft home-made leather shoes for children.

17. 'Rein Arisches unternehmen' – Gross-versandhaus Quelle fürth i. Bayern #61 c. 1937.

18. *Knitting for All Illustrated*.

19. Sir Ralph Kohn, interviewed for the *Jewish Chronicle* , 14 May 2015.

CHAPTER 7: DRESSED IN AS MANY LAYERS AS POSSIBLE

1. Anita Lasker-Wallfisch, *Inherit the Truth 1939–1945*.

2. Details from a letter written to Dr Lasker's client Count Keunigl, 15 April 1942. Private papers of Mrs A. Lasker-Wallfisch, documents.2071 92/31/1 Imperial War Museum.

3. Letter to Marianne Lasker dated October 1941. Private papers of Mrs A. Lasker-Wallfisch, documents.2071 92/31/1 Imperial War Museum.

4. Lucie Adelsberger, *Auschwitz: A Doctor's Story*.

5. Letter from Mania Heidenstein to Rita Heidenstein dated 6 March 1940. Private collection.

6. Letter from Jock Heidenstein to a family tracing agent, 31 October 1967. Jock added, 'Unfortunately, due to the unsettled conditions during the war and numerous changes of address, I no longer have any of the correspondence.' Private collection.

7. Letter from Jock Heidenstein to Stella Heidenstein, dated 10 November 1941. Private collection.

8. Memorial designed by Volkmar Hasse, erected 1987.

9. Tauba Heidenstein, born 6 September 1888, departed Berlin 1 March 1943 and arrived at Auschwitz 2 March 1943. She did not survive selection at Auschwitz: only 150 men were chosen for work. The remaining people were murdered in the gas chambers.

10. Bayla Felsenbach née Heidenstein was born 19 January 1895 in Radymno, near Chaim Heidenstein's hometown of Przemysl. She was deported from Berlin on 27 November 1941 on Transport DA31. Her husband, Chaskel, born 26 July 1892, is memorialised at Belzec extermination camp.

11. Martha's husband, Isidor, died on 31 August 1940. Martha herself lasted only a few months in Lodz. At fifty-five years old, she wasn't considered essential for the Nazi work enterprises. She was murdered in Chelmno extermination centre on 9 May 1942.

12. Arek Hersh, *A Detail of History*.

13. Zahava Kohn, *Fragments of a Lost Childhood*.

14. Josef Zumerkorn written testimony, Yad Vashem Item ID 9698712 file number 8548 created 12.6.2011.

15. Josef Zumerkorn written testimony, Yad Vashem.

CHAPTER 8: WHAT LOVELY THINGS WE MADE IN THE GHETTO

1. Josef Zumerkorn video testimony, Yad Vashem YVA O.3/VT/6660.

2. Lola Schwartz née Weintraub testimony 6 May 1996. Shoah Visual History Foundation Interview code 42028.

3. Josef Zumerkorn video testimony.

4. Dvora's parents were Yitzhak Moshe Farber and Sara Hinda Farber. They had one and a half rooms upstairs from the Zumerkorns. Josef Zumerkorn testified post-war that Sara, a tailoress, died in the ghetto in 1941, and Yitzhak was murdered in Chelmno in 1942. David's parents were Nakhum Gershon and Ester Rakhel Gershon. They had only one room on the third floor of the building. Both were deported to Chelmno in September 1942 and murdered there.

5. Writer Wladyslaw Remont gives a picturesque account of the Old Market in Lodz, in his 1899 novel *The Promised Land*.

6. This public humiliation of mill owners in particular was witnessed by Gena Turgel, whose parents ran a textile business in Krakow.

7. Eva Libitzky, *Out on a Ledge*. Eva loved the pulse of urban life in pre-war Lodz and suffered with her family when the Germans took over.

8. Sara Zyskind, *Stolen Years*.

9. Oskar Singer, 'Quickly Walking through the Ghetto,' quoted in Joanna Podolska, *Traces of the Litzmannstadt Ghetto*.

10. In the 1931 listing full names are given as Chaim-Josef and Chana Jochweta. Josef was noted as eleven years old, Chana was ten and Nechama was just one year old. Księga ludności stałej m. Łodzi guberni piotrkowskiej nr

domu 225-228, Lodz State Archives 39/221/0/3.2.3/10049. The 1941 listing is from a compilation 'Lodz-names: a record of the 240,000 inhabitants of the Łódź Ghetto,' USHMM ID 20619. There is a faint image of Chana's mother among the Lodz State Archive files. It is cut from a roll of camera film and fixed to an Identity card application, marked 'Protokoll Nr 114.' On the form, Dvora Gitla Zumerkorn's identity is confirmed by two witnesses. Her address is Stary Rynek 2. Age 48. The application date is 19 June 1941 and the form was filed 23 July.

11. Diary entry dated 16 March 1942. Quoted in Michal Unger, ed., *The Last Ghetto*.

12. As an example, figures for January 1941 alone show output of five-to-six thousand earmuffs a week, with a total of nearly twenty-two thousand for that month. Lodz State Archives Strickerei Fabrikations-Abteiling Ref 39/221/0/5.1.10/30628.

13. Helmut Paulus, quoted in Nicholas Stargadt, *The German War. A Nation Under Arms, 1939-1945*. Helmut benefited from bales of knitwear distributed in early February 1942.

14. Lucille Eichengreen, née Celia Landau, *Rumkowski and the Orphans of Lodz*.

15. Lodz State Archives 39/221/0/5.1.10/30610, letter dated 14 October 1942.

16. Diary entry dated 16 March 1942. Quoted in Michal Unger, ed., *The Last Ghetto*.

CHAPTER 9: NOBODY MUST KNOW

1. Deborah Barton, *Writing and Rewriting the Reich: Women Journalists in the Nazi and Post-war Press*.

2. *Baedecker's – Generalgouvernement*, 1943.

3. Arnold Mostowicz, interviewed for *Photographer: Lodz Ghetto Through the Lens of Walter Genewein*, directed by Dariusz Jablonski (1998).

4. USHMM photograph number 74514A 1940–44.

5. Elizabeth Harvey, *Women in the Nazi East. Agents & Witnesses of Germanization*.

6. Walter Piller, second in command of the Sonderkommando, testified to circus tent c 80m long 15m wide and 8m high used for sorting victims' clothes, *Chelmno Witnesses Speak*.

7. Quoted in Laurence Rees, *Auschwitz: The Nazis and the Final Solution*, 91.

8. "The Extermination Centre for Jews in Chełmno-on-Ner, in the Light of the Latest Research," Symposium proceedings, 6–7 September (2004), District Museum in Konin. Zofia Szałek, interviewed in 1998 by representatives of the United States Holocaust Memorial Museum. Alina Skibinska, project coordinator.

9. 'Die Ausrottung des jüdischen Volkes,' Heinrich Himmler speech at Posen, 4 October 1943.

10. *Chelmno Witnesses Speak.*
11. Zofia knew of Szymon Srebrnik, who succeeded in breaking free and who survived the war to testify against the Nazis.
12. *Chelmno Witnesses Speak,*
13. Hans Biebow speech, 7 August 1944, Andrzej Strzelecki, *The Deportation of Jews from the Łódź Ghetto to KL Auschwitz and Their Extermination.*
14. Quoted in Zvi Szner and Alexander Sened, eds., *With a Camera in the Ghetto.* Over just two weeks in July 1942 there were nearly 800,000kg of clothes and rags delivered, nearly 70kg of used footwear, and 50kg of stockings and socks.
15. Reisswolf is now the name of a German company specialising in data destruction, archiving and digitisation – a different kind of fragmentation.

CHAPTER 10: WHO CAN KNIT?

1. Conversation with Miriam Kahanov, 24 June 2023.
2. Conversation with Eran Kahanov, 24 June 2023.
3. Thomas 'Toivi' Blatt interview with Karl Frenzel, 1984, 'The Confrontation with a Murderer,' Jewish Virtual Library, accessed 7 July 2023. Full audio interview USHMM Accession Number 2020.123.1 RG Number: RG-90.138.0001.
4. Riva/Rivka Feldman changed her name to Regina Wojcisyzn late in 1944 for survival reasons. 'Regina' has been used throughout this book for consistency.
5. 'Hat sich bestialisch benommen'; 'von bestlizlischer Brutalität' – German translation of Regina's testimony, 5 April 1963, Extermination Camp Sobibor 3.3.1 13-20 Witness statements and interviews of survivors of Sobibor 947-92, NIOD Institute for War, Holocaust and Genocide Studies.
6. Regina Zielinski interview with Jules Schelvis, 1983, www.sobiborinterviews.nl. Survivor and historian Jules Schelvis invited Regina to his home in the Netherlands to recover after the ordeal of bearing witness at the Frenzel trial in Frankfurt.
7. Johann Niemann album, Sobibor Perpetrator Collection, USHMM Accession Number: 2020.8.1.
8. Esther Terner, USHMM interview 18.2.1992 – interview code 3029.2
9. USHMM Sobibor Perpetrator Collection Accession No. 2020.8.1.
10. Regina Zielinski interview with Jules Schelvis, 1983.
11. A mini poll of experienced modern knitters, conducted by the author (who can barely knit a dishcloth, let alone turn the heel of a sock) suggests that three days per sock would be a comfortable knitting target. Knitters conclude that to knit a sock a day would need an early start and an all-day commitment.
12. Dr Jacob Presser, *Ashes in the Wind: The Destruction of Dutch Jewry.*
13. Dr Jacob Presser, *Ashes in the Wind.* Much of the social/welfare work of

the Displaced Persons Aid Bureau was headed by Gertrude von Tijn-Cohn. Her hundred-strong team of staff and volunteers gave aid to the departing– *Hulp aan Vertrekkenden* – and also cared for the dependents of deportees left without other support.

14. After the war a collection of eighteen pencil drawings sketched on paper scraps and newspaper fragments were discovered in Chelm, not far from Sobibor. They were dated 1942–43, and the work of artist Joseph Richter, a partisan. In one sketch two very elegant women at a carriage window are depicted, with classy up-dos and dangling earrings. Richter's caption reads, *Trains from Holland. They don't know anything. Pullman cars, comfort, in an hour they will die.* Ghetto Fighter's House Museum collection Art/2422.

15. Testimony of Hersh Cukierman at Karl Frenzel's trial 1965, quoted in Michael S. Bryant, *Eyewitness to Genocide.* The murderer in this instance was SS Sergeant Kurt Bolender. His dog called Bari. Bari was trained to attack Jewish inmates. Bolender was only arrested in 1961. He denied there was ever any such brutal method of loading of clothing at Sobibor. Cukierman's father was beaten to death by Frenzel, wrongly accused of taking a few kilos of meat.

16. Testimony in German submitted December 10, 1974, for criminal proceedings against Hubert Gomerski at the District Court in Frankfurt-am-Main, NIOD. Survivor Toivi Blatt remembers that the boy was fifteen years old, although he believed him to have been shot at the crematorium, "The Confrontation with a Murderer."

17. Andrew Zielinski, *Conversations with Regina.*

18. From 2007, archaeologists excavating the area of Sobibor extermination camp uncovered thousands of personal belongings, including hairpins, buttons, name tags . . . and a wedding ring. The Australian Broadcasting Corporation speculated in 2014 that this could have been the same ring hidden by Regina during her time in Sobibor. Regina was no longer alive to see the ring and confirm if it was Golda Felenbaum's.

19. Am 16.4.1943 wurden an die Bekleidungswerk, Lublin, Chopinstrasse 27 zum versand gebracht, quoted in Marek Bem, *Sobibor Extermination Camp 1942–1943.* There was a central record of processed goods destined for the SS Main Economic and Administrative Office that included women's hair, shorn before their murders.

20. Esther Terner-Raab, USHMM interview, 18 February 1992 – interview code 30292.

CHAPTER 11: AN IRRESISTIBLE URGE TO FLEE

1. Regina Zielinski 1983 interview with Jules Schelvis, www.sobiborinterviews.nl.

2. Conversation with Eran and Miriam Kahanov 24 June 2023.

3. Kurt Ticho correspondence, letter written 9 December 1985 NIOD. Fren-

zel apparently kept one of the artworks painted by Max Van Dam. It was destroyed by his family after his arrest in 1962, perhaps to deny Frenzel's connection with a crime-infested past, perhaps to purge him from the family. Either way, a piece of Max Van Dam was destroyed with it. Van Dam arrived in Sobibor in March 1943. Some sources say he was murdered in September that year, others say he maybe died in the uprising.

4. Zentrale Stelle der Landesjustizverwaltungen Ludwisburg Archives, case file 45 Js 27/61 file re. No 208 AR-Z 251/59 Holon/Israel May 1959. Quoted in Marek Bem, *Sobibor Extermination Camp 1942–1943.*
5. Toivi Blatt, 'The Confrontation with a Murderer.'
6. Regina Zielinski 1983 interview.
7. Andrew Zielinski, *Conversations with Regina.*
8. Gitta Sereny, *Into That Darkness.*
9. Ada Lichtman interview 1985, USHMM 1996.166 RG-60.5023.
10. Esther Terner Raab 1992 USHMM 18.2.1992 – interview code 30292.
11. Andrew Zielinski, *Conversations with Regina.*
12. Selma Wijnberg, quoted in Miriam Novitch, *Sobibor. Martyrdom and Revolt.*
13. Regina Zielinski 1983 interview.
14. Gitta Sereny, *Into That Darkness.*
15. Regina Zielinski 1983 interview.
16. Kalmen Wewryk, *To Sobibor and Back – An Eyewitness Account.*
17. Toivi Blatt, 'The Confrontation with a Murderer.
18. Richard Rashke, *Escape from Sobibor.*
19. Saartje Selma Engel née Wijnberg USHMM testimony 1994.A.0447.10 RG-50.042.0010. Selma was born in the Netherlands in 1922. She arrived Sobibor with over two thousand others on 9 April 1943. Selma's friend Ursula Stern found a knitted dress in the storehouse and took it to wear. Selma recognised it as her own dress, knitted by her mother,
20. Esther Raab née Terner USHMM interview.
21. Richard Rashke, *Sobibor. Martyrdom and Revolt.*
22. Regina Zielinski 1983 interview.
23. Esther Raab née Terner USHMM interview.
24. Regina Zielinski 1983 interview.
25. Hella Weiss née Felenbaum interview with Jules Schelvis 1983, www.sobiborinterviews.nl.
26. Andrew Zielinski, *Conversations with Regina.*

CHAPTER 12: I FEEL GOOD THAT I FOUGHT

1. Regina Zielinski née Feldman, 1983 interview with Jules Schelvis, www.sobiborinterviews.nl.
2. A similar escape took place in Treblinka extermination camp in September 1942, when Polish Jew Abraham Krzepicki hid in a train wagon of clothing

for three kilometres then jumped out of the train and made his way to the Warsaw ghetto, where his account of Treblinka's monstrosities was given to the Oneg Shabbat group.

3. Esther Raab née Terner, USHMM interview.

4. Yitzhak Arad, *Belzec, Sobibor, Treblinka.*

5. Hella Weiss née Felenbaum, 1983 interview.

6. Luka's fate following the uprising is unknown. The shirt she gifted Alexander Pechersky was cherished by his family for seventy years, and is on display in Rostov-on-Don. The blue dye is now faded; Pechersky's fame lives on undimmed.

7. Hella Weiss née Felenbaum, 1983 interview with Jules Schelvis, www.sobiborinterviews.nl.

8. Regina Zielinski née Feldman, 1983 interview.

9. Regina Zielinski née Feldman, 1983 interview.

10. Zelda narrowly missed a reunion with Regina in Wlodawa. Zelda was hidden by Polish peasants. She obtained false papers to pass as Aryan: 'I went to Lvov and resumed a normal life until the end of the war, as if Sobibor never existed.' *Dokumenty Zbrodni I Meczenstwa*, Documents of Crime and Martyrdom, Cracow 1945.

11. Regina Zielinski née Feldman, 1983 interview.

12. Conversation with Miriam and Eran Kahanov 24 June 2023.

13. Hella Weiss née Felenbaum, 1983 interview with Jules Schelvis.

14. Hella received four commendations between October 1944 and May 1945, in battles to liberate Czechoslovakia. She was first in the reconnaissance and sabotage detachment of the NKVD Okhotnicki detachment commanded by Nikolai Prokopyuk, then in rifle regiments. She continued duties as a medical officer at her regimental command post. Her full military service is detailed in "The Memory Book" at www.pechersky.org.

15. Miriam Kahanov in conversation with the author, 24 June 2023.

16. Hella Weiss née Felenbaum, 1983 interview.

CHAPTER 13: THE TRAIN SEEMED TO HAVE NO END

1. Regina Zielinski née Riva Feldman, 1983 interview with Jules Schelvis, www.sobiborinterviews.nl.

2. Army tailor Franz Suchomel was the man responsible for packing up Sobibor's plunder and his comrades' belongings. He was complicit in the T4 murder program, and murders at Treblinka. He gave testimony when prosecuted during the Treblinka trials in 1964–65.

3. In 2014 archaeologists uncovered a wedding ring in the sandy soil of the Sobibor site. Although it has no direct provenance, some speculated that it could be Golda Feldman's ring, recovered then hidden by Regina. 'Wedding ring found at Nazi concentration camp might have Adelaide connection,' www.abc.net.au, 24 October 2014.

4. Regina Zielinski née Riva Feldman, 1983 interview with Jules Schelvis, www.sobiborinterviews.nl.

5. Mania's name isn't on any deportation documents. Details of her destination were gleaned by Rita Heidenstein after the war, but cannot be confirmed – as is the case with so many people, despite Nazi bureaucracy.

6. Jochewet Heidenstein letter from Shefford, 17 February 1943; letter from Shefford 9 March 1943. Private correspondence.

7. The babies were always found then shot in the head. Helga Schneider's memoir, *Let Me Go: My Mother and the SS*, gives a searing account of mothers trying to hide children before entering the gas chambers. Schneider's mother was a fanatical SS guard in Ravensbrück and Auschwitz-Birkenau, entirely unrepentant post-war and still contemptuous of Jewish mothers lamenting the loss of their children.

8. Steven Paskuly, ed., *Death Dealer: The Memoirs of the SS Kommandant of Auschwitz*, Rudolf Höss testimony written post-war.

9. Letter from Mania Heidenstein to Rita Heidenstein, 3 June 1940. Private collection.

10. Jerzy Rawicz, ed., *KL Auschwitz as Seen by the SS*. Pery Broad's testimony is harrowing to read but a necessary insight into the reality of the genocidal process.

11. Visitors to the Auschwitz-Birkenau State Museum can see examples of children's clothes on display. The fabric may be fragile, but the emotions they carry are so strong. Conservationists do not attempt to restore them to their original pristine state. Eliminating their stains and tears would almost be like erasing their history.

12. The Auschwitz *Sterbebücher*, or book of death certificates, listed the details and death dates of prisoners registered in the concentration camp between 29 July 1941 and 31 December 1943. Ruth Krumme's death is noted as 25 February 1943, although Renate Lasker later recalled being in the dock with Ruth. Because Ruth's husband, Werner, was non-Jewish, once his Jewish wife was dead, he was legally considered eligible for compulsory drafting into the Wehrmacht. Werner had survived his stint in Auschwitz as one of the relatively privileged prisoner-clerks working in the SS Administration block.

13. Anita Lasker-Wallfisch, *Inherit the Truth 1939–1945*.

CHAPTER 14: IN AUSCHWITZ THEY STRIPPED US OF EVERYTHING

1. Anita Lasker-Wallfisch, BBC, *Desert Island Discs* interview, 25 August 1996.

2. On 29 November 1943, thirty-seven female prisoners arriving in a group transport were given numbers 69370–69406. This group included Anita Lasker. *Auschwitz Chronicle*.

3. Anita Lasker-Wallfisch, USC Shoah Foundation video testimony USHMM 1995.A.1285.53 RG-50.149.0053.

4. Anita Lasker-Wallfisch, USC Shoah Foundation video testimony.
5. Primo Levi, *If This Is a Man*.
6. Helena Dunicz Niwińska, *One of the Girls in the Band: The Memoirs of a Violinist from Birkenau*.
7. Fania Fénelon, *The Musicians of Auschwitz*.
8. One knitting work kommando made wool sweaters for Toebbens & Schultz, a Nazi-operated company based in the Warsaw ghetto. Magdalena Emilewicz-Pióro and Piotr M.A. Cywiński, *Auschwitz Legacies*.
9. Lucy Adlington, *The Dressmakers of Auschwitz*.
10. Jutta Pelz, born 1924, testimony in *Auschwitz – the Nazi Civilisation*, Dr Lore Shelley.
11. Correspondence with Faye Levinson, Perla Blass's daughter.
12. Eva Schloss, *Eva's Story*. Eva became Anne Frank's stepsister posthumously, when her mother married Anne's father, Otto. All were Auschwitz survivors.
13. Anita Lasker-Wallfisch, BBC, *Desert Island Discs* interview.
14. Gabriela (Ella) Truly née Braun, interview, USHMM Accession Number: 1997.A.0441.50, RG-50.462.0050.
15. Hermann Langbein, *People in Auschwitz*.
16. Comments reported by the Höss gardener Stanislaw Dubiel, quoted in Jerzy Rawicz, *KL Auschwitz as Seen by the SS*.
17. Gabriela Truly Braun, oral history interview, USHMM. Ella survived Auschwitz thanks to her friends, and her knitting skills. She was evacuated to Germany, liberated by Russians, and returned to Slovakia to find 'nobody was there.' Eventually she made a new home in New York, working as a finisher in a dress factory. 'And so life went on,' she concluded.
18. Anita Lasker-Wallfisch, USC Shoah Foundation video testimony 1995.A.1285.53 RG-50.149.0053.
19. Mary Thomas, *Mary Thomas's Book of Knitting Patterns* (1943).
20. Lucie Adelsburger, *Auschwitz. A Doctor's Story*.
21. Olga Lengyl, *Five Chimneys*.
22. Fania Fénelon, *The Musicians of Auschwitz*.
23. Sophie Sohlberg née Loewenstein, *Auschwitz–the Nazi Civilisation*.
24. Anita Lasker-Wallfisch, BBC, *Desert Island Discs* interview.
25. Quoted by Hilde Grünbaum Zimche in Kellie D. Brown, *The Sound of Hope*.
26. Survivor Guta Blumberg-Wohlmuth, quoted in Anna Eilenberg-Eibeshitz, *Preserved Evidence: Ghetto Lodz*, vol. II.

CHAPTER 15: BATTLING FOR SURVIVAL BY SHEER INSTINCT

1. Anita Lasker-Wallfisch, *Inherit the Truth 1939–1945*.
2. Hilda Grünham-Zimche was a violinist. Illness stopped her playing in the Auschwitz orchestra, so she became one of the music copyists, writing out

arrangements for the motley collection of instruments. Her red pillow-case bag (with very smart pockets and her name embroidered in pale blue chain stitch) is now in the Yad Vashem artefact collection, on loan from Hilda.

3. Steven Paskuly, ed., *Death Dealer*, Rudolf Höss's memoir, written during his post-war incarceration for war crimes.

4. Jósef Garliński, *Fighting Auschwitz*.

5. Kitty Hart-Moxon, *Return to Auschwitz*.

6. Charlotte Delbo, *Auschwitz and After*.

7. Anita Lasker-Wallfisch, *Inherit the Truth 1939–1945*.

8. Extract from Heinrich Himmler speech to the Gruppenführer at Posen, 4 October 1943, United States Chief Counsel for the Prosecution of Axis Criminality, *Nazi Conspiracy and Aggression*, vol. IV, Washington, DC: United States Government Printing Office (1946).

9. Harmęże was established in July 1942. From June 1943 the rabbits were exclusively cared for by women and girls. It was part of extensive agricultural enterprises in Auschwitz which included fisheries, animal husbandry and plant experimentation.

10. Gudrun Burwitz née Himmler, diary entry 22 July 1941, quoted in the *New York Times* obituary, 6 July 2018. Details of rabbit farming in Dachau by Harold Marcuse in *Horror and Human Tragedy Revisited: The Management of Sites of Atrocities for Tourism*, eds. Greg Ashworth and Rudi Hartmann.

11. Eva Schloss, *Eva's Story*.

12. Tanya Singer, 'Angora Rabbits in Auschwitz Concentration Camps.' Correspondent Sigrid Shultz worked for the *Chicago Tribune*. She donated the album to the Wisconsin Historical Society in 1965, item WHI 45276, *Die angora-zuchten des SS Wirtschafts-Verwaltung shauptamtes*, 1943.

13. Arek Hersh, deported from Lodz ghetto, describes this practice in his memoir *A Detail of History*.

14. Peter Hellman and Beate Klarsfeld, eds., *The Auschwitz Album*.

15. *Auschwitz Chronicle*, 27 November 1944 report from branch B of the WVHA, the SS main economic and administrative office, responsible for overseeing plunder. SS Captain Kersten, who submitted the report, was horrified by the wastage of clothes, but not by the piles of cadavers who once wore them.

16. Kitty Hart-Moxon, *Return to Auschwitz*.

17. Fania Fénelon, *The Musicians of Auschwitz*.

18. Manca Svalbova's 1964 memoir *Vyhasnuté oči*, (*Eyes Extinguished*) details her response to Alma Rosé's violin playing which she found very moving, saying, 'I too bleed, and hope for beauty.' This quote inspired the post-war commission of an orchestra score of the same title.

19. Anita Lasker-Wallfisch, *Inherit the Truth 1939–1945*.

20. Anita Lasker-Wallfisch, *Inherit the Truth 1939–1945*.

CHAPTER 16: WE HAD LEARNED TO BE RESOURCEFUL

1. Alice Kern, *Tapestry of Hope*.

2. Anita Lasker-Wallfisch testimony, USC Shoah Foundation 1995.A.1285.53 RG-50.149.0053.

3. Anita Lasker-Wallfisch, BBC, *Desert Island Discs* interview, 25 August 1996.

4. Anita Lasker trial testimony, *Law Reports of Trials of War Criminals Selected and Prepared by the United Nations War Crimes Commission*, English ed., vol. II: The Belsen Trial. UNWCC His Majesty's Stationery Office 1947.

5. Hitler's valet helped roll Hitler's body into a rug. During the Nuremburg trials another witness claimed to have seen the legs of Hitler's corpse sticking out from a short blanket: testimony of Edmund Glaise-Horstenau, 12 June 1946, USHMM film 2001.358.1/RG-60.2979.

6. Eric Somers and René Kok, *Jewish Displaced Persons in Camp Bergen-Belsen 1945–1950: The Unique Photo Album of Zippy Orlin*. Image of Zippy Orlin and child survivors at Bergen Belsen, USHMM 77843 courtesy of Izak Sagi.

7. Muriel Knox Doherty, *Letters from Belsen 1945: An Australian Nurse's Experiences with the Survivors of War*.

8. Renate Lasker letter to Marianne Lasker, 17 June 1945, quoted in Anita Lasker-Wallfisch, *Inherit the Truth 1939–1945*.

9. Agnes Seidel, diary entry 7 May 1945, quoted in Nicholas Stargadt, *The German War*.

10. Han Hogerzeil and Robert Collins, *Straight On: Journey to Belsen and the Road Home*.

11. Muriel Knox Doherty, *Letters from Belsen 1945*.

12. Footage from a 1945 British government project, German Concentration Camps Factual Survey, featuring in the 2014 documentary film directed by Andre Singer, *Night Will Fall*.

13. Gucia Wald Teiblum, born 1926 in Poland, transferred from Auschwitz to Bergen-Belsen, January 1945. Yad Vashem artefact collection.

14. Presented by the anonymous fifteen-year-old maker to Muriel Knox née Doherty. Now in the collection of the Imperial War Museum, London.

15. Berta Lebovitz was eighteen and suffering from typhus when she found the bag among the 'schmattes' – the rags. Item #6989068 Yad Vashem artefact collection.

16. Muriel Knox Doherty, *Letters from Belsen 1945*. The Lüneburg trials took place between 17 September and 17 November 1945. Of the forty-four men and women on trial, eleven were sentenced to death and executed in December of the same year.

17. Unsent letter from Rita Heidenstein to her parents, 8 May 1945. Private collection.

18. Unsent letter from Rita Heidenstein to her parents, 8 May 1945. Private collection.

19. Letter from Rita Heidenstein to Oscar Heidenstein, 10 December 1947. Private collection.

20. Unsent letter from Rita Heidenstein to her parents, 8 May 1945, from the White House, Jewish Secondary School, Shefford. Private collection.

21. Jock's grandmother Sara Schwartz, born 1870, one of seven siblings, died 22 December 1940, Mitcham Park, Surrey.

22. Card dated 9 November 1940, 'To the Clothing Department Polish Jewish Refugee Fund 14 Manette Street W1 HEIDENSTEIN BDF153 Please supply bearer with necessary clothing for man and wife.' Hartley Library special collections MS 190 AJ 390 Case Files & Papers of the Polish Jewish Refugee Fund.

23. A social worker visited Lottie Kapelner at 39 Petherton Road, London, in August 1943 and noted that 'the rooms are very poorly furnished, they are, however, kept very clean." The Heidensteins were referred to as a 'genuine and deserving case.' Hartley Library special collections, University of Southampton MS190 AJ 390 Case Files & Papers of the Polish Jewish Refugee Fund. Tragically, Lottie's husband, Jacob Kapelner – Jock's uncle – was deported from Malines-Mechelen camp in Belgium on 15 January 1943. There were 998 people on the transport, all alive when they arrived at Auschwitz on 18 January. He died not long afterwards.

24. Betty Young née Adler, private diary entry. Betty's diary also noted the liberation of Riga by the Allies and awareness that her relatives in the area had probably perished.

25. The V1 'doodlebug' hit Petherton road on 2 July 1944, destroying houses, breaking water mains and creating a huge crater. Josef Heidenstein was taken to the Royal Northern Hospital where he died, aged seventy-nine. He was buried 10 July 1944 in Enfield cemetery, which had been established by Dr Schonfeld's father.

26. This campaign was organised by the Joint Clothing Committee and Jewish Committee for Relief Abroad, based out of Endsleigh Place in London. It was established by the Central British Fund.

27. An example of a knitting pattern for a child aged fifteen months to two years is in the VADS archive 1945, Arts University Bournemouth Design Collection AIBDC002338.

28. Joint Relief of Clothing working party, part of the Joint Orthodox Refugee Committee. Details from meeting minutes, Hartley Library special collections, University of Southampton, MS Schonfeld MS 45/1; additional details from Rabbi Dr Solomon Schonfeld, *Message to Jewry*. Schonfeld also arranged for four rabbis with a mobile synagogue to visit Belsen DP camp.

29. Fania Fénelon, *The Musicians of Auschwitz*.

30. Anita Lasker letter to Marianne Lasker, 17 June 1945, 'Ich habe ein cello!'

IWM, Private papers of Mrs A Lasker-Wallfsich, 1988 Documents.2074 92/31/1.

31. Letter from Renate Lasker to Marianne Lasker, 19 June 1945, reprinted in *Inherit the Truth 1939–1945*.

32. Anita Lasker letter to Marianne Lasker, 8 June 1945. IWM, Private papers of Mrs A Lasker-Wallfsich, 1988 Documents.2074 92/31/1.

33. Anita Lasker-Wallfisch, *Inherit the Truth 1939–1945*.

34. Gena Turgel, *I Light a Candle*.

CHAPTER 17: MEMORIES BECOME YOUR POSSESSIONS

1. Anita Lasker-Wallfisch, *Inherit the Truth 1939–1945*.

2. Jock was on the committee of Ben Zakkai Youth Society, supporting study circles led by Rabbi Dr Spitzer. Sabbath afternoon celebrations attracted large numbers of old alumni from the Jewish Secondary School – *Jewish Chronicle*, 29 June 1946. Jock also spent more than six years taking classes at Walthamstow & Leyton Synagogue in London.

3. Letter to Rita Heidenstein, 12 October 1945. Private collection. At this time Rita was a house mother at 'Shalom' hostel, 194 Lordship Road London, linked with Rabbi Dr Solomon Schonfeld and the Adath Yisroel congregation. She later worked at Holm-Acre Jewish Care Home in Altringham.

4. Regina Zielinski, née Riva Feldman, 1983 video interview with Jules Schelvis, www.sobiborinterviews.nl.

5. Elizabeth Bowen, postscript to *The Demon Lover and Other Stories*.

6. Mathilde Wolff-Mönckeberg, *On the Other Side*.

7. Regina Zielinski, née Riva Feldman, 1983 video interview with Jules Schelvis.

8. Elaine Blond, *Marks of Distinction*.

9. Jock Heidenstein letter, 31 October 1967. Private collection.

10. Jock Heidenstein letter, 3 August 1967, to Rosa Roifer. Private collection.

11. Hart-Moxon, Kitty, *Return to Auschwitz*.

12. Anita Lasker-Wallfisch interview BBC *Desert Island Discs*, 25 August 1996.

13. From a poem by Old Sheffordian Hermina Wolf, recited at Rita's wedding, 23 September 1951. Private collection.

14. Stella is listed as Library Assistant in the *London Gazette*, 17 October 1947. In July of the same year she was naturalised as British. She also worked for Praeger Publishing.

15. Letter from Gil Park of Universe, 9 April 1969. Private collection.

16. Letter from Stella Heiden to Gil Park, 16 April 1969. Private collection.

17. Stella Heiden letter to Gil Park, 24 April 1969. Private collection.

18. Author in conversation with Stella's former colleagues Adele Ursone, Dorothy Caesar and Cynthia Cook, 28 October 2022.

19. Author conversation with Hepzibah Rudofsky, daughter of Sir Ralph and

Lady Zahava Kohn née Kanarek, 1 May 2022. Zahava Kohn's moving story is told in her memoir, *Fragments of a Lost Childhood*. The Kohn business was Advisory Services Medical Symposia Ltd.

20. The Zielinski family travelled from Germany to Italy, boarding the *Castelbianco* at Naples. It sailed 5 July 1949, arriving in Sydney 3 August 1949.

21. Josef Zumerkorn video testimony, Yad Vashem YVA O.3/VT/6660.

22. Yad Vashem Artifacts Collection, letter from Josef Zumerkorn, donated with the sweater for the 'Gathering the Fragments' project, Item ID 9698712, 12 June 2011.

23. Estelle Glaser Laughlin, *Transcending Darkness*.

CHAPTER 18: SO MANY MISSING THINGS

1. Jakob Henryk Speriegen created the unique brand of Kangol in England, 1938. Pringles knitted hosiery evolved into fabulous outwear thanks to Otto Weisz.

2. Anita Lasker-Wallfisch, *Inherit the Truth 1939–1945*.

3. This description given by Teresa Stangl, wife of Sobibor's first commandant, Franz Stangl. Gitta Sereny, *Into That Darkness*.

4. Miriam Kahanov, conversation with the author, 24 June 2023. The film *Escape from Sobibor*, directed by Jack Gold, was made for British television in 1987. It drew on testimonies of Stanisław Szmajzner, Esther Terner-Raab, Thomas Blatt and others.

5. Modern knitters can follow Heatherly Walker's pattern to create their own Lizkor socks via a pattern in *Piece Works' Knitting Traditions* magazine, Spring 2013, link via www.yarnyenta.com or the Ravelry website. Expanding this ethos, Tanya Singer dedicates her talents for crafting and research to run the Knitting Hope project, using re-created knitwear to inspire communities of memorialization, www.tanyasinger.com.

6. Andrew Zielinski, *Conversations with Regina*. Andrew collected fragments of his mother's stories into this book, adding his own family recollections and some of Regina's recipes. It is a beautiful memorial work. An article titled 'Volunteer View' in the August 1993 Sydney Jewish Museum newsletter introduced Regina Zielinski, noting that sharing her story with museum visitors 'was the reason she survived.'

7. Anita Lasker-Wallfisch Testimony, USHMM 1995.A.1285.53 RG-50.149.0053.

8. Anita Lasker-Wallfisch, conversation with the author, 13 June 2023.

9. The glass suitcase was revealed in 2003, but dismantled two years later and replaced with a bronze sculpture of two children with their luggage: Füer das Kind memorial, Flor Kent. The metal sculptures are echoed by similar compositions at Friedrichstrasse station in Berlin, Harwichport, Essex, UK and at other relevant sites.

10. Andrew Zielinski, *Conversations with Regin.a*

POSTSCRIPT

1. Tzvetan Todorov, *Facing the Extreme.*

2. Melanie Lowy, *A Childhood Memoir: A Double Childhood.* Another former JSS pupil, Hannah Spitzer, married Philip Chody, who would eventually become Jock's solicitor and near neighbour.

3. Tamar Abrams, in conversation with the author, 9 February 2023.

4. The museum became its permanent home when the glass suitcase display was dismantled, although it also goes out on loan to exhibitions, sometimes alongside the album of photographs gifted by her school friends in January 1939.

5. Jochewet Heiden last will and testament, 14 September 2004. Jock's bequests included money for Fradel Lodge on Schonfeld Square in London, run by Agudas Israel Housing Association – a nice reminder of Rabbi Dr Solomon Schonfeld, who had helped save her, her sisters and her cousins. Another bequest supported the Side by Side educational charity, perhaps in acknowledgement of the education and haven Jock received from the Jewish Secondary School evacuated to Shefford. Like her sister Stella, Jock formally changed her surname from Heidenstein to Heiden.

6. Celia Eisenberg, speaking at Stella Heiden's memorial service, 25 October 1993, audiocassette recording. Private collection. Stella was buried in Jerusalem.

7. Jock Heiden headstone, Har Ha Menuchot cemetery, Givat Shaul, Jerusalem.

8. Lore Shelley, *Auschwitz – The Nazi Civilisation.*

9. Mania Heidenstein letter to Rita Heidenstein, 1939. Private collection.

Bibliography and Online Sources

Adelsburger, Lucie, *Auschwitz. A Doctor's Story,* Robson Books (1997)

Anne Frank House, Anne Frank Stichting (2018)

Adlington, Lucy, *The Dressmakers of Auschwitz. The True Story of the Women who Sewed to Survive*, HarperCollins (2021)

Ancona-Vincent, Victoria, *Beyond Imagination*, Quill Press (2004)

Arad, Yitzhak, *Belzec, Sobibor, Treblinka*, Indiana University Press (1987)

Arad, Yitzhak, Yisrael Gutman, and Abraham Margaliot, *Documents on the Holocaust*, University of Nebraska Press (1999)

Ashworth, Greg and Rudi Hartmann eds., *Horror and Human Tragedy Revisited: The Management of Sites of Atrocities for Tourism*, Cognizant Communications (2005)

Auschwitz-Birkenau State Museum, *Preserving for the Future. Material from an International Preservation Conference Oświęcim, June 23–25, 2003* (2004)

Auschwitz-Birkenau State Museum, *The Architecture of Crime. The Security and Isolation System of the Auschwitz Camp* (2008)

Bardgett, Suzanne, 'The Material Culture of Persecution: Collecting for the Holocaust Exhibition at the Imperial War Museum,' in Graeme Were and J. C. H. King, eds., *Extreme Collecting: Challenging Practices for 21st Century Museums*, Berghahn Books (2012)

Baumel-Schwartz, Judith Tydor, *Never Look Back. The Jewish Refugee Children in Great Britain 1938–1945*, Purdue University Press (2012)

Baxter, Ian, *The Ghettos of Nazi-Occupied Poland: Rare Photographs from Wartime Archives*, Pen & Sword (2000)

Bazyler, Michael J. and Roger P. Alford, eds., *Holocaust Restitution: Perspectives on the Litigation and Its Legacy*, New York University Press (2006)

Bem, Marek, *Sobibor Extermination Camp 1942–1943*, Stichting Sobibor Amsterdam (2015)

Bide, Bethan and Lucie Whitmore, *Fashion City: How Jewish Londoners Shaped Global Style*, Philip Wilson Publishers (2023)

Birenbaum, Halina, *Hope Is the Last to Die*, Auschwitz-Birkenau State Museum (2016)

Blatt, Thomas, *From the Ashes of Sobibor*, Northwestern University Press (1997)

———, *Sobibor: The Forgotten Revolt*, Holocaust Education Project (1988)

———, 'Confrontation with a Murderer,' Jewish Virtual Library, accessed July 1, 2023, https://www.jewishvirtuallibrary.org/confrontation-with-a-murderer

Blond, Elaine, with Barry Turner, *Marks of Distinction: The Memoirs of Elaine Blond*, Vallentine Mitchell (1988)

Brown, Kellie D., *The Sound of Hope: Music as Solace, Resistance and Salvation During the Holocaust and World War II*, McFarland & Company (2020)

Bryant, Michael S., *Eyewitness to Genocide: The Operation Reinhard Death Camp Trials 1955–1966*, University of Tennessee Press (2015)

Buziarek, Marek ed., *Lodzer Judaica in Archiven und Museen*, Muzeum Historii Łodzi (1996)

Cohen, Susan, *Rescue the Perishing: Eleanor Rathbone and the Refugees*, Vallentine Mitchell (2010)

Collins, Peter, 'Sir Ralph Kohn, 9 December 1927–11 November 2016,' Biographical Memoirs of Fellows of the Royal Society, 5 September 2018, royalsocietypublishing.org, accessed 3 October 2022

Collins, Robert and Han Hogerzeil, *Straight On: Journey to Belsen and the Road Home*, Methuen & Co. (1947)

Czech, Danuta, *Auschwitz Chronicle 1939–1945. From the Archives of the Auschwitz Memorial and the German Federal Archives*, Owl Books (1997)

Delbo, Charlotte, *Auschwitz and After*, Yale University Press (1995)

District Museum in Konin, *Chełmno Witnesses Speak,* Council for the Protection of Memory of Combat and Martyrdom in Warsaw, Konin (2004)

———, *The Extermination Center for Jews in Chełmno-on-Ner In the Light of the Latest Research*, Symposium proceedings September 6–7, Konin (2004)

Dunicz Niwińska, Helena, *One of the Girls in the Band: The Memoirs of a Violinist from Birkenau*, trans., William Brand, Auschwitz-Birkenau State Museum (2017)

Economic Intelligence Service, *Wartime Rationing and Consumption*, League of Nations (1942)

Eichengreen, Lucille with Rebecca Camhi Fromer, *Rumkowski and the Orphans of Lodz*, Mercury House (2000)

Eilenberg-Eibeshitz, Anna, 'Preserved Evidence,' *Ghetto Lodz*, vol. II, H. Eibeshitz Institute for Holocaust Studies (2000)

Eischeid, Susan, *The Truth About Fania Fénelon and the Women's Orchestra of Auschwitz-Birkenau*, Palgrave Point (2016)

Emilewicz-Pióro, Magdalena and Piotr M. A. Cywiński, *Auschwitz Legacies*, Auschwitz-Birkenau State Museum (2015)

Farnell, Jeordy, 'Dressing for Integration: How Clothing Helped or Hindered Refugees in Wartime England and a Contemporary Case Study,' Costume Society, https://costumesociety.org.uk/blog/post/dressing-for-integration-how-clothing-helped-or-hindered-refugees-in-wartime-england-a-contemporary-case-study, accessed 13 March 2023.

Fazel, M. and A. Stein, 'The Mental Health of Refugee Children,' *Archives of Disease in Childhood* 87, issue 5

Fénelon, Fania, *The Musicians of Auschwitz*, Sphere Books (1977)

Fox, Anne, *My Heart in a Suitcase*, Vallentine Mitchell (1996)

Frank, Otto H. and Mirjam Pressler, eds., *Anne Frank, The Diary of a Young Girl*, trans., Susan Massotty, Puffin Books (1997)

Freud, Anna and Dorothy T. Burlingham, *War and Children*, Medical War Books (1943)

Fromm, Bella, *Blood & Banquets: A Berlin Social Diary*, Birch Lane Press (1990)

Gardner, Lin, 'Fleece to Fashion. Wool Reclamation During WWII: A Lesson for Us All,' gla.ac.uk, accessed 15 January 2023

Garliński, Jósef, *Fighting Auschwitz*, Fontana (1976)

Gershon, Karen ed., *We Came as Children: A Collective Autobiography*, Victor Gollancz (1966)

Gies, Miep & Alison Leslie Gold, *Anne Frank Remembered*, Pocket Books (2009)

Glaser Laughlin, Estelle, *Transcending Darkness: A Girl's Journey out of the Holocaust*, Texas Tech University Press (2012)

Grossman, Mendel, *With a Camera in the Ghetto*, Schocken Books (1977)

Grunfeld, Dr Judith, *Shefford: A Story of a Jewish School in Evacuation 1939–1945*, Feldheim Publishers (2004)

Guske, Iris, *Trauma and Attachment in the Kindertransport Context: German-Jewish Child Refugees' Accounts of Displacement and Acculturation in Britain*, Cambridge Scholars Publishing (2009)

Harris, Mark Jonathan and Deborah Oppenheimer, *Into the Arms of Strangers: Stories of the Kindertransport*, Bloomsbury (2017)

Hart-Moxon, Kitty, *Return to Auschwitz*, Sidgwick & Jackson (1981)

Harvey, Elizabeth, *Women and the Nazi East. Agents & Witnesses of Germanization*, Yale University Press (2003)

Hellman, Peter and Beate Klarsfeld, eds., *The Auschwitz Album*, Random House (1981)

Hersh, Arek, *A Detail of History*, Apostrophe Books (2015)

Horwitz, Gordon J., *Ghettostadt. Łódź and the Making of a Nazi City*, Belknap Press of Harvard University Press (2008)

Ingram, Susan and Katrina Sark, *Berliner Chic: A Locational History of Berlin Fashion*, University of Chicago Press (2001)

Jüdisches Museum Berlin, *Raub und Restitution. Kulturgut aus Jüdischem besitz von 1933 bis heute*, Wallstein Verlag (2008)

Kavanaugh, Sarah, *ORT, the Second World War and the Rehabilitation of Survivors*, Vallentine Mitchell (2008)

Kern, Alice, *Tapestry of Hope*, Limited Edition Books (1988)

Knauss, Ferdinand, 'Discussion About Schickedanz in the Nazi Era,' www.handelsblatt.com, 23 July 2009, accessed 10 February 2022

Knox Doberty, Muriel, *Letters from Belsen 1945: An Australian Nurse's Experiences with the Survivors of War,* ed., Judith Cornell and R. Lynette Russel, Allen & Unwin (2000)

Kohn, Zahava in Conversation with Ann Rosen, *Fragments of a Lost Childhood*, Quill Press (2009)

Korobkin, Frieda, *Throw Your Feet over Your Shoulders: Beyond the Kindertransport*, RoseDog Books (2012)

Krebs, Stefan and Heike Weber, eds., *The Persistence of Technology: Histories of Repair, Reuse and Disposal*, Bielefeld (2021)

Kreutzmüller, Christoph, *Final Sale in Berlin: The Destruction of Jewish Commercial Activity, 1930–1945*, Berghahn Books (2017)

Ladwig-Winters, Simone, 'The Attack on Berlin Department Stores (Warenhaeuser) After 1933,' Shoah Resource Centre, https://www.yadvashem.org/articles/academic/the-attack-on-berlin-department-stores.html, accessed 22 June 2023

Lasker-Wallfisch, Anita, *Inherit the Truth 1939–1945*, Giles de la Mare Publishers (1996)

Leene, Jentina E., ed., 'Textile Conservation,' *International Institute for Conservation of Historic and Artistic Works*/Butterworths (1972)

Lengyel, Olga, *Five Chimneys. A Woman Survivor's True Story of Auschwitz*, Ziff-Davis Publishing (1947)

Leverton, Bertha and Shmuel Lowensohn, eds., *I Came Alone: The Stories of the Kindertransports*, Book Guild (1996)

Levi, Primo, *If This Is a Man*, Penguin Books (1987)

Levy, Michael, *Get the Children Out! Unsung Heroes of the Kindertransport*, Lemon Soul (2021)

Lipszyc, Rywka, *Rywka's Diary*, HarperCollins (2015)

Lower, Wendy, *Hitler's Furies: German Women in the Nazi Killing Fields*, Vintage (2014)

Lowy, Melanie, *A Childhood Memoir: A Double Childhood*, AuthorHouse (2011)

Mahlendorf, Ursula, *The Shame of Survival: Working Through a Nazi Childhood*, Pennsylvania State University (2009)

Mendelsohn, Adam D., *The Rag Race: How Jews Sewed Their Way to Success in America and the British Empire*, New York University Press (2015)

Michna, Pawel, 'Jewish Dress as Raw Material: The Visual Branding of the Lodz Ghetto Textile Industry," online paper for *Jewish Dress, Migration and Persecution in Modern European History* symposium, 19 June 2023.

Morsch, Günter and Astrid Ley, ed., *Sachsenhausen Concentration Camp 1936–1945: Events and Developments*, Metropol Verlag (2008)

Murray, Margaret and Jane Koster, *Knitting for All Illustrated*, Odhams Press (1942)

———, *Practical Knitting Illustrated*, Odhams Press (undated)

Nicosia, Francis R. and David Scrase eds., *Jewish Life in Nazi Germany: Dilemmas and Responses*, Berghahn Books (2010)

Noe, Rain, 'Recycling Wool the Hard Way, Since the 19th Century,' Core 77, October 6 2014, www.core77.com, accessed 27 July 2022

Nomberg-Przytyk, Sara, *Auschwitz. True Tales from a Grotesque Land*, University of North Carolina Press (1985)

Novitch, Miriam, *Sobibor. Martyrdom and Revolt: Documents and Testimonies*, Holocaust Library (1980)

Nyburg, Anna, *The Clothes on our Backs: How Refugees from Nazism Revitalised the British Fashion Trade*, Vallentine Mitchell (2020)

Oldfield, Sybil, *The Working-Day World: Women's Lives and Culture(s) in Britain 1914–1945*, Taylor & Francis (1994)

Paskuly, Steven, ed., *Death Dealer: The Memoirs of the SS Kommandant of Auschwitz*, trans. Andrew Pollinger, Prometheus Books (1992)

Podolska, Joanna, with Julian Baranowski, Marek Budziarek and Hubert Rogoziński, *Traces of the Litzmannstadt-Getto: A Guide to the Past*, Piątek Trzynastego (2004)

Rashke, Richard, *Escape from Sobibor*, Delphinium Books (1995)

Rathbone, Eleanor F., *Rescue the Perishing: A Summary of the Position Regarding the Nazi Massacres of Jewish and Other Victims and of Proposals for Their Rescue*, Harrison & Sons (1943)

Rawicz, Jerzy, ed., *KL Auschwitz as Seen by the SS*, Auschwitz-Birkenau State Museum (1970)

Rayasam, Renuka, 'Old Jewish Girls' School Converted into Berlin Gallery and Restaurant,' *Der Spiegel*, 20 April 2012, https://www.spiegel.de/international/zeitgeist/old-jewish-girls-school-converted-into-berlin-gallery-and-restaurant-a-828763.html, accessed 2 March 2023

Rees, Laurence, *Auschwitz: The Nazis and the Final Solution*, BBC Books (2005)

Reitlinger, Gerald, *The Final Solution*, Vallentine Mitchell (1953)

Schelvis, Jules, *Sobibór*, Berg (2007)

Schloss, Eva, *Eva's Story: A Survivor's Tale by the Stepsister of Anne Frank*, William B. Eerdmans (2010)

Schmidt, Christine E. and Barbara Warnock, *A Bitter Road: Britain and the Refugee Crisis of the 1930s and 1940s*, Wiener Library (2016)

Schneider, Helgam *Let Me Go: My Mother and the SS*, Vintage (2005)

Schonfeld, Rabbi Dr Solomon, *Message to Jewry*, Jewish Secondary School Movement (undated)

Schubert, Linda, *Danger on My Doorstep: The Anita Flora Powitzer Story*, Brandy Lane Publishers (2012)

Sereny, Gitta, *Into That Darkness: From Mercy Killings to Mass Murder*, Andre Deutsch Ltd (1974)

Shapiro, Leon, *The History of ORT: A Jewish Movement for Social Change*, Schocken Books (1980)

Shelley, Dr Lore, *Auschwitz – The Nazi Civilisation: Twenty-Three Women Prisoners' Accounts*, University Press of America (1992)

———, *Secretaries of Death: Accounts by Former Prisoners Who Worked in the Gestapo of Auschwitz*, Shengold Publishers (1986)

Singer, Tanya, 'Angora Rabbits in Auschwitz Concentration Camp,' *Tablet*, 7 April, 2022, https://www.tabletmag.com/sections/community/articles/fluffy-bunnies-of-auschwitz, accessed 7 April 23

Somers, Eric and René Kok, *Jewish Displaced Persons in Camp Bergen-Belsen 1945–1950: The Unique Photo Album of Zippy Orlin*, University of Washington Press (2004)

Stargadt, Nicholas, *The German War: A Nation Under Arms, 1939–1945*, Bodley Head (2015)

Strzelecki, Andrzej, *The Deportation of Jews from the Łódź Ghetto to KL Auschwitz and Their Extermination*, Auschwitz-Birkenau State Museum (2006)

Sturdy Colls, Caroline, *Holocaust Archaeologies: Approaches and Future Directions*, Springer (2015)

Szász Stessel, Zahava, *Wine and Thorns in Tokay Valley: Jewish Life in Hungary: The History of the Abaújszántó*, Fairleigh Dickinson University Press (2014)

Tabor, Paul, *The Nazi Myth*, Pallas Publishing (1939)

Taylor, Derek, *Solomon Schonfeld: A Purpose in Life*, Vallentine Mitchell (2009)

Thomas, Mary, *Mary Thomas's Book of Knitting Patterns*, Hodder and Stoughton (1943)

Todorov, Tzvetan, *Facing the Extreme: Moral Life in the Concentration Camps*, Weidenfeld & Nicholson (1999)

Trunk, Isaiah, *Łódź Ghetto: A History*, United States Holocaust Memorial Museum/ Indiana University Press (2006)

Turgel, Gena, *I Light a Candle*, Library of Holocaust Testimonies, Vallentine Mitchell (2006)

Turner, Nan, *Clothing Goes to War: Creativity Inspired by Scarcity in World War II*, Intellect (2022)

Unger, Michal ed., *The Last Ghetto: Life in the Lodz Ghetto 1940–1944*, Yad Vashem (1995)

Urbach, L., 'Wyberlye Ladies Convalescent Home, Burgess Hill,' *Jewish Historical Studies* 51, UCL Press (2020)

Velasco, Raymond A., "*German Wool Fabric and Manufacturing of World War Two*," Lost Battalions, www.lostbattalions.com, accessed 27 April 2022 (2005)

Walker, Heatherly, 'The Sock Knitters of Sobibor,' *Knitting Traditions* (Spring 2013)

Weber, Heike, 'Nazi German Waste Recovery and the Vision of a Circular Economy: The Case of Waste Paper and Rags,' *Business History*, 18 May 2021, accessed 21 December 2022

Webb, Chris, *The Sobibor Death Camp: History, Biographies, Remembrance,* Ibidem Verlag (2017)

Weisz, George M., 'Ghetto Medicine: The Special Case of Ghetto Lodz, 1940–44,' *Israeli Medical Association Journal* 15 (April 2013)

Westphal, Uwe, *Fashion Metropolis Berlin*, Henschel (2019)

Wewryk, Kalemn, *To Sobibor and Back: An Eyewitness Account*, Włodawa (2008)

Wolff-Mönckeberg, Mathilde, *On the Other Side: To My Children from Germany: 1940–1945*, trans. and ed., Ruth Evans, Pan Books (1979)

Zielinski, Andrew, *Conversations with Regina*, Muzeum Pojezierza Łęczyńsko-Włodawskiego (2008)

Zyskind, Sara *Stolen Years*, Lerner Publications (1981)

Index

About the Author

LUCY ADLINGTON is a British novelist and clothes historian with more than twenty years' experience researching social history and writing fiction and nonfiction. She lives in Yorkshire, England.

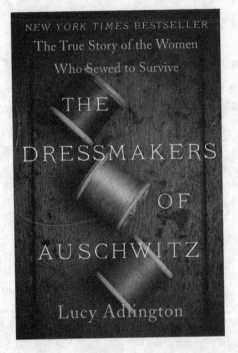